Fourth Edition

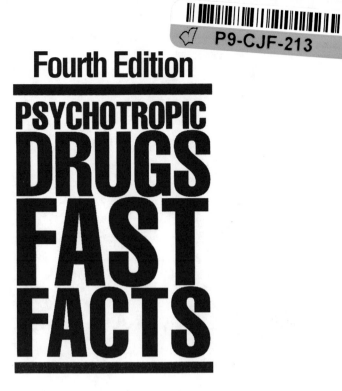

PSYCHOTROPIC DRUGS FAST FACTS

P9-CJF-213

A NORTON PROFESSIONAL BOOK

Fourth Edition

PSYCHOTROPIC DRUGS FAST FACTS

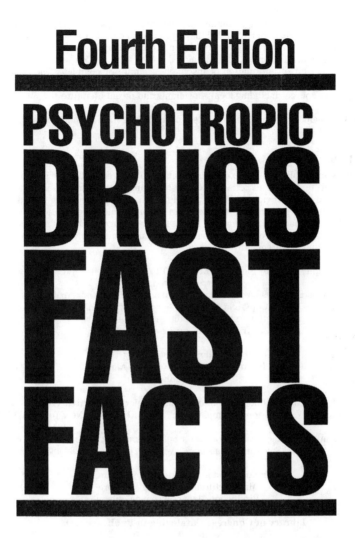

Jerrold S. Maxmen, MD
Sidney H. Kennedy, MD
Roger S. McIntyre, MD

W. W. Norton & Company
New York • London

NOTICE

We have made every attempt to summarize accurately and concisely a multitude of references. However, the reader is reminded that times and medical knowledge change, transcription or understanding error is always possible, and crucial details are omitted whenever such a comprehensive distillation as this is attempted in limited space. We cannot, therefore, guarantee that every bit of information is absolutely accurate or complete. The reader should affirm that cited recommendations are still appropriate by reading the original articles and checking other sources including local consultants and recent literature.

Note that all blank fields in tables indicate that the information is undetermined, unclear, or unknown.

DRUG DOSAGE

The authors and publisher have exerted every effort to ensure that drug selection and dosage set forth in this text are in accord with current recommendations and practice at the time of publication. However, in view of ongoing research, changes in government regulations, and the constant flow of information relating to drug therapy and drug reactions, the reader is urged to check the package insert for each drug for any change in indications and dosage and for added warnings and precautions. This is particularly important when the recommended agent is a new and/or infrequently used drug.

Copyright © 2008 by Sidney H. Kennedy, Roger S. McIntyre, and the Estate of Jerrold S. Maxmen.
Copyright © 2002, 1995 by Nicholas G. Ward and the Estate of Jerrold S. Maxmen.
Copyright © 1991 by Jerrold S. Maxmen.
Introduction to the Third Edition by Steven L. Dubovsky.
Copyright © 2002 by Steven L. Dubovsky.

All rights reserved
Printed in the United States of America
First Edition

For information about permission to reproduce selections from this book, write to Permissions, W. W. Norton & Company, Inc., 500 Fifth Avenue, New York, NY 10110.

For information about special discounts for bulk purchases, please contact W. W. Norton Special Sales at specialsales@wwnorton.com or 800-233-4830.

Composition and book design by Aptara, Inc.
Manufacturing by Courier Westford
Production Manger: Leeann Graham

Library of Congress Cataloging-in-Publication Data

Maxmen, Jerrold S.
Psychotropic drugs : fast facts / Jerrold S. Maxmen, Sidney H. Kennedy, Roger S. McIntyre.
—4th ed.
   p. ; cm.
"A Norton Professional Book."
Includes bibliographical references and index.
ISBN 978-0-393-70520-1 (paperback)
 1. Psychotropic drugs—Handbooks, manuals, etc. I. Kennedy, Sidney H. II. McIntyre, Roger S.
III. Title.
[DNLM: 1. Psychotropic Drugs—Handbooks. QV 39 M464p 2008]
RM315.M355 2008
615'.788—dc22

                                                                        2008001413

ISBN 13: 978-0-393-70520-1

W. W. Norton & Company, Inc., 500 Fifth Avenue, New York, N.Y. 10110
www.wwnorton.com
W. W. Norton & Company Ltd., Castle House, 75/76 Wells St., London W1T 3QT

1 3 5 7 9 8 6 4 2 0

To Yeeling, who has provided unending support to
me in this and related endeavors, and to those
who suffer from mental illness.
—Roger S. McIntyre, MD

To Nuala, Louise, Claire, Michael, and Laura.
—Sidney H. Kennedy, MD

Introduction
to the Fourth Edition

Major advances in psychopharmacology have necessitated a substantial revision to these *Fast Facts*. The new millennium has seen diagnostic refinement and significant advances in experimental clinical pharmacology, including new mechanisms of action for hypnotic and antidepressant agents (e.g., ramelteon and agomelatine act on melatonin receptors; memantine acts on NMDA receptors). However, most advances reflect modifications to current pharmacotherapies to provide better tolerability and, in some cases, enhanced efficacy. These include the isolation of stereoisomers (e.g., escitalopram, eszopiclone); the identification of principal active metabolites (e.g., paliperidone, desvenlafaxine succinate); and the availability of different drug delivery systems (e.g., transdermal selegiline).

The past decade has also seen an expansion of indications for many agents, notably the "second-generation" antipsychotic agents (SGAs; e.g., quetiapine, olanzapine). The SGAs, initially indicated for schizophrenia and related psychotic disorders, are now indicated for Tourette's Disorder and various phases of bipolar disorder, with anticipated approval for major depressive disorder and other mental disorders. The broad spectrum of efficacy offered by SGAs has fostered a clinical opinion that these agents are "panpsychotropics."

It is interesting to speculate what the next decade will bring. Substantive developments in psychopharmachology will require a refinement of the respective pathophysiological models subserving disparate psychopathologies. For example, emerging evidence indicates that alterations in neuronal plasticity and intracellular signaling are salient to the pathophysiology of mood and psychotic disorders. These observations have provided the basis for intensified efforts to evaluate mechanistically unique agents that target intracellular signaling cascades, transcription factors, immuno-inflammatory activation, peptidergic systems (e.g., a vaccine for Alzheimer's disease), insulin/insulin-growth factor (and other nerve-growth factors), as well as glutamatergic excitotoxicity. It seems within grasp that future treatments for mental disorders will not only suppress symptoms but also exert a salutary effect on the underlying disease process. We hope that in the next 5 years there will be sufficient progress in these directions to dramatically influence the fifth edition of *Psychotropic Drugs: Fast Facts*.

This edition would not have been possible without Candy W. Y. Law, whose exhaustive review of the literature and careful editing work produced a new edition for a new millennium. We are also grateful to colleagues who provided comments on individual chapters: Tim Bilkey, Len Cortese, Ron Keren, Kevin Kjernisted, Claire O'Donovan, and Arun Ravindran.

Sidney H. Kennedy, MD, FRCPC
Roger S. McIntyre, MD, FRCPC
May, 2008

Organization

Each chapter contains 13 sections—with occasional deviations according to circumstances.

INTRODUCTION TO DRUG CLASS

This section presents the general category of medications, their broad indications, and the disorders they treat in this and other chapters.

DOSING, DOSE FORM, AND COLOR

The book inlcudes only those drugs currently available in the United States. Standard therapeutic ranges, dosage adjustment for geriatric populations, drug delivery system, and appearance are discussed.

PHARMACOLOGY

This section is divided into pharmacokinetic and pharmacodynamic topics with an overview, where appropriate, of general classification.

Pharmacokinetics describes absorption, distribution, metabolism, and elimination. Several terms are often employed:

- *Bioavailability* is the percentage of an administered dose of unchanged drug that reaches the systemic circulation.
- *Plasma binding* is the percentage of drug bound clinically to plasma proteins.
- *Half-life*, usually expressed in hours, refers to the time period when 50% of the drug has been eliminated. The book's figures usually represent the drug's major active fractions, including metabolites; the broader numbers in parentheses are ranges.
- *P450 system enzymes* refer to the major routes of liver metabolism.

• *Excretion* is typically the percent of drug unchanged in the urine and/or feces.

Pharmacodynamics addresses the mechanisms of action and physiological effects of the drugs.

CLINICAL INDICATIONS

This section describes the clinical conditions that have received FDA approval for each medication.

SIDE EFFECTS

This section provides a reasonably comprehensive description of side effects for each drug class and their management. Although these effects are discussed under organ categories, this does not suggest that each side effect belongs exclusively to a single system. Categories are used for convenience. Because drugs within a class are rarely all compared in the same study, it is difficult to establish relative rates for each side effect across a class of agents.

DRUG AND FOOD INTERACTIONS

This section includes both drug–drug and drug–food interactions. Although not extensive, each list focuses on the clinically significant interactions. Food–drug interactions with MAO inhibitors are also included.

EFFECTS ON LABORATORY TESTS

This section outlines how these medications influence laboratory tests of blood and urine.

DISCONTINUATION

In the past decade, the potentially harmful effects of abrupt drug discontinuation have been increasingly recognized, particularly among antidepressants. This section highlights drug discontinuation emergent symptoms, preventive approaches, and where necessary, management of emergent symptoms.

OVERDOSE: TOXICITY, SUICIDE, AND TREATMENT

This section describes symptoms and signs associated with drug overdose, emphasizing high-risk overdoses (e.g., lithium carbonate) and optimal management.

SPECIAL POPULATIONS

This section addresses drug use in children and adolescents, women during pregnancy and lactation, and older adults.

The following table provides a summary of FDA-defined category ratings for drug safety during pregnancy.

Pregnancy Rating Category	Interpretation
A	Adequate, well-controlled studies in pregnant women have not shown an increased risk of fetal abnormalities in any trimester of pregnancy.
B	Animal studies have revealed no evidence of harm to the fetus; however, there are no adequate and well-controlled studies in pregnant women.
	OR
	Animal studies have shown an adverse effect, but adequate and well-controlled studies in pregnant women have failed to demonstrate a risk to the fetus in any trimester.
C	Animal studies have shown an adverse effect, and there are no adequate and well-controlled studies in pregnant women.
	OR
	No animal studies have been conducted, and there are no adequate and well-controlled studies in pregnant women.
D	Adequate well-controlled or observational studies in pregnant women have demonstrated a risk to the fetus. However, the benefits of therapy may outweigh the potential risk. For example, the drug may be acceptable if needed in a life-threatening situation or serious disease for which safer drugs cannot be used or are ineffective.
X	Adequate, well-controlled, or observational studies in animals or pregnant women have demonstrated positive evidence of fetal abnormalities or risks. The use of the product is contraindicated in women who are, or may become, pregnant.

O
R
G
A
N
I
Z
A
T
I
O
N

PRECAUTIONS

This section addresses relative and absolute contraindications.

KEY POINTS TO COMMUNICATE TO PATIENTS AND FAMILIES

This book is written for professionals rather than consumers of mental health-care. The information provided in this section represents the most pertinent issues presented in lay terms, including recommendations about when to take the medication, what side effects to expect, what to do if a dose is missed, and when to contact the doctor.

THERAPEUTIC APPLICATION

This section addresses sequential aspects of treatment (e.g., when a patient cannot tolerate the first drug or fails to respond). It includes optimization, switching, augmentation, and combination strategies.

ABBREVIATIONS

ACA	anticholinergic agents
Ach	acetylcholine
AD	antidepressant
ADR	adverse drug reaction
AV	atioventricular
bid	twice a day
CBC	complete blood count
CPK	creatine phorphokinase
d	days
D/S	dextrose and saline
D/W	dextrose and water
DST	dexamethasone suppression test
ECG	electrocardiogram
ECT	electroconvulsive therapy
EEG	electroencephalogram
EPS	extrapyramidal side effects
EUCD	emotionally unstable character disorder
FGA	first-generation antipsychotics
g	gram
GABA	gamma-aminobutyric acid
GAD	generalized anxiety disorder
h	hours
Hg	mercury
h/o	history of
HCAs	heterocyclic antidepressants (includes TCAs, maprotiline, and amoxapine)
hs	at sleep
IM	intramuscular injection
IV	intravenous injection
kg	kilogram
LBD	Lewy body dementia
LFT	liver function tests (SGOT, SGPT, LDH, bilirubin, alkaline phosphotase)
MAOI	monoamine-oxidase inhibitor
mEq/l	milliequivalents/liter
μg	microgram (10^{-6} grams)
mg	milligrams (10^{-3} grams)
MI	myocardial infarction
NDI	nephrogenic diabetes insipidus
ng	nanograms (10^{-9} grams)
NIMH	National Institute of Mental Health
NMS	neuroleptic malignant syndrome
NSAID	nonsteroidal anti-inflammatory drug
OCD	obsessive-compulsive disorder
PDD	Parkinson Disease-associated dementia

PTSD	posttraumatic stress disorder
po	oral dose
prn	as needed (pro re nata)
q	every
qd	once a day; daily
qhs	each night at bedtime
qid	four times a day
qod	every other day
RBC	red blood cells
RCT	randomized controlled trial
r/o	rule out
SC	subcutaneous
SGA	second-generation antipsychotics
SGOT/AST	aspartate aminotransferase
SGPT/ALT	alanine aminotransferase
SSRI	selective serotonin reuptake inhibitor
T_3	triiodothyronine
T_4	thyroxine
TCAs	tricyclic antidepressants
TD	tardive dyskinesia
tid	three times a day
TSH	thyroid-stimulating hormone
WBC	white blood cells

ORGANIZATION

Contents

C
O
N
T
E
N
T
S

Expanded Contents

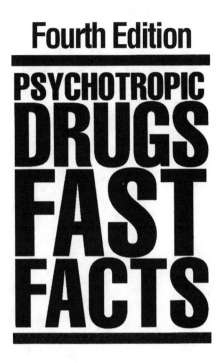

Fourth Edition

PSYCHOTROPIC
DRUGS
FAST
FACTS

1. Antipsychotics

INTRODUCTION TO DRUG CLASS

The introduction of the first-generation antipsychotic (FGA), chlorpromazine, ushered in the modern era of psychopharmacology. The FGAs were initially prescribed for their ataraxia-inducing effects and became widely prescribed for psychotic, mood, and other serious mental disorders. The widespread availability of FGAs provided a safer and more acceptable treatment avenue when compared to interventions that were commonplace in the early 20th century and prior. Coinciding with the dissemination and widespread availability of FGA treatment was a significant reduction in hospitalization rates reflective of a broader deinstitutionalization of the mentally ill in the latter 20th century. Furthermore, antipsychotics may have contributed to the lowering of mortality in some psychiatric presentations such as lethal catatonia and the consequence of psychotic excitement and impulsivity.

Paralleling these observations was an increasing awareness of the hazards posed by acute and long-term exposure to FGA treatment. The overarching safety concern was the risk of neurological toxicity manifested as abnormal motor movements (previously referred to as extrapyramidal side effects [EPS] and tardive dyskinesia). Abnormal involuntary movements engendered and/or exacerbated by FGAs was often disfiguring to affected individuals, amplifying the stigma associated with mental illness and its treatment. It is inexorably true that antipsychotic-associated abnormal movements are frequently irreversible, and hitherto there remains no reliable antidote.

Although FGAs are highly efficacious in treating aspects of psychopathology (e.g., positive symptoms, agitation, behavioral dyscontrol), they are insufficient at abrogating other commonly encountered symptomatic presentations such as negative and affective symptoms. This deficiency, as well as the concerns related to neurological toxicity, reduces the overall therapeutic index of FGAs. Taken together, these issues provided the impetus for the development and widespread usage of the second-generation antipsychotics (SGAs), which are prescribed more commonly than FGAs in North America and many other regions of the world. The SGAs, when appropriately dosed, confer a lower risk of neurological toxicity versus FGAs and may offer a broader spectrum of effectiveness across the panoply of psychiatric symptoms. Nevertheless, initial enthusiasm for SGAs has been tempered by effectiveness results from large naturalistic studies in mixed populations and by a different set of tolerability concerns (e.g., metabolic).

Although SGAs are distinctly differently from FGAs and from each other in their pharmacological efficacy and tolerability profile, all agents have dopamine D2 blockade as a point of commonality. Differences in their overall therapeutic index likely relate to differences between agents in their in vivo affinity for, and engagement of, various neurochemical systems.

First- and Second-Generation Antipsychotics by Chemical Class

Chemical Class	Generic Name	Trade Name
FIRST GENERATION		
Butyrophenone	Haloperidol	Haldol
Dibenzazepine	Loxapine	Loxitane
Dihydroindolone	Molindone	Moban
Diphenylbutylpiperidine	Pimozide	Orap
Phenothiazine		
—Aliphatic	Chlorpromazine	Thorazine
—Piperazine	Fluphenazine	Permitil
		Prolixin
	Perphenazine	Trilafon
	Trifluoperazine	Stelazine
—Piperidine	Thioridazine	Mellaril
Thioxanthene	Flupenthixol	Fluanxol
	Thiothixene	Navane
SECOND GENERATION		
Benzisoxazole	Risperidone	Risperdal
	Paliperidone	Invega
Dibenzodiazepine	Clozapine	Clozaril
Dibenzothiazepine	Quetiapine	Seroquel
	Ziprasidone	Geodon
Dihydrocarbostyril	Aripiprazole	Abilify
Thienobenzodiazepine	Olanzapine	Zyprexa

FIRST-GENERATION ANTIPSYCHOTICS

Dosing, Dose Form, and Color

Profile of First-Generation Antipsychotics

Generic Names	Therapeutic Dose Range (mg/day)	Geriatric Dose (mg/day)	Dose Form (mg)[a]	Color
BUTYROPHENONES				
Haloperidol	2–10	0.5–6	t: 0.5/1/2/5/10/20 o: 2 mg/ml p: 5 mg/ml p: 50/100 mg/ml	t: white/yellow/pink/ green/aqua/salmon
Haloperidol decanoate	50–300 mg q 4 wk		p: 50/100 mg/ml	

Generic Names	Therapeutic Dose Range (mg/day)	Geriatric Dose (mg/day)	Dose Form (mg)[a]	Color
DIBENZAZEPINE				
Loxapine	15–50		c: 5/10/25/50 o: 25 mg/ml p: 50 mg/ml	t: dark green/yellow–green/light green–dark green/blue–dark green
DIHYDROINDOLONE				
Molindone	50–75	50–150	t: 5/10/25/50/100 o: 20 mg/ml	t: orange/lavender/light green/blue/tan o: cherry
DIPHENYLBUTYLPIPERDINES				
Pimozide	2	10–50	t: 2	t: white
PHENOTHIAZINES				
Aliphatics				
Chlorpromazine	100–500	25–200	t: 10/25/50/100/200 sr: 30/75/150/200/300 o: 10/30/100 p: 25 mg/ml s: 10 mg/5 ml sp: 25/100 mg/ml	t: all orange
Piperazines				
Fluphenazine	2.5–10	2–10	t: 1/2.5/5/10 e: 0.5 mg/ml o: 5 mg/ml p: 2.5 mg/ml	t: white/blue/pink/orange
Fluphenazine decanoate	12.5–100 mg q 2–4 wk		p: 25 mg/ml	
Fluphenazine enanthate	25 mg q 1–3 wk		p: 25 mg/ml	
Perphenazine	4–16	4–48	t: 2/4/8/16 o: 3.2 mg/ml p: 5 mg/ml	t: all gray
Trifluoperazine	4–20	2–15	t: 1/2/5/10 o: 10 mg/ml p: 2 mg/ml	t: all blue
Piperidines				
Thioridazine	150–300	25–200	t: 10/15/25/50/100/150/200 o: 30/100 mg/ml su: 25/100 mg/5 ml	t: chartreuse/pink/tan/white/green/yellow/pink o: straw yellow/light yellow
THIOXANTHENES				
Flupenthixol	3–6	0.5–1	t: 0.5/3	t: both ochre-yellow
Thiothixene	4–13	2–15	c: 1/2/5/10/20 o: 5 mg/ml p: 2/5 mg/ml	c: orange–yellow/blue–yellow/orange–white/blue–white/dark blue–light blue

[a]c = capsule; e = elixir; o = oral concentrate; p = parenteral concentrate; s = syrup; sp = suppository; sr = sustained-release spansules; su = suspension; t = tablets.

Pharmacology

PHARMACOKINETICS

• Rapidly absorbed from the gastrointestinal tract and undergo extensive first-pass metabolism.

- Highly lipophilic, which results in ready transport across the blood–brain barrier.
- Metabolized by the cytochrome P450 enzyme system.
  - √ The isozyme systems predominately involved are CYP2D6, CYP1A2, and CYP3A4.
  - √ Medications that inhibit or compete for these substrates can increase antipsychotic blood levels.
- Parent compounds and their metabolites are glucuronidated in the liver and excreted by the kidney in the urine or feces.
- The average plasma half-life is approximately 20–24 hours, allowing for once-daily dosing.
- Haloperidol and fluphenazine are available in long-acting intramuscular injectable preparations.
  - √ This allows for less fluctuation in plasma level compared to oral formulations, bypasses first-pass metabolism, and can improve patient compliance.

Pharmacokinetic Properties of First-Generation Antipsychotics

				P450 Systems		
Generic Names	Bioavailability (%)	Protein Binding	Half-Life (h)	Substrate of	Inhibits	Excretion (%)[a]
Chlorpromazine	32 ± 19	95–98	16–30	1A2, 2D6	2D6	25 ± 15 R/70–80 F
Fluphenazine	40–50	80–90	15–30			
Flupenthixol	30–70	99	26–36		2D6	
Haloperidol	70 ± 18	91 ± 1.4	12–36	3A4	2D6	40 R
Loxapine	30	90	8–30	1A2, 2D6, 3A4		61 R/22 F
Molindone		98	1.5			
Perphenazine	low	high	9–21			
Pimozide	>50	99	55			38–45 R
Thioridazine	30	70–99	16	1A2, 2D6, 3A4		
Thiothixene			34			
Trifluoperazine		>80	9.3			

[a]F = fecal; R = renal.

PHARMACODYNAMICS

- Bind to numerous neurotransmitter receptor subtypes, including those of dopamine, norepinephrine, epinephrine, acetylcholine, serotonin, and histamine.
  - √ Act to antagonize the endogenous ligands at these receptors.
- Both therapeutic effects and movement disorders can be attributed to the antagonism of dopamine at D_2 receptors, with actions at the other neuroreceptors associated with side effects.
- The FGAs can be classified according to high (e.g. haloperidol), mid (e.g. loxapine), and low (e.g. chlorpromazine) potency on the basis of their degree of affinity for D_2 receptors at therapeutic dose range.

Relative Neuroreceptor Affinities for First-Generation Antipsychotics at Therapeutic Doses

Generic Names	D_2	H_1	α_1	α_2	5-HT_{1A}	5-HT_{2A}	5-HT_{2C}
Chlorpromazine	+++	++	++++	0	0	++	+
Fluphenazine	++++	+	++	+	0	+	0
Haloperidol	+++	0	++	+	0	0	0
Loxapine	++	++	+	0	0	++	++
Molindone	0	0	0	0	0	0	0
Perphenazine	+++	++	++	0	0	++	0
Pimozide	++++	0	0	0	0	+	0
Thioridazine	++	+	+++	0	0	++	0
Thiothixene	++++	+++	++	0	0	0	0
Trifluoperazine	+++	0	+	0	0	++	0

Note. + to ++++ = low to marked affinity; 0 = minimal to none.

Clinical Indications

SCHIZOPHRENIA

- Effective in the acute and maintenance treatment of psychotic episodes.
- Broadly efficacious in treating schizophrenic symptomatology with differential efficacy in positive symptoms (e.g., thought disorder, hallucinations, delusions).
- Limited therapeutic effects in the treatment of negative (e.g., restricted emotional experience, low social drive, alogia, anhedonia, anergia) as well as affective symptoms.

ACUTE MANIA AS PART OF BIPOLAR DISORDER

- The FGAs are highly efficacious in the treatment of acute mania, particularly for agitation, psychoses, and behavioral dyscontrol.
- Onset of therapeutic effect sooner than lithium.
- Clinical experience and empirical data suggest that FGAs may intensify and/or engender depressive symptoms during acute propholytic treatment.
- Hazard for movement disorders may be greater in individuals with bipolar disorder vs. schizophrenia.

DELUSIONAL DISORDER

- Historical reports suggest the efficacy of pimozide in delusional disorder of various types: somatic, erotomanic, jealous, and persecutory.
- Extant literature with pimozide is comprised largely of case reports and uncontrolled, nonrandomized studies.
- Efficacy of other FGAs unproven.

AGITATION AND AGGRESSIVE BEHAVIOR

- Haloperidol has been used frequently as an intramuscular as-needed medication for agitation and aggressive behavior in emergency departments.
  √ However, it is no longer a reasonable choice due to its side effect profile.

TOURETTE'S DISORDER

- Haloperidol is effective in treating the symptoms of Tourette's syndrome in both adults and children.
- Pimozide is only recommended for patients with severe symptoms who are intolerant of, and/or nonresponsive to, haloperidol.

OTHER INDICATIONS

FGAs are also prescribed (off-label) as/for:

- Antiemetic
- An adjunct to anesthesia and analgesia
- Delirium
- Major depressive disorders with psychotic features
- Treatment-resistant obsessive–compulsive disorder
- Autism and pervasive developmental disorder in childhood
- Eating disorders (e.g., anorexia nervosa to provide ataraxia)
- Personality disorders

Side Effects

The three phenothiazine groups have different side effect profiles:

- Aliphatic—chlorpromazine causes more hypotension, sedation, dermatitis, and convulsion, but less movement disorders.
- Piperidines—thioridazine causes more ECG effects, retinal toxicity, and ejaculatory problems, but *least* movement disorders.
- Piperzines—perphenazine, fluphenazine, and trifluoperazine cause more movement disorders but less sedation, hypotension, and lens opacities.

ANTICHOLINERGIC EFFECTS

Anticholinergic actions affect many systems and may produce a variety of adverse effects:

- Hypotension
- Dry mouth
- Constipation
- Paralytic ileus
- Urinary hesitancy or retention
- Blurred near vision
- Dry eyes
- Narrow-angle glaucoma
- Photophobia
- Nasal congestion
- Confusion and decreased memory

Most anticholinergic symptoms decrease in 1–4 weeks but do not completely remit.

- Management
  - √ Bethanechol 10–50 mg po tid or qid can reverse peripheral but not central effects. Duration of action is 2–8 hours.
  - √ Switching to a less anticholinergic antipsychotic and/or switching to a non-anticholinergic extrapyramidal drug (e.g., amantadine) can reduce or eliminate anticholinergic side effects.

CARDIOVASCULAR EFFECTS

Nonspecific ECG changes and arrhythmias
- Especially with thiordazine and pimozide
  - √ Usually quinidine-like effects (prolonged QT and PR interval and wave).
- Get baseline ECG before initiating an antipsychotic and a repeat ECG every year thereafter.
  - √ Do not use high-risk agents
    - ◻ If congenital long QT syndrome seen
    - ◻ Or if taking other drugs that delay cardiac conduction (including some nonsedating antihistamines).
  - √ ECG is periodically recommended with pimozide during dose adjustment.
- In rare cases, "torsade de pointes" has occurred.
  - √ It is a form of ventricular tachycardia in which the amplitude and direction of QRS complexes change periodically.

Orthostatic hypotension
- Dizziness, lightheadedness, weakness, fainting, and syncope on standing up; worse at times of peak blood levels.
  - √ Highest risk with low-potency phenothiazines.
- Management
  - √ Hypotension is more frequent with low salt intake, low fluid intake, antihypertensive agents, hypothyroidism, or stimulant withdrawal.
    - ◻ Use least hypotensive antipsychotic drugs in these high-risk circumstances.
  - √ Suggest that patient stand up slowly over 15–60 seconds.
  - √ If more severe hypotension, lower head and elevate legs.
  - √ Use support stockings (nighttime is highest risk time; patient needs to wear stockings day and night).
  - √ Use divided doses to avoid high blood levels.
  - √ Try dihydroergotamine.
  - √ If medically serious, employ volume expanders and, if necessary,
    - ◻ Alpha-adrenergic pressor agents, such as metaraminol, phenylephrine, or norepinephrine.
    - ◻ *Do not use epinephrine or isoproteronol.*
  - √ Try fludrocortisone 0.1–0.2 mg/daily.
    - ◻ *Check electrolytes and BP regularly.*

Tachycardia
- (> 100 beats/minute)

- More often seen as isolated symptom without hypotension in young adults.
  - √ Optimal heart function often compensates for BP drop.
- Frequent occurrence on low-potency antipsychotics.
  - √ Manage by lowering antipsychotic dose or changing antipsychotic.
  - √ If persists, treat with peripheral β-blocker or propafenone (antiarrhythmic).

CENTRAL NERVOUS SYSTEM EFFECTS

- Low serum iron has been reported to be common in patients (particularly females) with akathisia, dystonic reactions, and neuroleptic malignant syndrome.
  - √ Anecdotal evidence suggests that measuring serum iron and, if indicated, correcting with supplemental iron, may improve movement disorders.

Types of Extrapyramidal Symptoms

Syndrome	Onset	Risk Groups	Clinical Course
Dystonia	1 h–5 days	Young males (under 30 y.o.) and females (under 25 y.o.)	Acute, spasmodic, painful; usually remits spontaneously in 10 days; can be prevented with ACA.
Parkinsonism	5 h–30 days	12–45% of patients; elderly, particularly women	Occurs throughout treatment
Akathisia[a]	2 h–60 days	20–50% of patients, elderly	There are two types: motor and psychological (inner restlessness). Persists during treatment; propranolol and amantadine may be more effective than ACA.
Neuroleptic malignant syndrome (NMS)*	weeks	0.5–1% of patients; 80% are under 40; affects 2 x men as women; high-potency antipsychotics	Mortality rate is 20–30%; symptoms typically persist 5–10 days on oral forms and 20–30 days after depot injections.
"Rabbit" syndrome	months–years	4% of patients untreated with ACAs	Usually reversible with ACAs
Tardive dyskinesia (TD)	month–years	20–30% of patients, with range of 0.5–60%; women, elderly, and patients with mood or CNS disorders	Treat best with prevention; 50% irreversible; vitamin E 400 mg tid or qid may help (~1600 IU per day). ACAs usually hurt.

*Risk is substantially increased by rapid dosage increase of antipsychotic.

Akathisia

- The least obvious but the most prevalent movement disorder.
- The most common side effect that causes patients to stop antipsychotics.
  - √ Erupts between 6 hours and 2 weeks after starting antipsychotic.
- Haloperidol-treated patients had higher treatment-emergent akathisia vs. olanzapine.

- Symptoms include
  - √ Subjective restlessness
  - √ "Jitters," fidgety
  - √ Tapping feet incessantly, "restless legs"
  - √ Rocking forward and backward in chair
  - √ Shifting weight from side to side when standing or sitting
- May present as a muscular discomfort in an agitated, frightened, dysphoric, pacing, hand-wringing, and weeping individual.
- Patient might not notice or be bothered by regular rhythmic leg jiggling.
- Can be misdiagnosed as anxiety, psychotic agitation, attention-deficit/hyper-activity disorder, or stimulant abuse.
  - √ Important to know patient's presentation before medication is started.
  - √ If diagnosis is unclear, ask patient if restlessness is a "muscle" feeling or a "head" feeling; the muscle feeling often experienced in the limbs suggests akathisia; the head feeling, anxiety.
  - √ Myoclonic jerks sometimes accompany akathisia.
  - √ May see voluntary movements to reduce symptoms.
  - √ May only be a subjective state with no observable behaviors.
- Differs from restless legs syndrome (RLS); frequent features of RLS, rarely seen in akathisia, include:
  - √ Restricted to legs
  - √ Unpleasant sensory symptoms in calves
  - √ Myoclonic jerks
  - √ Insomnia
  - √ Worse, or only occurs, in evenings
  - √ Worse lying down, relief with walking
  - √ Responds best to benzodiazepines, L-dopa, or bromocriptine.
- Management
  - √ Lower dose.
  - √ Treat with propranolol, amantadine, or benzodiazepine.
  - √ Anticholinergic agents are less effective.

Parkinsonism
- In parkinsonism tremor, the fingers, hands, and wrists move faster and as a unit; micrographia also appears.
- Physical symptoms and signs include:
  - √ Akinesia
    - □ Often the first sign
  - √ Decreased arm swing
  - √ Stiffness, stooped posture
  - √ Masklike face, bradykinesia
  - √ Shuffling, festinating gait (with small steps)
  - √ Cogwheel rigidity
  - √ Drooling, seborrhea
  - √ Tremor
    - □ The most common form is "postural tremor" (vs. resting tremor seen mostly in Parkinson's disorder).
  - √ Coarse pill-rolling of thumb and fingers at rest

- In older adults, check for signs of parkinsonism *before* treatment with antipsychotic.
  - √ The elderly are at most risk of parkinsonism (up to 75%).
    - ▫ 50% of elderly "parkinsonized" within 24 hours with low-dose, low-potency antipsychotic (e.g., chlorpromazine 50 mg).
  - √ Shuffling gait, stooped posture, bradykinesia, increased extremity tone, and decreased facial mobility are common baseline signs in this population.
- Parkinsonism contributes to inactivity (which can be misdiagnosed as catatonia), withdrawn and negative symptoms, schizophrenia, and depression.
- Management
  - √ Lower dose.
  - √ Switch to lower-risk agent (e.g., SGAs).
    - ▫ For example, risperidone, 1–6 mg qd.
  - √ Add anticholinergic agent.
  - √ Add amantadine.

Akinesia

- Symptoms include:
  - √ Paucity of spontaneous gestures or voluntary useful movements
  - √ Apathy
  - √ Rigid posture
  - √ Diminished (or total lack of) conversation
  - √ Arm swing decreased
  - √ Shorter stride walking
- May or may not be associated with parkinsonism.
  - √ Sedation 12 h after last dose suggests akinesia.
  - √ Absence of leg crossing also indicates akinesia.
- Management
  - √ Lower antipsychotic dose.
  - √ Add ACA drug or amantadine, if needed.

Neuroleptic malignant syndrome (NMS)

- Uncommon yet potentially fatal unless recognized and treated early.
- NMS affects 0.2–0.5% of patients treated with antipsychotics.
- Typical erupts in 24–72 h.
- Deaths, which usually occur within 3–30 days, occur in 10–20% of NMS patients.
  - √ Prior NMS episodes are a significant risk factor for future episodes.
    - ▫ About 17% of NMS patients have experienced a similar episode.
- Recurrence of NMS drops to 15% when low-potency FGAs are used and is probably lower, but still exists, when SGAs are prescribed.

Anticholinergic syndrome symptoms not seen in NMS (*see also* pp. 52–54 for further anticholinergic side effects).

- Dry skin
- Pupil dilation
- Hyperreflexia
- Muscle relaxation

Hyperthermia from drugs (e.g., lidocaine, meperidine, NSAID toxicity) or endocrinopathy (e.g., hyperthyroidism)

- No muscle effects

Autonomic hyperreflexia from CNS stimulants (e.g., amphetamine) not seen in NMS

- Hyperreflexia

A summary of the well-supported risk factors for NMS includes the following:

- Patients under 20 and over 60 y.o.
- Male sex
- Prior episodes of NMS
- High antipsychotics doses (e.g., > 600 mg chlorpromazine)
- Rapid dosage increase
- Depot antipsychotic agents (generate more symptoms of NMS but same number of deaths)
- High-potency antipsychotics

A summary of the potential risk factors for NMS includes the following:

- History of ECT
- Simultaneous use of lithium
  √ Risk factor may be bipolar mood disorder and not lithium itself.
- Low serum iron
  √ Cause vs. effect of NMS not resolved.
- High ambient temperatures
  √ More often in summer
- Dehydration
- Agitation
- Need for restrait

Fatalities from NMS, in percentage of patients who developed NMS on a specific FGA, are:

- Trifluoperazine (43%)
- Chlorpromazine (40%)
- Thiothixene (40%)
- Fluphenazine (depot) (33.3%)
- Fluphenazine (8.3%)
- Haloperidol (5.5%)
- Thioridazine (0%)

Supportive measures must be instituted immediately:

- Stop antipsychotic and anticholinergic agents.
- Maintain hydration by oral or IV routes.
- Correct electrolyte abnormalities.

- Use antipyretic agents.
- Cool body to reduce fever.
- Diagnose and treat pneumonia or pulmonary emboli.
- No drug treatment has been proven to be more effective than intensive supportive measures.
- One study compared supportive care with supportive care plus dantrolene alone, bromocriptine alone, or dantrolene–bromocriptine combined.
  √ All treatments showed improvement within 2–4 days after antipsychotics was stopped.
  √ Duration of NMS with supportive treatment was 5–14 days.
  √ Duration of NMS with drug treatments was longer, averaging 14 days.
    □ 20% lasted 4 weeks or more.
    □ 30% of bromocriptine-treated patients had recurrence of NMS signs when bromocriptine reduced.
- For patients not markedly better after a few days of intensive supportive treatment, consider drug treatments, including:
  √ Bromocriptine
    □ Safest drug treatment for NMS.
    □ Rigidity quickly disappears.
    □ Temperature, BP instability, and creatine kinase levels normalize after a few days.
    □ Failing bromocriptine, consider amantadine.
  √ Dantrolene
    □ Lowers hyperthermia and creatine kinase, while increasing muscle relaxation, often in hours.
    □ Initial dose may be 2–3 mg/kg/day.
    □ Hepatic toxicity occurs with doses > 10 mg/kg/day.
  √ Carbamazepine (CBZ)
    □ Reported effective within 8 h after first dose of 600 mg followed by 200 mg tid.
    □ Dose later titrated to establish therapeutic CBZ level.
  √ ECT has been successful, especially in the post-NMS patient.
- ACAs usually do not help and risk hyperthermia.
- Failing reasonable trial(s), consider plasmapheresis for NMS.
  √ When patient has recently had a decanoate preparation, consider plasmapheresis.

Antipsychotic rechallenge after prior NMS:

- High (> 80%) success rates reported.
- Best chances of success (no NMS) with
  √ 2-week or more wait after the last clinical sign of NMS.
  √ Start with low doses and very gradually increase.
    □ Low-potency antipsychotics may be safer.
    □ SGAs—for example, olanzapine (10–20 mg) or risperidone (2–5 mg) and especially clozapine (25–250 mg)—have significantly lower NMS rates and are therefore first choices for patients with h/o NMS.
  √ Plentiful hydration
  √ Cool room temperatures

√ Monitor temperature and other vital signs frequently.
√ Check WBC and CPK regularly.

Drugs Used to Treat NMS

Generic Name	Dose
Anticholinergic agents	
Bromocriptine	7.5–60 mg/day po
Dantrolene	0.8–10 mg/kg/IV; 50 mg qd–qid po
Levodopa	100 mg bid po
Carbidopa–levodopa	25 mg tid, 200 mg qid po
Amantadine	100 mg bid or tid po
Lorazepam	1.5–2 mg IV, then po

Paresthesia
• Burning paresthesia reported with risperidone.
   √ Seen more often on hands and feet.
   √ Severity dose-related.
   √ Incidence ~2%.

"Rabbit syndrome"
• Perioral tremor
• Arises late during antipsychotic treatment.
   √ Consists of rapid lip (typically a 5 Hz tremor) and buccal masticatory movements that mimic a rabbit.
• Sometimes mistaken for TD but unlike TD.
   √ Usually decreases with lower dose (whereas TD may increase).
   √ Does not involve tongue.
   √ Continues during sleep.
• Responds well to ACAs.
• Stops when antipsychotic is stopped.

Sedation
• Sedation declines during first 2 weeks of therapy.
• Management
   √ Prescribe full dose at bedtime.
   √ Diminish daytime doses.
   √ Switch to less sedation antipsychotics.
• Some impairment may be related to dopamine blockade.
   √ Increasing cognitive impairment seen.
   √ In one study nicotine transdermal patches reversed impairment.

Tardive dyskinesia
• Consists of involuntary face, trunk, and/or limb movements.
• Presents with three major types of symptoms.
   √ *Facial–lingual–oral involuntary hyperkinesis* (first appearance of TD and most common):
      ▫ Frowning, blinking, smiling, grimacing, puckering, pouting, blowing, smacking, licking, chewing, clenching, mouth opening, rolling and protruding ("fly catcher's") tongue, and spastic facial distortions.

√ *Limb choreoathetoid movements:*
  □ Choreiform movements that are rapid, purposeless, irregular, and spontaneous.
  □ Athetoid movements that are slow, irregular, complex, and serpentine.
  □ Tremors that are repetitive, regular, and rhythmic.
  □ Lateral knee movements.
  □ Foot tapping, squirming, inversion, and eversion.

√ *Trunk movements:*
  □ Movements of neck, shoulders, and dramatic hip jerks.
  □ Rocking, twisting, squirming, pelvic gyrations, and thrusts.

• TD patients
  √ May grunt.
  √ May suppress symptoms temporarily by intense voluntary effort and concentration.
  √ Evince movement disorders in toes, requiring shoeless examination.
  √ Often exhibit disappearance of TD symptoms while asleep.
  √ Experience exacerbation under stress.

• TD typically arises after 6–36 months of antipsychotics treatment.
  √ Initially appears milder in people on larger antipsychotics doses, which mask TD.
  √ Typically appears or worsens when antipsychotics are lowered or stopped, but often seen while still on full antipsychotic dose.

Drug-induced TD

• All antipsychotics can cause TD.
• SGAs have much lower TD risk.
  √ FGAs with 5–10% of patients per year at risk.
  √ Risperidone has lower risk in < 6 mg qd doses, with 0.34–0.5% of patients per year at risk.
  √ Olanzapine has similar risk, 0.52% per year.
  √ Quetiapine has low risk (0–3%) for, and may decrease, TD.
• Drug-induced rate may be lower than suspected because spontaneous dyskinesias occur in up to 15–20% of individuals with chronic never-treated schizophrenia.
  √ Risk factors for spontaneous dyskinesia include:
    □ Prominent negative symptoms, deficit form of schizophrenia
    □ Lower premorbid IQ
    □ Hebephrenic subtype (46% prevalence)
    □ Cigarettes and cannabis use
• Frequency varies enormously among studies.
  √ Probably closest to 15% (over spontaneous dyskinesia rate) in patients treated with antipsychotics for over 2 years.
    □ About 50% of these are reversible.
  √ Most cases are mild.
  √ 2–5% of patients get severe symptoms.
  √ Once TD syndrome manifests, it doesn't usually progress.
  √ Dyskinesia affects 1–5% of individuals without schizophrenia who have *never* been exposed to antipsychotics.

Antipsychotic-induced TD risk factors include:

• More interruptions in antipsychotics treatment.
• Longer use and higher dose equivalents of antipsychotics.
• Female patients over 40 y.o.
• Male patients over 30 y.o.
• Mood disorder
  √ May be due to intermittent antipsychotics use.
• African ethnicity
• Older age
• Brain impairment/mental retardation
• Diabetes (2x higher)
• Prior movement disorder symptoms
  √ However, TD can occur when EPS has never occurred.
• Make sure "TD" does not stem from ill-fitting dentures!

Prevention of TD

• Regularly monitor patients on antipsychotics with a standardized TD assessment scale, such as the Abnormal Involuntary Movement Scale (AIMS).
• Antipsychotics should not be used longer than 6 continuous months in patients without schizophrenia and who do not have chronic psychotic symptoms or significant risk of relapse.
• Assess long-treated patients at least every 6 months to see if antipsychotics can be reduced or stopped.
  √ Reduction is usually the most likely alternative, since long-treated patients rarely do well when off antipsychotics.
• If antipsychotic discontinued and TD emerges, allow at least 3–7 months for symptoms to disappear or lessen on their own.
  √ Spontaneous remission rate in 6 months about 50%.
  √ After 6 months spontaneous remission rate for 10 years about 2.5–5% a year.
  √ After 18 months, abnormal movements diminish by mean of 50%.
• ACAs do not usually alleviate TD and often aggravate it.
• Antipsychotics can temporarily mask TD, but symptoms eventually reemerge, frequently worse.

Agents for treating TD

• Vitamin E 1200–1600 mg qd
  √ Strongest evidence of efficacy, particularly in cases with TD under 5 years.
  √ Approximately 50% have clinically significant improvement.
  √ Not curative—symptoms may return within 12 weeks after Vitamin E discontinued.
  √ Minimal efficacy in TD > 5 years duration.
• Ondansetron
  √ May reduce TD.
  √ 30 inpatients with schizophrenia (mean age 69) with mild or worse TD that had persisted 3–45 years.

    □ Patients treated with 4–8 mg of ondansetron daily for 4 weeks.

    □ Mean reduction in total AIMS was 45%, and four patients showed a reduction of 50% or more.

    □ Significant improvement in the Positive and Negative Symptom Scale (PANSS).

  √ Another study with 6-week duration and 12 mg/day of ondansetron had "solid" results.

- Other drugs that might inhibit TD but lacking convincing evidence:

  √ Amantadine (100 mg bid–tid)—15% average improvement in very chronic (most > 5 yrs.) population, some with 25% improvement.

  √ Baclofen (5–20 mg tid)

  √ Benzodiazepines (e.g., diazepam, clonazepam)

  √ Bromocriptine (2.5 mg/day) helped in placebo-controlled trial.

    □ Perhaps by preferentially stimulating autoreceptors.

  √ Buspirone (45–120 mg/day)

  √ Calcium channel blockers

    □ Verapamil (16–320 mg qd), diltiazem (120–240 mg qd)

  √ Carbamazepine (100–800 mg/day)

  √ Choline (2–8 g/day)

  √ Lecithin (10–40 g/day)

  √ Levodopa (100–2000 mg/day)

  √ Lithium (300 mg tiq–qid)

  √ Reserpine (1–6 mg/day)

  √ Valproic acid (1000–1500 mg/day)

  √ Vitamin B6 (up to 200 mg bid)

  √ Tarvil (a long-branch amino acid that decreases phenylalanine in the brain)

ENDOCRINE EFFECTS

Prolactin elevation

- Increased blood prolactin can occur with all FGAs.
- Elevated prolactin may produce:

  √ Amenorrhea, menstrual irregularities, delayed ovulation

  √ Breast enlargement and tenderness in both women and men (gynecomastia)

  √ Breast cancer growth increased.

    □ In approximately one-third of breast cancers, increased prolactin increases growth rate.

    □ Changed to a lower-risk antipsychotic (i.e., clozapine, olanzapine, quetiapine).

  √ Galactorrhea

  √ Diminished libido

  √ Osteoporosis

- Management

  √ Bromocriptine, which inhibits prolactin secretion, comes in 2.5 mg tablets or 5 mg capsules.

    □ Start at 1.25–2.5 mg/day.

    □ Add 2.5 mg q 3–7 days as tolerated.

    □ Until optimal dose of 5–7.5 mg/day is reached, or

    □ The therapeutic range of 2.5–15 mg/day is satisfied.

- Bromocriptine occasionally worsens psychoses.
  - √ Amantadine sometimes can substitute.

Priapism
- Occurs more often with α_1-adrenergic blockade (e.g., low-potency antipsychotics).

EYES, EARS, NOSE, AND THROAT EFFECTS

Blurred vision
- Difficulty with close vision, not distance.
  - √ Most often an anticholinergic side effect.
- Management
  - √ Pilocarpine 1% eye drops, or
  - √ Bethanechol 5–30 mg po effective for 2–8 h.
  - √ Eye glasses can be used temporarily, but they need frequent changing.

Dry bronchial secretions and strained breathing
- Aggravate patients with respiratory disorder.

Dry eyes
- This anticholinergic disturbance particularly bothers older adults or those wearing contact lenses.
- Management
  - √ Artificial tears
    - □ Employ cautiously with soft contact lenses, or
    - □ Apply patient's usual wetting solution or comfort drops.
  - √ Bethanechol 5–30 mg po.

Narrow-angle glaucoma
- Highly anticholinergic antipsychotics can trigger narrow-angle glaucoma.
- A h/o eye or facial pan, blurred vision, or halos circling outside lights suggest acute narrow-angle glaucoma.
  - □ When shining a penlight across the eye's anterior chamber, if the entire eye does not illuminate, suspect narrow-angle glaucoma.

Nasal congestion, dry throat

Photophobia
- Pupils dilated by anticholinergic effects.

Pigmentation
- Long-term antipsychotics use, especially chlorpromazine, places granular deposits chiefly in the back of the cornea and the front of the lens.
- Star-shaped opacities in front of the lens indicate a more advanced case.
- Pigmentation probably dose-dependent.
- Vision usually unimpaired.
  - √ Eye pigmentation often coexists with antipsychotic-induced skin pigmentation or photosensitivity reactions.

• Eye pigmentation dose not require slit-lamp examination,
  √ But if shining a light into the eye displays an opaque pupil, patient should consult ophthalmologist.

Pigmentary retinopathy
• Caused almost always by chronic use of > 800 mg/day of thioridazine.
• Causes reduced visual acuity and blindness.
• Management
  √ Stop thioridazine.
  √ Symptoms may disappear if caught early.
  √ *Never prescribe* > 800 mg/day of thioridazine.

Hallucinations
• Visual
• Auditory

GASTROINTESTINAL EFFECTS

Allergic obstructive hepatitis
• This cholestatic jaundice is much less common now than when chlorpromazine (and its impurities) was introduced.
• Occurs in < 0.1% of patients in first month of treatment.
• Rarely leads to hepatic necrosis or permanent damage.
• Reversible if drug stopped.
• Routine LFTs do not predict.
• Lower risk with higher-potency antipsychotics.

Anorexia, nausea, vomiting, dyspepsia

Constipation
• Management
  √ Increase bulk (e.g., bran, salads) and fluids (e.g., water, milk).
  √ Improve diet (e.g., prunes).
  √ Add stool softener (e.g., docusate), fiber (e.g., psyllium), or
  √ Bethanechol 10–50 mg tid–qid.

Dry mouth
• Management
  √ Use sugar-free gum and sugarless candy to reduce dental cavities, thrush, and weight gain.
  √ Make use of cool drinks (minimal sugar, e.g., Gatorade, or drinks with sugar substitues).
  √ Biotène—sugar-free cool mints
  √ Ice chips
  √ Frequent brushing
  √ Wash mouth with
    ▫ Pilocarpine 1% solution, or
    ▫ Gradually dissolve cholinergic agonist bethanechol 5–10 mg tablets.

Diarrhea (occasionally)

Excessive salivation

Hepatic transaminase enzymes
• Mild transient increase seen with many FGAs.

Paralytic ileus

Weight gain
• Usually due to increased appetite and decreased activity.
• More common with chlorpromazine and thioridazine.

Weight loss
• Molindone does not cause significant weight gain.
  √ Molindone average weight loss at 100 mg dose is 4.8 lbs in 2 months.

HEMATOLOGIC EFFECTS

Agranulocytosis (Schultz syndrome)
• Agranulocytosis is a granulocyte count (polys 4 bands) $< 500/mm^3$.
• Occurs suddenly, often within hours, usually in the first month of treatment, but can erupt any time during the initial 12 weeks of therapy.
• Arises in $< 0.02\%$ of patients on antipsychotics.
• Results most frequently with chlorpromazine (0.7%).
  √ $<1\%$ with frequent monitoring.
  √ Extremely rarely with high-potency antipsychotics.
• Statistically more frequent in white females over 40 y.o.
• Common signs and symptoms are
  √ Acute sore throat
  √ High fever
  √ Mouth sores and ulcers
• Also possible are
  √ Upset stomach
  √ Weakness, lethargy, malaise
  √ Lymphadenopathy
  √ Asthma
  √ Skin ulcerations
  √ Laryngeal, angioneurotic, or peripheral edema
  √ Anaphylactic reactions
• Management
  √ Do not start any patient on low-potency antipsychotics if WBC is < 3000–$3500/mm^3$.
  √ With onset of sore throat and fever, *stop* all non-life-sustaining drugs (e.g., antipsychotics).
  √ Routine or frequent CBCs do not help.
• Treatment of agranulocytosis
  √ Hematopoietic growth factors—granulocyte colony stimulating factor and granulocyte–macrophage colony stimulating factor (GM CSF), given 48 h after onset.
    □ Both accelerate recovery in mean of 8 days.

Leukopenia
- WBC 2000–3500/mm^3
- Usually gradual and without symptoms, and
- More common than agranulocytosis.
  - √ Usually transient.
- Management
  - √ Symptoms may be similar to agranulocytosis.
  - √ If no symptoms and not severe, wait and repeat labs.
  - √ May be prevented with lithium addition if mainly neutropenia.
  - √ If more severe, reduce or stop antipsychotic.

RENAL EFFECTS

Polydipsia and hyponatremia
- Polydipsia (compulsive water drinking) frequently occurs in chronic schizophrenia, particularly during psychotic exacerbations.
  - √ 25–50% of patients with polydipsia develop hyponatremia.
  - √ 3–5% of patients with chronic schizophrenia are hyponatremic and may experience episodes of life-threatening water intoxication accompanied by impaired water excretion, usually related to inappropriate antidiuretic hormone secretion.
- Signs and symptoms of acute water intoxication include lethargy, nausea, confusion, blurred vision, vomiting, ataxia, myoclonus, cramps, large diurnal weight gain, and seizures.
- Water intoxication can cause delirium, seizures, coma, irreversible neurological deficits, and death.
  - √ Usually seen with acute water intoxication and < 120 nmol sodium.
  - √ Chronic cases may experience headache, constant thirst, anorexia, and excretional dyspnea.
- Detection of self-induced water intoxication includes:
  - √ Consumption of water > 3–4 liters qd.
  - √ Greater than a 3–5% weight gain from A.M. to P.M.
  - √ Urine-specific gravity < 1.01.
- Management
  - √ Fluid restriction—usually too difficult to enforce.
  - √ Furosemide
  - √ Salt tablets
  - √ Demeclocycline 600–1200 mg qd

Urinary hesitancy or retention
- Urinary retention increases risk of urinary tract infections, which require periodic urinalyses and cultures. Urinary retention
  - √ Occurs equally often in males and females.
  - √ Usually caused by anticholinergic effects.
- Management
  - √ Reduce anticholinergic exposure by moving to less anticholinergic antipsychotics and switching to amantadine or propanolol if on an anticholinergic for movement disorder.

√ Prescribe bethanechol 10–25 mg tid–qid or 5–10 mg qd until symptom abates.

√ May prescribe IM/SC bethanechol 5–10 mg for more serious cases.

SEXUAL EFFECTS

Retrograde ejaculation/erectile dysfunction
- May be physically painful.
- Occurs with patients on all antipsychotics, but especially common with thioridazine.
- Management
  - √ Cyproheptadine 2–8 mg po prn 2 hours before intercourse or tid to allow spontaneous sex.
  - √ Yohimbine 2.7–8.1 mg prn 2 hours before intercourse or tid to allow spontaneous sex.
    - □ Yohimbine (5 mg tid) may reduce impotence.
    - □ May aggravate psychosis.
  - √ Amantadine 100–400 mg qd.
  - √ Bupropion 75–225 mg day in divided doses.
    - □ May aggravate psychosis.

SKIN, ALLERGIES, AND TEMPERATURE

Hypothermia more common than hyperthermia
- Management
  - √ Warn patients in advance so they can protect themselves.
  - √ Proper heated (or cooled environment).
  - √ Avoid overexercising or working in hot places.
  - √ Ensure adequate hydration.

Decreased sweating
- May cause a secondary, and sometimes fatal, hyperthermia.
- Be careful with patients who
  - √ Work in hot weather.
  - √ Take antipsychotics with high anticholinergic effects.
  - √ Drink excessive alcohol.
  - √ Suffer from CNS disease

Photosensitivity
- Chlorpromazine and other antipsychotics foster severe sunburn after 30–60 minutes of direct sunlight.

Skin rashes
- Seborrheic dermatitis highly associated with parkinsonian signs.
- Management
  - √ Treat with appropriate soaps, lotions, and shampoos.
  - √ Check nature and distribute to exclude contact dermatitis.
  - √ Stop antipsychotic if not contact dermatitis.

Drug and Food Interactions

Drug Interactions with First-Generation Antipsychotics

Drug (X) Interacts with:	First-Generation Antipsychotics (A)[a]	Comments
Anesthetic (general)	X↑	CNS depression, hypotension
Antiarrhythmic (e.g., quinidine)	X↑ A↑	Increased quinidine-like effects with dysrhythmias, especially phenothiazines
Anticholinergic	X↑	Added anticholinergic effect. Consider amantadine; variable effects seen on metabolism, plasma level, and efficacy of antipsychotic.
Anticoagulant (warfarin)	X↑ A↑	Increased PT ratio or INR response with haloperidol
Anticonvulsant	X↑	Increased level of carbamazepine and metabolite with loxapine and haloperidol
Antidepressant		
MAO inhibitor	X↓	Hypotension may result; MAO inhibitors may trigger movement disorder.
SSRI	A↑	May increase EPS and plasma levels. Fluvoxamine least likely to increase antipsychotic level.
TCA	X↑ A↑	Possible toxicity or hypotension; TCAs may diminish movement disorders.
Antihypertensive	X↑	Increased hypotension, particularly with low-potency antipsychotics
β-blocker (e.g., propranolol)	X↑ A↑	Hypotension, toxicity, and seizures. Monitor serum levels; decrease dose.
Caffeine	A↓	Increased psychosis in high doses, 600–1000 mg
CNS depressant (e.g., alcohol, antihistamines, hypnotics)	X↑ A↑	CNS depression
Estrogen	A↑	Potentiates hyperprolactinemic effect.
Grapefruit juice	A↑	Increased plasma level of pimozide due to inhibited metabolism via CYP3A4. *Avoid*.
Lithium	X↑ A↑	Rarely causes movement disorders. Acute neurotoxicity at normal serum levels. Increased plasma level of molindone and haloperidol.
Nicotine	A↓	Decreased blood levels
Sympathomimetic (e.g., epinephrine, norepinephrine)	X↓	Hypotension

[a]↑ = increase; ↓ = decrease.

Special Populations

CHILDREN AND ADOLESCENTS

• Compared with adults, children and adolescents are especially vulnerable to adverse effects, including movement disorders, sedation, weight gain, and prolactin elevation.

• They should, therefore, be monitored on a consistent and frequent basis for any changes and encouraged to exercise as a means of intervention.

WOMEN: PREGNANCY AND POSTPARTUM

Pregnancy Rating   • Category C

Teratogenicity (1st trimester)   • No proven risk of increased anomalies.

                                • Low-potency phenothiazines may increase malformations if administered during weeks 4–10.

Direct Effect on Newborn (3rd trimester)	• Movement disorders (may last 6 months), excessive crying, hyperreflexia, hypertonicity, and vasomotor instability may occur.

• Neonatal jaundice may occur.

• Up to 18% of patients on chlorpromazine have had a marked fall in BP during last 10 days of pregnancy; this can harm both mother and newborn.

• Although chlorpromazine is usually safe during pregnancy, other antipsychotics are preferred.

Lactation • Present in breast milk in concentrations equal to plasma.

LATE LIFE

• Use only one antipsychotic agent at a time.
• Gradual dosage reduction should be attempted every 6 months after therapy begins.
  √ Target to the lowest possible dosage to control symptoms.
• Older adults are particularly vulnerable to the drug-induced movement disorders.
  √ Movement disorders can cause stiffness, immobility, and falls and are associated with significant morbidity.
  √ SGAs should be considered first choices in this older population.
• Drug interactions, especially those involving the cytochrome P450 system, must be considered.

Effects on Laboratory Tests

Effects of First-Generation Antipsychotics on Blood/Serum and Urine Tests

Generic Name[†]	Blood/Serum Tests		Urine Tests	
	Marker	Results[a]	Marker	Results[a]
Chlorpromazine	LFT[b]	↑	VMA	↓
	Glucose	↑↓	Urobilinogen	↑
Fluphenazine	LFT	↑	VMA	↓
	Cephaline Flocculation	↑	Urobilinogen	↑
Haloperidol	Only prolactin		None	
Loxapine	LFT	↑	None	
Molindone	LFT	↑		
	Eosinophils	↑		
	Leukocytes	↓		
	Fatty acids	↑		
Perphenazine	Glucose, PBI	↑↑	Pregnancy test	False ↓
Thioridazine	None			
Thiothixene	LFT	↑	None	
	Uric acid	↓		
Trifluoperazine	LFT	↑	VMA	↓
	Glucose	↑↓	Urobilinogen	↑

[a]↑ = increases; ↓ = decreases; ↑↓ = increases and decreases.
[b]LFT = liver function tests (AST/SGOT, ALT/SGPT, alkaline phosphatase, bilirubin, and LDH); PBI = protein bound iodine; VMA = vanillylmanaelic acid.
[†]All can elevate prolactin.

Discontinuation

- Abrupt cessation of high doses may produce:
  √ Flu-like symptoms without a fever
  √ Insomnia and nightmares
  √ Gastritis, nausea, vomiting, diarrhea
  √ Headaches
  √ Diaphoresis, increased sebaceous secretion, restlessness, and general physical complaints
  √ Supersensitivity psychosis (acute relapse) has been described after acute withdrawal in some patients.
- These symptoms
  √ Begin 2–4 days after discontinuation and may persist up to 2 weeks.
  √ Can cease by reducing the dose gradually over 1–2 weeks.
- Tardive neurological symptoms may emerge.
- A transient withdrawal dyskinesia also may arise occasionally.
  √ Withdrawal dyskinesia resembles a tardive dyskinesia with abnormal movements of the neck, face, and mouth.
  √ Antiparkinsonian drugs do not relieve it.
  √ Withdrawal dyskinesia stops with
    □ Re-establishing maintenance antipsychotic dose, and
    □ Reducing antipsychotics more gradually (1–3 months).

Overdose: Toxicity, Suicide, and Treatment

- Antipsychotic drug overdose is associated with low morbidity and mortality.
- Fatal overdose more common with less potent FGAs (e.g., chlorpromazine).
  √ The therapeutic index ranges from
    □ 25–200 for low-potency phenothiazines, to
    □ > 1,000 for high-potency piperazines and haloperidol.
- Symptoms of toxicity are extensions of common adverse effects: anticholinergic, extrapyramidal, and CNS stimulation followed by CNS depression.
- Postural hypotension may evolve into shock, coma, cardiovascular insufficiency, myocardial infarction, or arrhythmias.
- Convulsions appear late.
- Management
  √ Obtain ECG, temperature, vital signs, and, if needed, establish an airway.
  √ Arousal may not occur for 48 h.
  √ Observe awake patient for 8–12 h after ingestion.
  √ Ascertain other drugs ingested during past 2–10 days.
  √ Speak soon with family or friends who might afford life-saving information.
  √ Begin gastric lavage as soon as possible.
    □ Before initiating gastric lavage, employ cuffed endotracheal intubation to prevent aspiration and pulmonary complications.
    □ Stop convulsions before passing stomach tube.

√ Avoid emetic because an acute dystonic reaction of the head or neck could cause aspiration.

√ Lavage best if overdose transpired within 4 h, yet it can remove drugs consumed 24–36 h earlier.

√ *After* lavage, supply activated charcoal (40–50 g in adults, 20–25 g in children) by mouth or through lavage tube to prevent further absorption.

√ Loss of consciousness can be reversed with stimulants.

  □ Use amphetamine, dextroamphetamine, or caffeine with sodium benzoate.
  □ Avoid drugs that can cause convulsions (e.g., picrotoxcin or pentylene tetrazol).

√ If hypotension is present, place patient in Trendelenburg's position while saline is infused.

  □ *Do not use epinephrine;* may result in lower blood pressure.

√ Treat seizures with IV diazepam.

  □ Avoid barbiturates due to risk of respiratory depression.
  □ Avoid pentylenetrazol, picrotoxin, and bemegride.

Precautions

• Hypotension occurs most with parenteral use, especially with high doses.
• Use antipsychotics cautiously with
  √ Narrow-angle glaucoma
  √ Prostatic hypertrophy
  √ Bone marrow depression blood dyscrasias
  √ Parkinson's disease
  √ Antipsychotic hypersensitivity
  √ Extreme hypotension or hypertension
  √ Acutely ill children (e.g., chickenpox, measles, Reye's syndrome, gastroenteritis, dehydration)
    □ Increased movement disorders, particularly dystonias and akathisias
    □ Increased hepatotoxicity risk
  √ Elderly who have
    □ Hepatic disease
    □ Cardiovascular illness (especially low-potency)
    □ Chronic respiratory disease
    □ Hypoglycemia
    □ Seizures (especially low-potency)
• Prior to prescribing thioridazine or pimozide, a baseline ECG and serum potassium should be done, and monitored periodically during the course of therapy.
  √ *Do not use* these agents in patients with QT_c interval > 450 ms.

Key Points to Communicate to Patients and Families

Patient and family should notify doctor if

• Patient has a sore throat during first several months of treatment.

- NMS appears.
- Patient is having general or dental surgery.

Tell patients and families:

- Antipsychotics treat psychotic symptoms, including hallucinations, delusions, confused thinking, paranoia, and oversensitivity to stimuli.
  - √ Many patients who deny that their symptoms are psychotic will try antipsychotic medication to treat insomnia, poor concentration, overworrying (paranoia), and/or short temper.
- Particularly if on low-potency antipsychotic, patients may have
  - √ Anticholinergic side effects (e.g., dry mouth, constipation, blurred vision, fuzzy thinking)
  - √ Sedation that should wear off and can help with sleep and anxiety
  - √ Low blood pressure with dizziness when standing up
  - √ May see similar symptoms on high- or mid-potency antipsychotics.
- The three main forms of movement disorders are
  - √ Dystonia, a sudden and often sustained pull of a muscle group
  - √ Akathisia, a feeling of physical (not necessarily mental) restlessness
  - √ Parkinsonism, involving stiff muscles, slowed movements, tremor, and drooling
- TD not necessarily discussed during acute treatment phase while patient actively psychotic.
  - √ TD won't occur in that phase and there is no assurance that drug will be taken chronically.
- Discuss TD *before* 3 months of antipsychotics treatment elapse.
  - √ Best to do it when patient and physician are beginning a chronic course of treatment.
  - √ Inform patients that they will be evaluated for TD annually (e.g., AIMS).
- When starting antipsychotics, carefully drive cars, work around machines, and cross streets.

Patient initially should check for psychomotor impairments.

- May drink alcohol with antipsychotics, but "one drink often feels like two drinks."
- Avoid overexposure to sun; use sunscreen.
- Do not keep medication at bedside to avoid accidental ingestion.
  - √ Keep safely away from children.
- If forget a dose, patient can take up to 3 h late, but
  - √ If more than 3–4 h late, wait for next scheduled dose.
  - √ Do not double the dose.
- Do not suddenly stop medication.
  - √ Even if there is no immediate return of symptoms, there is a very high risk of relapse in the weeks and months after medication has been stopped.

SECOND-GENERATION ANTIPSYCHOTICS

Dosing, Dose Form, and Color

Profile of Second-Generation Antipsychotics

Generic Names	Therapeutic Dose Range (mg/day)	Geriatric Dose (mg/day)	Dose Form (mg)[a]	Color
BENZISOXAZOLE				
Risperidone	t: 2–6 p: 25–50 mg q 2 wk	t: 0.5–4	t: 1/2/3/4 p: 25/37.5/50 mg/vial	t: white/orange/ yellow/green
Paliperidone	3–12		t: 3/6/9	t: white/beige/pink
DIBENZODIAZEPINE				
Clozapine	300–900	100–400	t: 25/100	t: all yellow
DIBENZOTHIAZEPINE				
Quetiapine	300–800+	50–300	t: 25/100/200/300 sr: 200/300/400	t: peach/yellow/ white round/white capsule sr: yellow/pale yellow/white
Ziprasidone	20–40	20–80	c: 20/40/60/80	c: blue/white– blue/blue–white/ white–blue–white
DIHYDROCARBOSTYRIL				
Aripiprazole	10–30		t: 2/5/10/15/20/30	t: green/blue/pink/ yellow/white/pink
THIENOBENZODIAZEPINE				
Olanzapine	10–20	3–15	t: 2.5/5/7.5/10/15 t: 5/10	t: white (2.5–10 mg)/blue (15 mg) t: yellow (orally distintegrating)

[a]c = capsule; p = parenteral concentrate; sr = sustained-release spansules; t = tablets.

Pharmacology

PHARMACOKINETICS

- The pharmacokinetics of SGAs are similar to those of first-generation (*see* pp. 3–4).
- Aripiprazole and its active metabolite dehydroaripiprazole have exceptionally long half-lives of 75 and 94 hours, respectively.
  - √ Steady-state concentrations are achieved after 14 days.
- Quetiapine and ziprasidone have shorter half-lives, which suggest twice-daily administration.
  - √ However, with repeated dosing the pharmacodynamic effects may extend beyond the period, allowing the consolidation of dosing to once daily.

- Among the SGAs, olanzapine and ziprasidone are available in a parenteral form for acute use in agitated patients, giving the benefits of a more rapid onset of action and the ability to bypass the extensive first-pass metabolism that these agents undergo.
- Risperidone is also available in long-acting injectable form to allow for less fluctuation in plasma level compared to oral formulations.

Pharmacokinetic Properties of Second-Generation Antipsychotics

Generic Names	Bioavailability (%)	Protein Binding (%)	Half-Life (h)	P450 Systems Substrate of	P450 Systems Inhibits	Excretion (%)[a]
Aripiprazole	87	99	75–94	3A4, 2D6		
Clozapine	50–60	95	5–16	1A2, 3A4, 2D6		50 R/30 F
Olanzapine	60	93	21–54	1A2, 2D6		57 R/30 F
Paliperidone	28	74	23	2D6, 3A4		80 R/11 F
Quetiapine	90 ± 9	83	6–7	3A4		73 R/20 F
Risperidone	70	90	20–24	2D6	2D6	70 R/15 F
Ziprasidone	60	99	7	3A4		20 R/66 F

[a]F = fecal; R = renal.

PHARMACODYNAMICS

- SGAs are distinguished as a class by
  - √ A higher ratio of 5-HT$_2$ to D$_2$ receptor blockade, and
  - √ Rapid dissociation from D$_2$ receptor (rate varies across agents).
- The combination of 5-HT$_{2A}$ and D$_2$ receptor blockade facilitates the release of dopamine in the limbic system, striatum, and prefrontal cortex.
  - √ This may explain the lower incidence of movement disorders while maintaining clinical effectiveness.
- SGAs have specific regional effects on DA receptors (e.g., selective blockade of A10 cells of the mesolimbic regions).
- Aripiprazole is currently the only antipsychotic that acts as a partial agonist at D$_2$ and 5-HT$_{1A}$ receptors and an antagonist at the 5-HT$_{2A}$ receptor.
- Quetiapine and ziprasidone block NE transporter.

Relative Neuroreceptor Affinities for Second-Generation Antipsychotics at Therapeutic Doses

Generic Names	D$_2$	H$_1$	α_1	α_2	5-HT$_{1A}$	5-HT$_{2A}$	5-HT$_{2C}$
Aripiprazole	++++	+	+	0	+++	+++	+++
Clozapine	+	+++	++++	+++	0	+++	+++
Olanzapine	++	+++	0	0	0	+++	+++
Quetiapine	+	++	+	0	0	0	0
Risperidone	+++	+	++	0	0	++++	++++
Ziprasidone	+++	+	+	+	+	++++	++++

Note. + to ++++ = low to marked affinity; 0 = minimal to none.

Clinical Indications

SCHIZOPHRENIA

- SGAs are effective in relieving both the positive and negative symptoms of schizophrenia.
- A majority of patients taking SGAs are likely to have
  √ Positive symptom improvement that tends to plateau at 3–6 months.
  √ Negative symptoms improve most rapidly in 2–3 months, with continued gradual improvement.
  √ Improved neuropsychological function
    □ Verbal memory (e.g., remembering instructions and names)
    □ Recognition of affect (e.g., ability to sense how another person feels)
    □ Executive function (e.g., ability to make plans)
    □ Reaction time (e.g., safety operating equipment)
    □ Attention (e.g., ability to stay on task or listen to others)
    □ Visuospatial memory (e.g., ability to remember how something appeared or where something should go)

BIPOLAR DISORDER

- SGAs are efficacious in the treatment of acute mania as monotherapy or combination therapy with lithium or valproate.
- Onset of therapeutic effect sooner than lithium.
- Olanzapine is used for maintenance treatment of bipolar disorder and, in a combination pill with fluoxetine, for treatment of patients with depressive episodes associated with bipolar disorder.
- Early data suggest that clozapine may help relieve severe or refractory symptoms of bipolar disorder and prevent recurrences of mania.

AGITATION AND AGGRESSIVE BEHAVIOR

- Intramuscular olanzapine is as efficacious as intramuscular haloperidol in reducing acute undifferentiated agitation.
  √ Olanzapine has a superior movement disorders safety profile to that of haloperidol and involves a very low risk of both acute dystonia and QT_c prolongation.
- The antiaggressive characteristics of clozapine are well established in chronically psychotic patients.
  √ However, clozapine initiation is contraindicated in the psychiatric emergency setting because of its serious potential side effects, including seizures and arganulocytosis.

Side Effects

ANTICHOLINERGIC EFFECTS

Anticholinergic actions affect many systems and produce a variety of symptoms:

- Hypotension
- Dry mouth

Adverse Events Associated with Second-Generation Antipsychotics Compared to First-Generation

Side Effects	First-Generation Agents	Aripiprazole	Clozapine	Olanzapine	Paliperidone	Quetiapine	Risperidone	Ziprasidone
CNS								
EPS	+ to +++	+	0	+	0	0	++	+
TD	+ to +++	+	0	+	0	0	++	+
NMS	+		+	+	0		+	+
Sedation	+ to +++	+	+++	++	+	+++	+	+
Seizures	0 to +	0 to +	+++	0 to +	0	0 to +	0	0 to +
CARDIOVASCULAR								
Myocarditis/ cardiomyopathy		0	0 to +	0	0	0	0	0
QT$_c$ prolongation	+ to +++	0	0	0	+	+	+	++
Hypotension	+ to ++	+	+++	++	0	++	+	+
Sinus Tachycardia	+ to +++	0	+++	++	+	++	+	+
METABOLIC								
Weight gain	+	0	+++	+++	+	+	+	0
Dyslipidemia	+	0	++	+++	+	+	+	0
HORMONAL								
Prolactin elevation	+++	0	0	0 to +	+++	0	+++	0 to +

Note. + to +++ = active to strongly active; 0 = minimal to none; EPS = extrapyramidal side effects; TD = tardive dyskinesia; NMS = neuroleptic malignant syndrome.

- Constipation
- Paralytic ileus
- Urinary hesitancy or retention
- Blurred near vision
- Dry eyes
- Narrow-angle glaucoma
- Photophobia
- Nasal congestion
- Confusion and decreased memory

Most anticholinergic symptoms decrease in 1–4 weeks but do not completely remit.

- Management
  - √ Bethanechol 10–50 mg po tid or qid can reverse peripheral but not central effects. Duration of action is 2–8 h.
  - √ Switching to a less anticholinergic antipsychotic and/or switching to a non-anticholinergic extrapyramidal drug (e.g., amantadine) can reduce or eliminate anticholinergic side effects.

CARDIOVASCULAR EFFECTS

Nonspecific ECG changes and arrythymia
- ECG changes reported with ziprasidone at higher doses but rarely with risperidone and quetiapine.
- Ziprasidone increased the QT_c interval by a mean of 10 msec at the 160 mg daily dosage.
  - √ Ziprasidone should be avoided in patients with QT prolongation, recent acute MI, uncompensated heart failure or cardiac arrhythmia, or if persistent QT_c measurements > 500 msec.
  - √ Patients with symptoms that could indicate the occurrence of torsade de pointes—e.g., dizziness, palpitations, or syncope—should receive further medical evaluation.

Orthostatic hypotension
- Syncope reported in 0.6% of patients treated with ziprasidone.
- Management
  - √ Suggest that patient stand up slowly over 15–60 seconds.
  - √ If more severe hypotension, lower head and elevate legs.
  - √ Use support stockings (since middle of the night is highest risk time, patient needs to wear hose day and night).
  - √ Use divided doses to avoid high blood levels.
  - √ Try dihydroergotamine.
  - √ If medically serious, employ volume expanders and, if necessary,
    - ▢ Alpha-adrenergic pressor agents, such as metaraminol, phenylephrine, or norepinephrine.
    - ▢ *Do not use epinephrine or isoproteronol.*
  - √ Fludrocortisone 0.1–0.2 mg/daily
    - ▢ *Check electrolyte and BP regularly.*

Tachycardia (> 100 beats/min)
- Especially common on clozapine.
  - √ Manage by lowering antipsychotic dose or changing antipsychotic.
  - √ If persists, treat with peripheral β-blocker or propafenone (antiarrhythmic).

CENTRAL NERVOUS SYSTEM EFFECTS

Extrapyramidal symptoms
- SGAs infrequently cause movement disorders and have significantly lower NMS rates.
- Switching to clozapine in antipsychotic-resistant patients with coexisting TD, parkinsonism, or akathisia can improve the movement disorder.
  - √ At mean final dose of 200 mg after 18 weeks, improvement rate was 50–74% for TD, 69% for parkinsonism, and 78% for chronic akathisia.
- Risperidone can cause movement disorders at lower doses in high-risk patients, including
  - √ Geriatric patients
  - √ Parkinson's patients

√ Adolescent patients
√ Bipolar patients on lithium
√ Patients on SSRIs
- Olanzapine can cause movement disorders in doses over 20 mg (especially in women), but symptoms usually mild.
- Tardive dyskinesia has been observed following risperidone and olanzapine treatment (~0.4–0.5% per year on med).
  √ However, patients with schizophrenia who have never been on a antipsychotic have a lifetime hazard for TD up to 15%.

Sedation
- Declines during first 2 weeks of therapy.
- Management
  √ Prescribe full dose at bedtime.
  √ Diminish daytime doses.
  √ Switch to less sedating antipsychotics.

Seizures
- Uncommon
- More common with clozapine.
  √ Dose-related:
    □ 1–2% with < 300 mg qd
    □ 3–4% with 300–500 mg qd
    □ 5% with 600–900 mg qd
  √ In patients on > 300 mg clozapine, 65% have abnormal EEGs.
  √ Increased risk with large single doses and/or rapid dose titration.
    □ Lower risk with tid or qid dosing.
    □ Lower risk with increased dosing of 12.5–25 mg every 2–4 days.
  √ Increased risk with high plasma levels (> 450 μg/ml).
    □ Obtain plasma levels in patients with high seizure risk.
- Management
  √ Reduce dose by half if possible.
  √ Get neurology consult.
  √ Get EEG.
  √ Begin valproate or other appropriate anticonvulsant.
    □ Do not use carbamazepine with clozapine.
  √ After blood level stabilized, increase clozapine 25 mg/day to desired dose.
  √ After 6 months wean anticonvulsant.

ENDOCRINE EFFECTS

Prolactin elevation
- Elevated prolactin may produce
  √ Amenorrhea, menstrual irregularities, delayed ovulation
    □ Risperidone may have the highest risk, with prolactin levels routinely as high as, or higher than, in patients on haloperidol.
  √ Breast enlargement and tenderness in both women and men (gynecomastia)
  √ Breast cancer growth increased.

□ In approximately one-third of breast cancers, increased prolactin increases growth rate.

□ Change to a lower-risk antipsychotic (i.e., clozapine, olanzapine, quetiapine).

√ Galactorrhea

√ Diminished libido

√ Osteoporosis

• Management

√ Bromocriptine, which inhibits prolactin secretion, comes in 2.5 mg tablets or as 5 mg capsules.

□ Start at 1.25–2.5 mg/day

□ Add 2.5 mg q 3–7 days as tolerated,

□ Until optimal dose of 5–7.5 mg/day is reached, or

□ The therapeutic range of 2.5–15 mg/day is satisfied.

• Bromocriptine occasionally worsens psychoses.

√ Amantadine sometimes can substitute.

Hyperglycemia, glycosuria, high or prolonged glucose tolerance tests

• Risk highest and greatest increases seen with clozapine and olanzapine.

• Disturbances in glucose metabolism increase the potential for hyperinsulinemia and peripheral insulin resistance.

• The development of diabetes has been reported to occur within 6 months after starting therapy.

Dyslipidemia

• Elevated levels of triglycerides and low-density lipoprotein as well as reduced levels of high-density lipoprotein reported.

• Increases the risk for cardiovascular disease and insulin resistance.

• Management

√ Lipid screening total cholesterol, low- and high-density lipoprotein cholesterol, and triglycerides at baseline and every 6 months thereafter.

Hypothyroidism

• Slight decrease in total T_3, total T_4, and free T_4 without increase of TSH.

Priapism

• Occurs more often with α_1-adrenergic blockade.

EYES, EARS, NOSE, AND THROAT EFFECTS

Blurred vision

• Difficulty with close vision, not distance.

√ Most often an anticholinergic side effect.

• Management

√ Pilocarpine 1% eye drops, or

√ Bethanechol 5–30 mg po effective for 2–8 h.

√ Eye glasses can be used temporarily, but they need frequent changing.

Dry bronchial secretions and strained breathing

• Aggravate patients with respiratory disorder.

A
N
T
I
P
S
Y
C
H
O
T
I
C
S

Dry eyes
- This anticholinergic disturbance particularly bothers older adults and those wearing contact lenses.
- Management
  - √ Artificial tears
    - □ Employ cautiously with soft contact lenses, or
    - □ Apply patient's usual wetting solution or comfort drops.
  - √ Bethanechol 5–30 mg po.

Narrow-angle glaucoma
- Highly anticholinergic antipsychotics can trigger narrow-angle glaucoma.
- A h/o eye or facial pain, blurred vision, or halos circling outside lights suggest acute narrow-angle glaucoma.
  - √ When shining a penlight across the eye's anterior chamber, if the entire eye does not illuminate, suspect narrow-angle glaucoma.

Nasal congestion, dry throat

Photophobia
- Pupils dilated by anticholinergic effects.

Hallucinations
- Visual
- Auditory

GASTROINTESTINAL EFFECTS

Allergic obstructive hepatitis
- Occurs in < 0.1% of patients in first month of treatment.
- Rarely leads to hepatic necrosis or permanent damage.
- Reversible if drug stopped.
- Routine LFTs do not predict.

Anorexia, nausea, vomiting, dyspepsia

Constipation
- Management
  - √ Increase bulk (e.g., bran, salads) and fluids (e.g., water, milk).
  - √ Improve diet (e.g., prunes).
  - √ Add stool softener (e.g., docusate), fiber (e.g., psyllium), or
  - √ Bethanechol 10–50 mg tid–qid.

Dry mouth
- Management
  - √ Sugar-free gum and sugarless candy to reduce dental cavities, thrush, and weight gain.
  - √ Cool drinks (minimal sugar, e.g., Gatorade, or drinks with sugar substitues).
  - √ Biotène—sugar-free cool mints
  - √ Ice chips

√ Frequent brushing
√ Wash mouth with
  □ Pilocarpine 1% solution, or
  □ Gradually dissolve cholinergic agonist bethanechol 5–10 mg tablets.

Diarrhea (occasionally)

Excessive salivation

Hepatic transaminase enzymes
• Mild transient increase.

Paralytic ileus

Weight gain
• Usually due to increased appetite and decreased activity.
• High risk with clozapine and olanzapine.
• Pooled results from monotherapy trials with olanzapine at 15 mg/day indicate a mean weight increase of 11.8 kg after 1 year of treatment.
• Management
  √ Check BMI every visit for 6 months, and quarterly thereafter.

HEMATOLOGIC EFFECTS

Agranulocytosis
• Most frequent with patients on clozapine (0.85–1.3%).
• High risk-groups/factors include:
  √ Women twice as often as men
  √ Lower baseline WBC counts
  √ Over 40 y.o. but may be under 21 y.o.
  √ Ashkenazi Jews with specific HLA haplotype.
  √ Co-administration of drugs at risk for agranulocytosis.
• Incidence on clozapine
  √ 0.75% first 6 months, 0.05% second 6 months, 0.06% third 6 months
  √ Should get labs, including agranulocytosis, weekly for 6 months and then decrease to biweekly if stable.
• Starting clozapine contraindicated if
  √ WBC $< 3500/m^3$ or neutrophils $< 1500/m^3$.
  √ These limitations include those with benign neutropenia, cancer chemotherapy, or HIV infection.
• Treatment of agranulocytosis
  √ Hematopoietic growth factors—that is, granulocyte colony stimulating factor and granulocyte–macrophage colony stimulating factor (GM CSF), given 48 h after onset.
  □ Both accelerate recovery in mean of 8 days.

Eosinophilia
• Occurs at 3–5 weeks after clozapine administration and usually disappears after 4 weeks.
  √ 10–60% of patients experience this.

√ Eosinophil may reach as high as 55% of total WBC count.

√ Clozapine should be stopped if eosinophils reach 1400/μl–3000/μl.

• Do not immediately switch to olanzapine, due to reports of prolonged (mean, 21 days) granulocytopenia in some patients.

Leukopenia
• WBC 2000–3500/mm^3
• 41% risk with clozapine
• Usually transient.
• Management
 √ Symptoms may be similar to agranulocytosis.
 √ If no symptoms and not severe, wait and repeat labs.
 √ May be prevented with lithium addition if mainly neutropenia.
 √ If more severe, reduce or stop antipsychotic.

RENAL EFFECTS

Polydipsia and hyponatremia
See page 20.

Urinary hesitancy or retention
See pages 20–21.

Urinary incontinence
• Incontinence develops in > 20% of patients 2 weeks to 7 months after starting clozapine.
 √ Associated with female gender and concomitant treatment with FGAs.
 √ A majority of cases spontaneously resolve.
 √ Alpha-adrenergic blockage probable cause.
 √ Rare with other antipsychotics.
• Management
 √ Ephedrine 25–150 mg/day.
 √ All incontinence resolves spontaneously early in treatment.

SEXUAL EFFECTS

Retrograde ejaculation/erectile dysfunction
• May be physically painful.
• Management
 √ Cyproheptadine 2–8 mg po prn 2 hours before intercourse or tid to allow spontaneous sex.
 √ Yohimbine 2.7–8.1 mg prn 2 hours before intercourse or tid to allow spontaneous sex.
  ▫ Yohimbine (5 mg tid) may reduce impotence.
  ▫ May aggravate pschosis.
 √ Amantadine 100–400 mg qd.
 √ Bupropion 75–225 mg a day, in divided doses.
  ▫ May aggravate psychosis.

SKIN, ALLERGIES, AND TEMPERATURE

Hypothermia more common than hyperthermia
See page 21.

Decreased sweating
See page 21.

Photosensitivity
See page 21.

Skin rashes
See page 21.

Drug and Food Interactions

Drug Interactions with Second-Generation Antipsychotics

Drugs (X) Interacts with:	Second-Generation Anti-psychotics (A)[a]	Comments
Antiarrhythmic (e.g., quinidine)	X↑ A↑	Increases quinidine-like effects with dysrhythmias; increases clozapine and risperidone levels.
Anticholinergic	X↑	Added anticholinergic effect. Consider amantadine; variable effects seen on metabolism, plasma level, and efficacy of antipsychotic.
Anticoagulant (warfarin)	X↑ A↑	Increased PT ratio or INR response with quetiapine
Anticonvulsant	A↓	Increased clearance and decreased antipsychotic plasma level with carbamazepine
Antidepressant		
MAO inhibitor	X↓	Hypotension may result; MAO inhibitors may trigger movement disorders.
SSRI	A↑	May increase movement disorders and plasma levels. Fluvoxamine least likely to increase antipsychotic level.
TCA	X↑ A↑	Possible toxicity or hypotension; TCAs may diminish movement disorders.
Antihypertensives	X↑	Increased hypotension
Caffeine	A↓	Increased psychosis in high doses, 600–1000 mg; increased plasma levels of clozapine.
CNS depressant (e.g., alcohol, antihistamines, hypnotics)	X↑ A↑	CNS depression
Estrogen	A↑	Potentiates hyperprolactinemic effect
Grapefruit juice	A↑	Increased plasma level of quetiapine due to inhibited metabolism via CYP3A4. *Avoid.*
Lithium	X↑ A↑	Possibly increased risk of agranulocytosis and seizures with clozapine
Nicotine	A↓	Decreased blood levels
Sympathomimetic (e.g., epinephrine, norepinephrine)	X↓	Hypotension

[a]↑ = increase; ↓ = decrease.

Special Populations

CHILDREN AND ADOLESCENTS

- Adverse effects may be more prevalent and more severe in children and adolescents than in adults.
- The prevalence of movement disorders is much lower in children treated with SGAs than in those given FGAs.
- Sedation can be minimized through gradual dose escalation.
- The relative propensities for producing weight gain in children and adolescents are olanzapine > risperidone > quetiapine.

WOMEN: PREGNANCY AND POSTPARTUM

Pregnancy Rating	• Category C (clozapine is category B)
Teratogenicity (1st trimester)	• Maternal adiposity associated with medication use lead to a greater risk of neural tube defects in infants.
Direct Effect on Newborn (3rd trimester)	• Neonatal jaundice • Clozapine has been associated with sedation, irritability, and seizures in infants.
Lactation	• Present in breast milk in concentrations equal to or greater than plasma.

LATE LIFE

- Use only one antipsychotic agent at a time.
- To minimize side effects, these medications should be started at low dosages that are increased incrementally.
- Drug interactions, especially those involving the cytochrome P450 system, must be considered.

Effects on Laboratory Tests

Effects of Second-Generation Antipsychotics on Blood/Serum and Urine Tests

	Blood/Serum Tests		Urine Tests	
Generic Name	Marker	Results[a]	Marker[a]	Results[a]
Clozapine	Prolactin	↑		
	WBC	↓		
	LFT[b]	↑		
Risperidone	Prolactin	↑	Pregnancy test	False ↑

[a] ↑ = increases; ↓ = decreases; ↑↓ = increases and decreases.
[b] LFT = liver function tests (AST/SGOT, ALT/SGPT, alkaline phosphatase, bilirubin, and LDH).

Discontinuation

- Abrupt cessation of high doses may produce:
  √ Flu-like symptoms without a fever (may reflect cholinergic rebound)
  √ Insomnia and nightmares
  √ Gastritis, nausea, vomiting, diarrhea
  √ Headaches
  √ Diaphoresis, increased sebaceous secretion, restlessness, and general physical complaints
  √ Supersensitivity psychosis (acute relapse) has been described after acute withdrawal in some patients.
- These symptoms
  √ Begin 2–4 days after discontinuation and may persist up to 2 weeks.
  √ Can cease by reducing the dose gradually over 1–2 weeks.
- Tardive neurological symptoms may emerge.
- A transient withdrawal dyskinesia also may arise occasionally.
  √ Withdrawal dyskinesia resembles a tardive dyskinesia with abnormal movements of the neck, face, and mouth.
  √ Antiparkinsonian drugs do not relieve it.
  √ Withdrawal dyskinesia stops with
    □ Reestablishing maintenance antipsychotic dose, and
    □ Reducing antipsychotics more gradually (1–3 months).
- Rapid clozapine and quetiapine withdrawal can differ.
  √ Symptoms include delirium, pschosis, severe agitation, and abnormal movements.
  √ Suggested to taper clozapine by 25–100 mg/week and quetaipine by 50–200 mg/week.

Overdose: Toxicity, Suicide, and Treatment

- Antipsychotic drug overdose is associated with low morbidity and mortality.
- Toxic effects begin within 1–2 h and peak by 4–6 h following ingestion.
- The toxic effects in adults and children are similar.
- Symptoms of toxicity are extensions of common adverse events: anticholinergic effects, sedation, miosis, and orthostatic hypotension.
- Major toxicity manifests primarily in cardiovascular and central nervous systems.
- Management
  √ Primarily supportive.
  √ Obtain ECG, temperature, vital signs, and if needed, establish an airway.
  √ If ECG changes occur, such as prolonged QT_c, cardiac monitoring should continue for at least 24 h.
  √ Perform a complete blood count on any patient that takes clozapine and presents with a fever.
  √ Administer activated charcoal if within 1 hour of ingestion and no contraindications exist.
  √ If hypotension is present, place patient in Trendelenburg's position while saline is infused.
    □ *Do not use epinephrine;* may result in lower blood pressure.

√ Treat seizures with IV diazepam.
  □ Avoid barbiturates due to risk of respiratory depression.
  □ Avoid pentylenetrazol, picrotoxin, and bemegride.

Precautions

• Use antipsychotics cautiously with
  √ Narrow-angle glaucoma
  √ Prostatic hypertrophy
  √ Bone marrow depression blood dyscrasias
  √ Parkinson's disease
  √ Antipsychotic hypersensitivity
  √ Extreme hypotension or hypertension
  √ Diabetes
  √ Acutely ill children (e.g., chickenpox, measles, Reye's syndrome, gastroen-
    teritis, dehydration)
    □ Increased movement disorders, particularly dystonias and akathisias
    □ Increased hepatotoxicity risk
  √ Elderly who have
    □ Hepatic disease
    □ Cardiovascular illness
    □ Chronic respiratory disease
    □ Hypoglycemia
    □ Dementia
    □ Seizures

Key Points to Communicate to Patients and Families

Key points for SGAs are the same as those discussed in the previous section for
FGAs (*see* pp. 25–26).

However, note the following for clozapine:

• Clozapine may cause a low white blood cell count, which can put patient at
  risk for infection.
  √ Although serious, it affects less than 1% of people.
  √ If this happens and it goes undetected, it can result in a serious problem and
    may be fatal.
  √ Therefore, under current clozapine guidelines, frequent blood tests are required.
• Patient and family should notify doctor if any of the following side effects occur:
  √ Sore throat or mouth
  √ Fever
  √ Cold or flu
  √ Other signs of infection
  √ Skin rash or itching

A
N
T
I
P
S
Y
C
H
O
T
I
C
S

THERAPEUTIC APPLICATION

Initiation of Treatment

Start with a sufficiently high dose to squelch symptoms but low enough to minimize side effects. The equivalent of 300–600 mg chlorpromazine is a reasonable target dose for a majority of schizophrenia patients, then wait 2 weeks. Exceeding a patient's own antipsychotic threshold doesn't speed recovery. Generally less sedating, more potent antipsychotics are preferred because they have fewer side effects during the maintenance phase than the highly sedating ones (e.g., chlorpromazine or thioridazine).

- The use of "neuroleptic threshold" (NT) is sometimes used.
  √ Not expected to work with risperidone, clozapine, olanzapine, ziprasidone, or quetiapine.
  √ May work best with high-potency antipsychotics.
    □ Low-potency antipsychotics with intrinsic anticholinergic effects may mask threshold movement disorders.
- The NT guides initial dosing.
  √ The NT is defined as a slight increase in cogwheel rigidity after starting the antipsychotic.
    □ This can be tested by flexing and extending the patient's arms at the elbow and the wrist.
    □ If patient is unable to relax the tested arm, have patient perform and concentrate on rapid, alternating movements with the other arm.
  √ Others have argued that the fine motor signs of micrographia or decreased arm swing while walking are more sensitive indicators of threshold.
- To establish baseline rigidity
  √ The patient should be evaluated for 1–3 days before medications are started.
  √ Initially haloperidol 2 mg qd (or its equivalent) is given, and if no increase in rigidity occurs, this is increased by 2 mg every other day.
  √ If rigidity is equivocal, wait 1 or 2 days to see if it increases, and if not, increase by one more 2 mg dose.
- Effective antipsychotic dosing in the 3–5 mg range of haloperidol can sometimes be achieved.
  √ However, sickness, missing one or more doses, and other risks can result in a quick return of psychotic symptoms.
- 86 inpatients with chronic schizophrenia on maximum doses fixed at 6 mg/day of risperidone or 300 mg/day of clozapine at endpoint (8 weeks) were clinically improved:
  √ 67% of the risperidone group and 65% of the clozapine group showed reduction of 20% or more in total PANSS scores.
  √ Risperidone had faster onset than clozapine.
- This approach may be particularly helpful in certain problematic populations, including
  √ Adolescents
  √ Older adults (use 0.5 or 1 mg equivalents of haloperidol)
  √ Patients who have never been on antipsychotics

POOR OUTCOME PREDICTORS FOR SCHIZOPHRENIA

- Earlier age of onset
- Long duration of illness
- Slow onset
- Poor premorbid functioning and social competence
- Emotional blunting
- Unsystematized and unfocused delusions
- Clear sensorium
- No precipitating factors
- No family h/o affective disorder
- Family with h/o schizophrenia
- Treatment naïve movement disorders
- CAT scan changes (i.e., cortical atrophy and enlarged ventricles)

Since the efficacy among FGAs is roughly equivalent, choosing the "right" antipsychotic can be elusive. SGAs have much lower risks for movement disorders and are more potent at reducing negative symptoms. In general, the SGAs are a first choice.

- Select an agent that has previously helped the patient, but if none exists:
  - √ If the first dose seems to be tolerated by the patient, continue it.
  - √ If not (e.g., patient is dangerously woozy), try a much lower dose or consider another antipsychotic.
- If patient is not agitated, give a less sedating antipsychotic (e.g., risperidone or fluphenazine) in a single dose 30 minutes before bedtime.
  - √ Risperidone usually effective in 3–5 mg range for healthy adults.
  - √ For elderly or patients with significant medical problems, 0.5–2 mg qd is often useful.
  - √ After 4 weeks treatment, greater overall improvement in patients receiving risperidone than haloperidol.
  - √ When patient is switched from clozapine to risperidone or olanzapine, will need prolonged cross-titration > 1 month.
- Bedtime doses lessen the experience of side effects because peak levels occur only during sleep.
- If the patient is agitated and requires sedation
  - √ Choose a more sedating antipsychotic (e.g., olanzapine or perphenazine).
    - ▫ Olanzapine 15 mg is superior to 10 mg on most negative symptoms.
  - √ Rapidly increase target antipsychotic dosage.
  - √ Take advantage of sedating effects by using tid or qid doses.
  - √ Make sure patient is getting medication: Give IM antipsychotic (e.g., haloperidol 5 mg) if rapid effect is needed, or give liquid form and observe patient taking it.
  - √ If at target dose, to avoid unnecessary further risks for movement disorders, add benzodiazepines (e.g., lorazepam 1–2 mg/po or IM, diazepam 5 mg IM).
    - ▫ Beware of disinhibition at low and intermediate benzodiazepine doses.

- Special precautions with clozapine
  - √ Do not rapidly increase clozapine; increases seizure risk.
  - √ Monitor clozapine for sedation and hypotension and beware of rare (1:3,000) respiratory or cardiac arrest.
  - √ Start at 12.5 mg qd or bid and increase by 25–50 mg qd every 2 days.
  - √ Little clinical gain in prolonging exposure to clozapine beyond 8 weeks at any dose, if no response is seen.
- In cases of severe refractory psychotic agitation, IM droperidol 2.5–1.5 mg (1–6 ml) can be considered.
  - √ 0.15–0.25 mg/kg can be started in physically healthy adults (< 65 y.o.).
  - √ Duration of action usually under 5 h but can be as high as 12 h.
  - √ Shows rapid onset (3–10 minutes) and peak action (20–30 minutes).
  - √ Can be very sedating/tranquilizing.
  - √ Low risk of prolonged oversedation.
  - √ Occasionally doses up to 50 mg required.
  - √ Less hypotensive than low-potency sedating phenothiazines.
  - √ Increases risk for movement disorders of other drugs.
  - √ Prolongs QTc interval.

Treatment Resistance

What happens if patient does not improve sufficiently?

- Psychotic symptoms may resolve in days, but many require 2–12 weeks (or more) to disappear.
- If all symptoms remain unchanged after initial 2 weeks, consider:
  - √ Is patient taking the medication?
    - □ If patient dose not have a common side effect (e.g., dry mouth), probably is *not* ingesting the medication.
  - √ To be certain, obtain a plasma level by drawing blood 12 h after an oral dose.
    - □ Overly high levels may interfere with antipsychotic effect.
    - □ Overly low levels may suggest noncompliance or rapid metabolism of drug.
  - √ Liquid medication is more readily swallowed than pills, which can be graciously "cheeked."
- If patient is taking pills but without a good response, then:
  - √ Reconsider diagnosis and make sure there are clear target symptoms.
    - □ Raise (or lower) the dose of the same antipsychotic.
    - □ Try an IM form.
    - □ Switch to depot medication; this may particularly help patients with extensive first-pass metabolism.
    - □ Brief Psychotic Rating Scale (BPRS) at 4 weeks was significantly better for risperidone (24%) than haloperidol (11%), but very little improvement after the first 4 weeks of treatment.
    - □ If on high doses (e.g., 50 mg/qd haloperidol), gradual reduction to 30–50% of this dose may help.
- If prominent negative symptoms remain, consider risperidone, olanzapine, ziprasidone, clozapine, or possibly quetiapine.

√ Effects of clozapine usually seen within 12 weeks.
  □ At 100 mg/day of clozapine, tapering of FGA can be started as dose of clozapine is increased.
√ Fluvoxamine, fluoxetine, desipramine, and probably other ADs can augment clozapine-resistant schizophrenia.
√ If patient is on high-potency antipsychotic with only partial response, clozapine can be added safely, with an eventual goal to take only clozapine.
• If prominent positive symptoms remain, consider a different class of antipsychotic.
• If patient is treatment-resistant to two or more FGAs, consider risperidone, olanzapine, ziprasidone, or clozapine.
• If partial response observed, consider augmentation.
• Depressive symptoms with schizophrenia improve in larger percentage of patients and to greater extent with olanzapine than with haloperidol.
• If negative symptoms are worse, consider antipsychotic-induced akinesia and lower dose and/or add ACA.

Augmentation

• Benzodiazepines can improve positive and negative symptoms.
  √ 50% response rate
  √ 2–3 mg qd alprazolam typical dose
  √ Clonazepam may diminish agitation and possibly psychosis, although findings are unclear.
    □ Start dose at 0.5 mg bid–tid.
    □ Increase 0.5–1.0 mg q 3 days until stabilization occurs.
    □ Dose may reach 3 mg/day.
• Adding lithium can help "good prognosis" in patients with schizophrenia as well as those with schizoaffective bipolar disorder (symptoms of a mood disorder and schizophrenia).
• Anticonvulsants may help
  √ If "atypical" features, seizure-like, organic symptoms (e.g., olfactory, tactile, or kinesthetic hallucinations).
  √ With prominent negative symptoms (e.g., affective flattening).
  √ If symptoms of bipolar disorder observed.
• Bromocriptine 2.5 mg/qd
  √ Case reports positive in treatment-resistant psychosis.
• Propranolol in doses > 800 mg qd
  √ May function as anticonvulsant at this dose.
  √ May also aggravate or cause psychosis.
• Eicosapentaenoic acid (EPA) can sustain remission of positive and negative symptoms of schizophrenia.
  √ In study of 20 patients with schizophrenia, reduction of both positive symptoms and TD occurred.
  √ All were on their regular antipsychotic medication.
  √ Average symptom response about 25%.
• Clozapine augmentation with ondansetron 8 mg q 8 h.
  √ Decreased delusions and hallucinations.

Augmentation with negative symptoms:

- Glycine, a potentiator of NMDA neurotransmission for negative symptoms of schizophrenia, dissolved in water and given orally tid, was titrated to 0.8 mg/kg/day (mean dosage 60 mg/day).
  √ 19 patients on glycine showed a decrease of negative symptoms as measured on PANSS, a significant improvement (30% ± 18%, $p < .001$) in the BPRS total scores, and a 50% reduction in scores on Simpson–Angus Scale for Extrapyramidal Symptoms.
  √ 15 (79%) subjects showed a 20% or greater improvement in PANSS scores.
  √ Total BPRS scores decreased by 30% during glycine treatment.
- D-serine treatment, 30 mg/kg/day, added to stable antipsychotic regimen, resulted in significant improvement in positive, negative, and cognitive symptoms.
  √ These results support the hypothesis of NMDA receptor hypofunction in schizophrenia because D-serine is an NMDA receptor complex co-agonist.
- D-cycloserine given 50 mg/day resulted in 61% of D-cycloserine-treated patients responding and 26% of the placebo group.
  √ Gains were greatest in the area of blunted affect, with improvements also in anhedonia and associativeness, but no differences in apathy, attention, or alogia.
  √ Mean improvement on Alzheimer's Disease Assessment Scale, cognitive subscale, with 100 mg of D-cycloserine, was 3 points.
- Trazodone 100–500 mg (mixed results; used for negative symptoms).
  √ Essentially no positive effects.
- Famotidine (Pepcid), a potent lipophylic histamine-2 blocker, 20 mg bid, improved negative symptoms in small ($N = 18$) open trial.
  √ Patients experienced reduction of 14% in BPRS, 18% in Schedule for the Assessment of Negative Symptoms (SANS) scores, and improvement in Clinical Global Impression (CGI).
- ACAs may worsen positive symptoms and improve negative symptoms.
  √ Might be useful adjunct in patients with mostly negative symptoms.
- Pimozide 4–20 mg qd may have more effect on refractory negative symptoms and refractory delusional disorder.
  √ In seven cases, five with schizophrenia and two with schizoaffective disorder
    ▫ Pimozide's average dose was 4 mg (range 2–8 mg).
    ▫ All patients had consistent clinical improvement while on pimozide (mean baseline BPRS = 51; after pimozide use BPRS = 27).
- Selegiline 5 mg po bid taken for 1 month in an open trial significantly reduced negative symptoms (e.g., affective flattening, alogia, avolition/apathy, anhedonia/asociality).
  √ No effect on positive symptoms.
  √ Negative symptoms continued to improve over several months.
- Antidepressants may help negative symptoms/depression.
  √ Risk of exacerbating positive symptoms of psychosis has been overestimated.

• Amantadine 50 mg 3 times daily resulted in 23% responders who had negative symptoms without exacerbation on positive symptoms.

Maintenance

After the initial schizophrenic break:

• Qd dosing for most patients; divided dosing only if side effect problem (e.g., orthostatic hypotension) or if short half-life (e.g., 5–8 h) of antipsychotic requires dosing two or three times a day.
  √ At beginning of treatment risperidone is recommended in bid dosing, but if there is no hypotension, it can be given qd.
• From 6–9 months after discharge (or point of maximum improvement), consider tapering to 20–50% of the highest dosage.
  √ If symptoms begin to recur, increase dose.
• If patient will be under high stress (e.g., new job), do not alter medication until stressor has past.
• Some studies suggest that serum prolactin predicts relapse risk.
  √ In fluphenazine decanoate study
    ▫ ≥ 16 ng/ml level was proactive.
    ▫ ≤ 6 ng/ml level was high relapse risk.
• In patients who unilaterally stop medication, 15% can be expected to relapse per month.

Depot antipsychotics that provide 2–4 weeks therapeutic efficacy are employed for maintenance therapy, particularly for patients with poor or inconsistent compliance.

• They are effective treatment for chronic psychoses.
• Their advantages are:
  √ Patient does not have to remember to take pills every day.
  √ Certainty that drug is in the patient.
  √ Less staff surveillance.
  √ Lower relapse rates than with oral meds.
• Their disadvantages:
  √ Following injection, adverse consequence such as movement disorders are more difficult to prevent until drug clearance.
  √ They are not very effective for negative symptoms.
• Be aware of the following precautions.
  √ Do not start any treatment with depot antipsychotics unless usual medications have already been tried, without good results.
  √ Suddenly switching from oral to depot forms can radically alter serum level.
    ▫ For instance, 4 weeks of fluphenazine 10 mg/day po was stopped, replaced by fluphenazine decanoate 12.5 mg IM; 2 weeks later the serum level dropped from 0.51 ng/ml to 0.08 mg/ml and symptoms reappeared.
    ▫ Oral antipsychotics can reach steady state in 3–7 days.

- Safety factors
  - √ Gradually shift from oral to depot forms, and
  - √ Test dose.
- Method
  - √ No depot form is clearly better than another in controlling psychosis.
    - ▫ Fluphenazine enanthate has significantly higher side effects, especially movement disorders, and is not recommended.
  - √ First, stabilize the patient on a dose of oral fluphenazine, haloperidol, or risperidone; ensure adequate blood level and side effect tolerance.
  - √ To detect rate sensitivity to vehicle (sesame oil) or side effects, inject 6.25 mg (by insulin syringe for acute measurement) of fluphenazine decanoate (or any depot form).
  - √ Dose schedules include:
    - ▫ Fluphenazine decanoate, with a 7- to 10-day half-life, allowing depot injections about q 2 weeks.
    - ▫ Haloperidol decanoate dose should equal 10–20 times the daily dose of haloperidol orally. If not on any antipsychotic, the initial dose is usually 20 times oral dose; the next dose, approximately 1 month later, 15 times oral dose; and the final maintenance dose 1 month later, closer to 10 times the oral dose.
    - ▫ IM risperidone, with a 3- to 6-day half-life, should be administered q 2 weeks at a recommended dose of 25 mg IM. Although dose response for effectiveness has not been established, some patients not responding to 25 mg may benefit from a higher dose of 37.5 mg or 50 mg.
  - √ Maintain stable blood level.
    - ▫ If needed, continue oral medication.
    - ▫ Gradually taper oral medication as depot levels increase.
    - ▫ Example of schedule: Give full po dose on first day of IM; decrease po dose 20% of original dose each day; add more po medication if clinically indicated; po medication may accompany IM for 1 or 2 months until proper IM dose is determined.
- After being stabilized on fluphenazine decanoate 25 mg, some patients continue to do well with much lower doses (as low as 5–10 mg).
- Depot antipsychotics have not been approved for children under 12.

Pimozide as an alternative to depot antipsychotics in low-compliance patients:

- Frequently patients refuse deport antipsychotics because they do not want IM.
  - √ Check with patient to see if it is the site of administration and not IM that is reason for refusal.
  - √ Some patients resist buttocks IM but tolerate thigh or shoulder.
- If patient refuses IM medication and is part of a program that cannot monitor daily oral meds but can oversee three to five doses a week, then consider pimozide.
  - √ Pimozide's 55-h half-life allows dosing q 2–3 days.
  - √ However, pimozide is rarely, if ever, administered in this way.

Indications for long-term antipsychotic therapy:

- After two psychotic episodes, probably need antipsychotics for multiple years (if not indefinitely), always weighing the risks of psychosis against those of TD and other side effects.
  - √ Consider risperidone, olanzapine, or quetiapine (but beware of its 6-h average half-life).
  - √ If minimal or no response to these, try clozapine.
- Maintenance antipsychotic therapy over 2 years is superior to placebo.
  - √ Averts schizophrenic relapses in 40–70% of patients.

2. Agents for Treating Movement Disorders

INTRODUCTION TO DRUG CLASS

Since the original introduction of conventional neuroleptics, much has been learned about the pathophysiology, risk factors, preventive strategies, course, and outcomes of adverse neurological events. Collectively, extrapyramidal side effects (EPS) are prevalent and hazardous side effects originally associated with first-generation antipsychotic (FGA) agents. Extrapyramidal side effects were categorized as acute and included dystonia, parkinsonism, akathisia, as well as tardive (e.g., tardive dyskinesia). The presence of EPS has greatly diminished patient acceptability of antipsychotic agents and has provided the rationale for prophylactic usage of antiparkinsonian agents. The development and introduction of second-generation antipsychotics (SGAs) provided an opportunity for treatments that confer a lower hazard for EPS. Nevertheless, commercially available SGAs remain associated with EPS, and different liability is attributed to each agent. This chapter provides an up-to-date review of EPS associated with both FGA and SGA agents as well as a summary of primary and secondary prevention strategies.

Drugs Used to Treat EPS by Chemical Class

Chemical Class	Generic Name	Trade Name
Anticholinergic agent	Benztropine	Cogentin
	Biperiden	Akineton
	Procyclidine	Kemadrin
	Trihexyphenidyl	Artane
Antihistamine	Cyproheptadine	Periactin
	Diphenhydramine	Benadryl
	Orphenadrine	Norflex

Chemical Class	Generic Name	Trade Name
Benzodiazepine	Clonazepam	Klonopin
	Diazepam	Valium
		Diazepam Intensol
		Diastat
		Dizac
	Lorazepam	Ativan
		Lorazepam Intensol
β-blocker	Propranolol	Inderal
Dopaminergic agonist	Amantadine	Symmetrel

Dosing, Dose Form, and Color

Profile of Drugs Used to Treat EPS

Generic Names	Oral Dose (mg)	IM/IV Dose (mg)	Dose Form (mg)[a]	Color
Amantadine	100 bid–tid		c: 100	c: red
			s: 50 mg/5 ml	
Benztropine	1–3 bid	1–2	t: 0.5/1/2	t: all white
			p: 1 mg/ml	
Biperiden	2 tid–qid	2	t: 2	t: white
			p: 5 mg/ml	
Clonazepam	1–4 mg/day		t: 0.5/1/2	t: yellow/blue/white
Cyproheptadine	4 tid; up to		t: 4	t: white
	32 mg/day		s: 2 mg/5 ml	
Diazepam	5 qid	5–10	t: 2/5/10	t: white/yellow/blue
			p: 5 mg/ml	
Diphenhydramine	25–50 tid–qid	25–50	c: 25/50	
			p: 10/50 mg/ml	c: all pink–white
Lorazepam	1–2 qid	1–2	t: 0.5/1/2	t: all white
			p: 4 mg/ml	
Orphenadrine	50 tid; up tp		er: 100	er: white
	400 mg/day		p: 30 mg/ml	
Procyclidine	2.5–5 tid		t: 5	t: white
Propranolol	10 tid; up to		t: 10/20/40/80/120	t: orange/blue/
	120 mg/day			green/yellow/red
			sr: 60/80/120/160	sr: blue/orange/
			o: 4/8/80 mg/ml	blue pink
			p: 1 mg/ml	
Trihexyphenidyl	2–5 tid		t: 2/5	t: all white
			e: 2 mg/5 ml	

[a]c = capsule; e = elixir; er = extended-release tablets; o = oral concentrate; p = parenteral concentrate; s = syrup; sr = sustained-release capsules; t = tablets

Pharmacology

PHARMACOKINETICS

Pharmacokinetic Properties of Drugs Used to Treat EPS

Generic Names	Time to Peak Concentration (h)	Half-Life (h)	P450 Systems	
			Substrate	Inhibitor
Amantadine	1–6	16		
Benztropine		12–24	2D6	
Biperiden	1–1.5	18–24		
Clonazepam	1–4	19–60	2B4, 2E1, 3A4	2B4
Cyproheptadine		1–4		

Generic Names	Time to Peak Concentration (h)	Half-Life (h)	P450 Systems	
			Substrate	Inhibitor
Diazepam	0.5–2	14–80 (parent drug) 30–200 (metabolites)	3A4, 2C9, 2C19, 2B6	
Diphenhydramine		2–8	2D6	2D6
Lorazepam	1–6	8–24		
Orphenadrine	2	13–20	2D6, 2B6, 3A4, 1A2	1A2, 2A6, 2D6, 2B6, 3A4, 2C8/9, 2C19, 2E1
Procyclidine	1–2	12		2D6
Propranolol	1–1.5 (immediate release); 6 (long-acting)	2–6	1A2, 2D6, 2C19, 3A4	1A2, 3A4. 2D6
Trihexyphenidyl	1.2	6–10		

PHARMACODYNAMICS

The basal ganglia, which mediate involuntary movements, have a critical ratio of

$$\frac{Dopamine}{\text{Acetylcholine}}$$

When antipsychotics block these dopamine receptors, they lower this ratio and generate EPS.

By reducing acetylcholine, ACAs help to restore this balance. By releasing dopamine in the basal ganglia system, amantadine also helps restore this balance.

For akathisia there may be a critical ratio of

$$\frac{Dopamine}{\text{Norepinephrine}}$$

By reducing norepinephrine, β-blockers may restore this balance.

For EPS there may also be a critical ratio of

$$\frac{Dopamine}{\text{Serotonin}}$$

Because serotonin $5HT_2$ receptors mediate psychosis and reduce dopamine release in basal ganglia, SGA agents, which block these receptors, ameliorate psychosis and decrease abnormal movements caused by dopamine receptor antagonists. Selective serotonin reuptake inhibitors (SSRIs), which increase serotonin stimulation of $5HT_2$ receptors, further reduce the dopamine release that can cause EPS.

Clinical Indications

Influence of Drug on EPS

Generic Names	Akathisia	Akinesia	Dystonia	Rabbit	Rigidity	Tremor
Amantadine	3	3	2	2	3	2
Benztropine	2	2	3	3	3	3
Biperiden	1	2	3	3	3	3
Diazepam	2	0	1–2	1	1–2	0–1
Diphenhydramine	2	1	2–3	3	1	2

Generic Names	Akathisia	Akinesia	Dystonia	Rabbit	Rigidity	Tremor
Lorazepam	2	0	1–2	1	1–2	0–1
Procyclidine	1	2	3	3	3	3
Propranolol	3	0	0	1	0	1–2
Trihexyphenidyl	2	2	3	3	3	3

Note. 0 = no effect; 1 = some effect (20% response); 2 = moderate effect (20–40% response); 3 = good effect (> 40% responsible).

Side Effects

The side effects of diazepam, lorazepam, and propranolol are listed in Chapter 6 (*see* pp. 154–155, 165–167). Side effects of ACAs and amantadine are listed below.

In order of frequency, the most common (> 3%) side effects of

- ACAs include
  - √ Memory impairment
  - √ Dry mouth, nose, and throat
  - √ Blurred vision
  - √ Light sensitivity
  - √ Urinary hesitancy
  - √ Constipation
  - √ Appetite loss/nausea
  - √ Listlessness
  - √ Excitement
- Amantadine
  - √ Blurred vision
  - √ Dry mouth
  - √ Urinary hesitancy
  - √ Nausea
  - √ Insomnia
  - √ Depression
  - √ Psychosis

Amantadine's side effect frequencies are only slightly more than placebo. In experimental trials in healthy volunteers, ACAs interfered with learning new material in adults of all ages and caused ratings of fatigue-inertia, tension-anxiety, and depression-dejection. Amantadine had none of these effects.

Since the side effects of ACAs are anticholinergic, manage them by

- Eliminating or reducing the ACA.
- Changing to a less anticholinergic antipsychotic.
- Substituting the non-anticholinergic amantadine for the ACA.

CARDIOVASCULAR EFFECTS

Palpitations, tachycardia

Dizziness

CENTRAL NERVOUS SYSTEM EFFECTS

Confusion, delirium, disturbed concentration, disorientation

Restlessness, tremors, ataxia

Weakness, lethargy

Numb fingers, inability to move particular muscles, slurred speech, incoherence
• More common in the elderly and in high doses.

Stimulation, nervous excitement, insomnia, depression
• All may be more common with trihexyphenidyl (see Precautions).

Psychosis
• Occurs especially with amantadine (0.5% psychosis, 3% hallucinations). Rate for ACA is lower in the absence of overdose. Before changing an antipsychotic in a "treatment-resistant" psychotic patient, first try taking the patient off amantadine.

ENDOCRINE EFFECTS

Amantadine may reduce glactorrhea provoked by neuroleptic-induced increased prolactin.

EYES, EARS, NOSE, AND THROAT EFFECTS

Blurred vision
• *See* page 17 in Chapter 1.

Dry bronchial secretions and strained breathing

Dry eyes
• *See* page 17 in Chapter 1.

Narrow-angle glaucoma
• ACAs can trigger narrow-angle glaucoma.
• If patient has a h/o glaucoma, test intraocular pressure before giving ACAs, tricyclic antidepressants (TCAs), or antipsychotics.
• If narrow-angle glaucoma becomes a problem, discontinue all ACAs and antipsychotics.

Nasal congestion, dry throat

Photophia
• From dilated pupils.

GASTROINTESTINAL EFFECTS

Dry mouth
• *See* page 18.

MOVEMENT AGENTS

Constipation
• *See* page 34.

Nausea, vomiting
• Reduce ACA.

Paralytic ileus

RENAL EFFECTS

Urinary hesitancy or retention
• See page 20.

SKIN, ALLERGIES, AND TEMPERATURE

Diminished sweating

Skin flushing

Skin rashes
• Stop ACA.
• Check nature and distribution of rash
  √ To exclude contact dermatitis.
  √ If only on neck or wrists, probably need new soap.
  √ Stop neuroleptic if not contact dermatitis.

Fever
• Apply ice bags.

Drug Interactions

Drug Interactions with Anti-EPS Agents

Drugs (X) interact with:	Anticholinergics (A)[a]	Comments
Acetaminophen	X↓	May increase acetaminophen use.
Amantadine	X↑A↑	Increased amantadine and ACA effects.
Antidepressants		
MAO inhibitor	A↑	May increase anticholinergic effects.
TCAs	A↑X↑	May diminish EPS; increased risk of anticholinergic toxicity.
Antihistamines	X↑A↓	Increased anticholinergic effects.
Antipsychotics	X↓A↑	ACAs may slow antipsychotic actions. ACAs enhance anticholinergic effects of antipsychotics, particularly low-potency phenothiazines.
Cocaine	A↓	Decreased anticholinergic effects
Digoxin	X↑	Increased bioavailability of digoxin tablets
Levodopa (L-dopa)	X↓	May reduce L-dopa's availability; when ACAs stopped, L-dopa's toxicity may erupt.
Methotrimeparazine	A↓	Combination may increase EPS.
Nitrofurantoin	X↑	ACA may increase nitrofuratoin effects.
Primidone	X↑	Excessive sedation

Drugs (X) interact with:	Anticholinergics (A)[a]	Comments
Procainamide	X↑	Increased procainamide effect
Propranolol	X↓	ACAs anatagonize the bradycardia effect of β–blocker.
Tacrine	X↓A↓	Interfere with each other's effects

Drugs (X) interact with:	Amantadine (A)	Comments
Alcohol	X↑	Increased alcohol effect; possible fainting
Anticholinergics	X↑A↑	Increased amantadine and ACA effects
Antiemetics	X↓	Possible decreased efficacy
Antipsychotics	X↓	May interfere with antipsychotic effect
Cocaine	X↑	Major overstimulation
Sympathomimetics	X↑	Increased stimulation and agitation
Trimethoprim, sulfamethoxazole (Bactrim, Septa)	X↑A↑	May increase each other's levels; CNS toxicity possible.
Quinidine	A↑	Modest increase in amantadine levels due to decreased renal clearance
Quinine	A↑	Modest increase in amantadine levels due to decreased renal clearance
Triametrene (in Dyazide)	A↑	Modest increase in amantadine levels

[a]↑ = increases; ↓ = decreases.

Special Populations

CHILDREN AND ADOLESCENTS

• Doses up to 80 mg trihexyphenidyl have been employed in the treatment of dystonic movements in children. Side effects were less frequent in children than in adults.

WOMEN: PREGNANCY AND POSTPARTUM

Pregnancy Rating	• Cyproheptadine and diphenhydramine: Category B
	• Diazepam and lorazepam: Category D
	• Others: Category C
Teratogenicity (1st trimester)	• Limited human data with many of these agents
	• Amantadine is contraindicated during first trimester.
	• No apparent fetal risk from trihexyphenidyl
	• No reports on biperiden
Direct Effect on Newborn (3rd trimester)	• A few cases of paralytic ileus with mother on chlorpromazine and benztropine

- Use of propranolol is associated with decreased fetal and placental weight.

Lactation
- Amantadine secreted in breast milk.
  √ Amantadine blood levels are useful to determine if a safe and low enough level has been reached to avoid potentially problematic effects on the baby.

LATE LIFE

- Older adults are more sensitive to the side effects of anticholinergic agents than younger adults.
  √ Monitor for constipation, urinary retention, increased confusion, memory loss, and disorientation.
- Caution when combining two or more drugs with anticholinergic properties.

Effects on Laboratory Tests

Effects of Drugs Treating EPS on Blood/Serum and Urine Tests

Generic Names	Blood/Serum Tests		Urine Tests	
	Marker	Results[a]	Marker[a]	Results
Amantadine	WBC, leukocytes	↓↓		
Benztropine	None		None	
Biperiden				
Diphenhydramine	WBC, RBC, platelets[b]	↓↓ ↓		
Procyclidine				
Trihexyphenidyl	None		None	

[a]↑ = increases; ↓ = decreases; ↑↓ = increases and decreases.
[b]WBC = white blood cells; RBC = red blood cells.

Discontinuation

ACAs do not cause:

- Dependence (but abuse is possible)
- Tolerance
  √ Some tolerance with amantadine occurs after 8 weeks.
- Addiction

ACA WITHDRAWL

Yet, even more than with antipsychotic agents, abruptly discontinuing ACAs can induce, in 2–4 (up to 7) days, a flu-like syndrome without a fever.

- Nausea, vomiting, diarrhea
- Hypersalivation

- Headaches
- Insomnia
- Nightmares

Less often develop

- Rhinorrhea
- Increased appetite
- Giddiness
- Dizziness
- Tremors
- Warm or cold sensations

These symptoms

- Represent cholinergic rebound.
- May persist 2 weeks.
- Are not life-threatening.
- Can diminish substantially by more gradually tapering off neuroleptics and ACAs.
- This approach also decreases risk of rebound EPS.

AMANTADINE WITHDRAWAL

Stopping amantadine abruptly can result in rebound EPS with "parkinsonian crisis" in patients with Parkinson's disease and a severe worsening of neuroleptic-induced EPS.

Overdose: Toxicity, Suicide, and Treatment

Symptoms of toxicity are extensions of common adverse effects (*see* pp. 52–54 in this chapter).

- Management
  - √ Stop all drugs with anticholinergic activity.
  - √ Physostigmine 1–2 mg IV q 1–2 h may decrease CNS toxicity for both ACA and amantadine.
  - √ For amantadine overdose, acidifying the urine may speed elimination.
  - √ Blood pressure, pulse, respiration, and temperature should be monitored.
  - √ The patient should be observed for the possible development of arrhythmias, hypotension, hyperactivity, and convulsions.
    - □ If required, appropriate therapy should be administered.

Precautions

Be alert to growing reports of ACA abuse.

- Occurs in 0–17.5% of patients taking ACAs.
- Occurs with all ACAs.

- Most common with trihexyphenidyl
  - √ Energizing
  - √ Induces euphoria
  - √ Sedating
  - √ Enhances socializing
  - √ Affords psychedelic and psychotogenic experiences

ACAs contraindicated in patients with

- Urinary retention, prostatic hypertrophy
- Paralytic ileus, bowel obstruction, megacolon
- Hyperthermia, heat stroke
- Congestive heart failure
- Narrow-angle (i.e., acute angle-closure) glaucoma
- Hypersensitivity to ACAs
- Dry bronchial secretions (especially in the elderly)
- Delirium and dementia
- Cardiac patients with hypertension

Use ACAs with extreme caution in patients with

- Cardiac arrhythmias
- Hypotension
- Liver or kidney disorders
- Geriatric conditions
- Peripheral edema

Key Points to Communicate to Patients and Families

GENERAL INFORMATION

- If blurred vision occurs or alertness is lowered, do not drive or work in situations that require close-up focusing or quick reflexes.
- For dry mouth, avoid calorie-laden beverages and candy; they foster caries and weight gain. Increase sugar-free fluid intake and try sugar-free candy.
- To avoid accidental ingestion, do not keep medication at bedside; keep safely away from children.
- To prevent or relieve constipation, increase bulk-forming foods, water (2,500–3,000 ml/day), and exercise. Stool softeners are okay, but laxatives should be avoided if possible.

ACA INFORMATION

- Most common side effects of ACAs are dry mouth and throat, blurred vision, light sensitivity, urinary hesitancy, constipation, depression, and mild memory impairment.
- Take ACAs with meals to reduce dry mouth and gastric irritation.
- ACAs may potentiate the effect of alcohol—one drink feels like two or three.

• Use extra caution in hot weather; heat stroke more likely.
• If a dose is missed by 2 h, skip the dose and resume medication at the next regularly scheduled time. *Do not double the dose.*
• Do not stop ACAs or amantadine until a week after antipsychotic agents have been stopped.

AMANTADINE INFORMATION

• Side effects reported include blurred vision, dry mouth, urinary hesitancy, nausea, and insomnia.
  √ Most people don't get these side effects.
• Take it once a day (up to 200 mg), but if side effects become a problem, divide the dosage into a twice-a-day regimen. Taking it with food may reduce nausea.

THERAPEUTIC APPLICATION

Initiation of Treatment

Effects of ACAs depend on the symptom. Therefore, when should one use ACAs or other extrapyramidal drugs (EPDs)?

• The *pro* arguments include:
  √ EPS are uncomfortable.
  √ EPS can induce patients to stop taking neuroleptics.
  √ High-potency neuroleptics cause EPS.
  √ ACAs especially help patients under 45 y.o.
  √ ACAs clearly relieve some EPS (e.g., dystonia, akinesia, pseudoparkinsonism).
• The *con* arguments include:
  √ Low-potency neuroleptics less frequently produce EPS.
  √ Patients without EPS initially can receive EPDs if EPS arise later.
  √ ACAs have side effects that compound neuroleptic side effects (e.g., dry mouth, confusion).
  √ ACAs are not very effective for other EPS (e.g., akathisias).
  √ Avoid ACAs in children under 3 y.o.
• In general, prophylactic ACAs are indicated for
  √ Males under 30 y.o. and females under 25 y.o. starting high-potency neuroleptics (e.g., haloperidol) (dystonia rate without ACA over 70%), and
  √ Patients with dystonia (or have h/o dystonia).
    □ Tolerance to dystonia usually develops in 1–3 weeks.
    □ Douses can then be increased to usual levels.
  √ Patients with a past history of EPS with neuroleptics.
• When depot antipsychotics peak after 2–14 days, patient may need ACAs.
• Whether to use ACAs in other circumstances depends on the seriousness of symptoms and the preferences of patients.

MOVEMENT AGENTS

Starting Oral Doses of Antiparkinsonian Drugs

Symptom	Medication
Akathisia	Propranolol or other lipophilic β-blocker (e.g., metoprolol, pindolol, or nadolol, but not atenolol) are first choices if akathisia is an isolated symptom.
	Amantadine or benzodiazepines (lorazepam or diazepam) are second choices.
	ACAs are third choices. If other EPS also occur, which are better treated with ACA, use ACA first.
	If patient has not improved, double-check the diagnosis. May help in chronic or "tardive" akathisia.
Dystonia	Diphenhydramine 25–50 mg IV/IM as first choice; often provides complete relief in minutes and reduces patient anxiety.
	Hydroxyzine is alternative.
	Benztropine 1–2 mg IV/IM is the second choice, and always works quickly.
	If patient does not respond to the above, question the diagnosis.
	Prevent future dystonias with any ACA.
Parkinsonism	Reduce antipsychotics to lowest effective dose.
	Try any ACA.
	Prescribe amantadine if troublesome anticholinergic symptoms already exist.
	Consider amantadine in older adults and to preserve new memory acquisition in any age group.
Rabbit syndrome	Responds well to any ACA.

GENERAL CONSIDERATIONS OF EXTRAPYRAMIDAL DRUGS (EPDS)

- β-blockers, clonidine, and benzodiazepines (e.g., clonazepam 1 mg q A.M.) mostly limited for use in akathisia and perhaps tremor.
  - √ Clonidine's effect may be secondary to sedation and not a specific effect.
  - √ β-blockers are first choice for akathisia alone.
- Amantadine is well tolerated, broadly effective (including on akathisia), does not affect memory, protects from type-A influenza, is expensive, and occasionally may worsen psychosis.
- Anticholinergics are broadly effective (except on akathisia), have highest side effects, including on memory, and probably don't cause psychosis unless in toxic range.
- Buspirone 5–10 mg tid may help akathisia.
  - √ Only a few case reports but no controlled studies.

SPEED OF RESPONSE

- Only dystonia routinely responds in minutes to hours.
- Other symptoms (including akathisia) may take 3–10 days to respond significantly, although responses after 1–2 doses are not rare.
- Do not keep increasing daily dose just because effect is not yet visible.
- Pick a target dose and stay with it for 3–4 days.

ACA Dosage Adjustment

- Benztropine drug levels can vary 100-fold with comparable dosing.
  - √ Both under- and overdosing is common.
  - √ This may also be true of other ACAs.
- Some patients can become very toxic at very low doses.

- Poor correlation between ACA dosage and control of EPS.
- High correlation between ACA blood levels (> 7 pmol of atropine equivalents) and control of EPS.
- 25% of patients on normal doses of ACA (usually 4 mg/qd benztropine) have very low blood levels.
  √ Most of these patients responded when dose was increased to 6–12 mg/day.
  √ If this is done, carefully monitor patient for ACA effects (e.g., dry mouth, constipation, memory impairments).
- Dry mouth often early sign of clinically significant ACA activity.
  √ If patient has poor control of EPS and no dry mouth, might try increasing ACA dose.
  √ If patient has good control of EPS but severe ACA symptoms, try lowering ACA dose.
- Once-a-day dosing is often possible with long half-life ACAs (i.e., benztropine, biperiden).
  √ This should be tried only after optimal dose for patient has been established.
- After 1–6 months of antipsychotic therapy, ACAs often can be discontinued.
  √ About 15% of patients reexperience clear neurological side effects, whereas about 30% will feel "better"—less anxious, depressed, sleepy—on continued ACAs.
  √ Because antipsychotics have longer half-lives than ACAs, prescribe ACAs for several days *after* discontinuing antipsychotics.

MOVEMENT AGENTS

3. Antidepressants

INTRODUCTION TO DRUG CLASS

All currently available antidepressants can be categorized into one of three pharmacological classes. The first class of enzyme inhibitors was developed in the 1950s and has evolved to include reversible and selective inhibitors of monoamine oxidase A and B.

The second class is a group of drugs that predominately inhibits the monoamine transporters. Tricyclic antidepressants (TCAs) are the prototypes for this class, followed by selective serotonin reuptake inhibitors (SSRIs) and dual reuptake inhibitors of both serotonin and norepinephrine (SNRIs). Bupropion also belongs to this class as a norepinephrine and dopamine reuptake inhibitor (NDRI).

The third class of receptor-acting drugs predominately inhibits the serotonin -2 and -3 receptors ($5\text{-}HT_{-2/-3}$). These include mirtazapine, trazodone, and more recently the combined melatonin agonist and $5\text{-}HT_{-2}$ antagonist, agomelatine. Nefazodone potently and selectively blocks postsynaptic $5\text{-}HT_2$ receptors and is a week inhibitor of serotonin and norepinephrine reuptake. However, its use has been restricted in many countries because of concerns about liver toxicity.

Antidepressants by Chemical Class

Chemical Class	Generic Name	Trade Name
MONOAMINE OXIDASE (MAO) INHIBITOR		
	Isocarboxazid	Marplan
	Moclobemide	Manerix
	Phenelzine	Nardil
	Selegiline	Eldepryl, Emsam
	Tranylcypromine	Parnate

A
N
T
I
D
E
P
R
E
S
S
A
N
T
S

Chemical Class	Generic Name	Trade Name
TRANSPORTER INHIBITORS		
Tricyclic antidepressants (TCA)		
	Amitriptyline	Elavil, Endepryl
	Amoxapine	Asendin
	Clomipramine	Anafranil
	Desipramine	Norpramin
	Doxepin	Sinequan
	Imipramine	Tofranil, Janimine
	Maprotiline	Ludiomil
	Nortriptyline	Aventyl, Pamelor
	Trimipramine	Surmontil
	Protriptyline	Vivactil
Selective serotonin reuptake inhibitors (SSRI)	Citalopram	Celexa
	Escitalopram	Lexapro
	Fluoxetine	Prozac
	Fluvoxamine	Luvox
	Paroxetine	Paxil
	Sertraline	Zoloft
Serotonin and norepinephrine reuptake inhibitors (SNRI)	Desvenlafaxine	Pristiq
	Duloxetine	Cymbalta
	Milnacipran[a]	Ixel
	Venlafaxine	Effexor
Norepinephrine and dopamine reuptake inhibitors (NDRI)	Bupropion	Wellbutrin SR
RECEPTOR ANTAGONISTS/AGONISTS		
	Agomelatine	Valdoxan
	Mirtazapine	Remeron
	Trazodone	Desyrel

[a]Not available in the United States.

MONOAMINE OXIDASE INHIBITORS

Dosing, Dose Form, and Color

Profile of Monoamine Oxidase Inhibitors

Generic Names	Therapeutic Dose Range (mg/day)	Geriatric Dose (mg/day)	Dose Form (mg)[a]	Color
Isocarboxazid	10–30	5–15	t: 10	t: peach
Moclobemide[b]	300–600	300–600	t: 100/150/300	t: orange/pale yellow/white
Phenelzine	30–90	15–45	t: 15	t: orange
Selegiline[c]	t: 5–10 ts: 6–12	t: 5–10	t: 5 ts: 6/9/12	t: white
Tranylcypromine	20–80	10–30	t: 10	t: rose–red

[a]t = tablets; ts = transdermal system.
[b]Not available in United States.
[c]Selegiline tablets are primarily used for Parkinson's disease.

Pharmacology

- The MAO inhibitors can be classified in different ways:
  - √ Hydrazine (phenelzine, isocarboxazid) vs. nonhydrazine derivatives (tranylcypromine, selegiline).
  - √ Irreversible (phenelzine, isocarboxazid, tranylcypromine, selegiline) vs. reversible (moclobemide).
  - √ Selective for A (moclobemide) or B (selegiline) isoenzyme vs. nonselective (phenelzine, isocarboxazid, tranylcypromine).
  - √ MAO-A
    - □ Preferentially oxidizes norepinephrine and serotonin
    - □ Found primarily in the placenta, gut, and liver
    - □ Generally responsible for the antidepressant effect
  - √ MAO-B
    - □ Preferentially oxidizes phenylethylamine
    - □ Found mainly in the brain (80–95%), liver, and platelets
    - □ Generally responsible for the side effects.
- High concentrations of MAO in the blood–gut and blood–brain barriers suggest a protective or detoxifying role for MAO.

PHARMACOKINETICS

- Well absorbed from the gastrointestinal tract
- Short half-life of 1–5 hours is not particularly relevant, particularly when irreversible MAO binding occurs.
- Thus, the activity of these drugs depends less on pharmacokinetics and more on the synthesis of new MAO to restore normal enzyme activity.
- This synthesis requires approximately 2 weeks.

Pharmacokinetic Properties of Monoamine Oxidase Inhibitors

Generic Names	Bioavailability (%)	Protein Binding (%)	Half-Life (h)	P450 Systems Substrate	P450 Systems Inhibitor	Excretion (%)[a]
Isocarboxazid			1.5–4			
Moclobemide[b]	55	50	1–3	2C19	2C19, 2D6, 1A2	95 R
Phenelzine			1–4	2E1	2D6, 2C19, 2C9	
Selegiline	75	99.5	2	2B6, 2C19, 2D6, 1A2, 3A4	2D6, 3A4	73 R/15 F
Tranylcypromine			2–4		2C19, 2D6, 2A6, 2C9	

[a]F = fecal; R = renal
[b]Not available in United States.

PHARMACODYNAMICS

- The MAO enzymes metabolize and therefore deactivate endogenous pressor amines (e.g., norepinephrine, epinephrine, dopamine, and serotonin) as well as ingested pressor amines (e.g., tyramine).
- MAO inhibitors block the activity of MAO, resulting in an increase in availability of these amines in the synapse.

PHARMACOGENETICS

- There is a wide interindividual variation in platelet MAO activity, with as much as 50-fold difference among individual subjects.
- Low MAO-B activity has been associated with stimulus-seeking, suicidal behavior and alcoholism.
- Increased MAO-B activity is associated with aging and neuronal loss.

Clinical Indications

GENERAL INFORMATION

- Although no longer first-line agents, the MAO inhibitors continue to serve as a valuable third-line alternative when other classes of agents are ineffective or intolerable.
- As with other antidepressant classes, MAO inhibitors may require 10–30 days to achieve therapeutic benefits.
- Some studies suggest that women respond better to MAO inhibitors than men.
- Phenelzine has been effective in the treatment of "atypical depression."
- Tranylcypromine was historically recommended for "anergic bipolar depression" and continues to be recommended for "treatment-resistant depression."
- Isocarboxazid is often the most tolerated of nonselective MAO inhibitors but is rarely prescribed in most countries (hence, not manufactured).
- Selegeline (l-deprenyl) is available in the United States as a transdermal preparation.
  √ By avoiding first-pass hepatic metabolism, dietary precautions are not required at the lower dose range for selegiline.

ATYPICAL DEPRESSION

- This is depression characterized by preservation of mood reactivity accompanied by two or more of the following symptoms:
  √ Extreme sensitivity to rejection or interpersonal loss
  √ Increased appetite
  √ Weight gain
  √ Hypersomnia
- Based on early treatment studies, phenelzine is frequently recommended for patients with atypical depression.
- Moclobemide and several SSRIs have also been shown to be effective in this population.

- There is considerable overlap between atypical depression and borderline personality disorder, for which phenelzine and tranylcypromine have both been effective.

ANERGIC BIPOLAR DEPRESSION

- Tranylcypromine was initially recommended for low energy depression. Subsequent evidence in support of lamotrigine, quetiapine, olanzapine-fluoxetine combination, and other bipolar antidepressants relegates the use of tranylcypromine to a third-line choice.

ANXIETY DISORDERS AND EATING DISORDERS

- Phenelzine and moclobemide are effective in anxiety disorders (particularly social anxiety disorder and panic disorder).
- Phenelzine and isocarboxazid are effective in treating bulimia nervosa.

Side Effects

- The two main limitations of MAO inhibitors are the high side-effect burden and concerns about food and drug interactions.
- MAO inhibitors have fewer anticholinergic side effects than TCAs.
- Dizziness and orthostatic hypotension are common to all nonselective MAO inhibitors, are dose related, and may result in drug discontinuation.
- Insomnia and sexual dysfunction are also frequently encountered.
- Common long-term effects:
  √ Weight gain (74%); ankle edema (13%); sexual dysfunction (20–70%)

CARDIOVASCULAR EFFECTS

Hypotension
- Orthostatic and dose related
- Complaints of dizziness are common (20–50%).
- Increased risk of falls and fractures—special caution in the elderly.
- Patients with preexisting hypertension are more likely to be susceptible.
- Primary management
  √ Sit for 60 seconds, or longer, if at all lightheaded.
  √ Stand slowly while holding onto stable object (e.g., bed).
  √ Highest risk time is getting out of bed in middle of night.
  √ Wait for at least 30 seconds before walking.
  √ Consider support stockings or corsets at night.
  √ Ensure adequate fluid intake.
- Ancillary management
  √ Consider presence of low-sodium diet, antihypertensives; if so, increase sodium or reduce antihypertensive dose.
  √ Try less hypotensive antidepressant (AD).
  √ If BP problems persist in patients without a cardiac illness or edema, may add sodium chloride (500–650 mg bid–tid) or yohimbine (5 mg tid).
  √ Hydrate with up to 8 glasses of fluid a day; patient must also have adequate sodium intake for this to work.

√ Add methylphenidate or d-amphetamine.

√ Greater BP drops may be treated with fludrocortisone (0.1 mg qd–bid), but this is only a short-term measure until an alternative AD is prescribed.

Cardiac conduction
• Minimal effect on heart rate, cardiac conduction, or myocardial function.

Hypertension
• Rare, but may occur spontaneously, 1–3 hours after ingestion of MAO inhibitor, or as a result of interaction with tyramine foods (see Drug–Drug Interactions).
• Spontaneous hypertension subsides 3–4 hours after dose.
• Most reports with tranylcypromine.

Peripheral edema
• Particularly with phenelzine.
• Management with support stockings or diuretic.
• Rare reports of pericardial edema.

CENTRAL NERVOUS SYSTEM EFFECTS

Agitation/mania
• Stimulation is most common with tranylcypromine.
• Hypomania especially in bipolar-prone patients.
• Management
  √ Reduce dose or switch agent.
  √ Add lithium or other mood stabilizers if evidence of bipolar risk.

Nocturnal myoclonus
• Often reported by sleeping partner.
• Indicative of excessive dose.
• Management
  √ Reduce or spread out dosing.
  √ Switch to another MAO inhibitor or other AD.
  √ Add clonazepam, carbamazepine, or valporate.

Sleep disturbance and day-time sedation
• Increased prevalence at higher doses (e.g., phenelzine > 60 mg daily).
• Insomnia is associated with REM sleep suppression.
• Abrupt discontinuation often results in REM rebound and disturbing nightmares.
• Management
  √ Avoid nighttime dosing.
  √ Decrease dose if possible.
  √ Consider alternative MAO inhibitor.
  √ Warn about increased risk of accidents (e.g., machinery, driving).

Toxicity
• Confusion/ataxia; patient may appear intoxicated.
• Seizures; seizure threshold lowered in patients with epilepsy.

- Management
  - √ Discontinue MAO inhibitor therapy.

Vitamin B6 (pyridoxine) deficiency
- Associated with isocarboxazid or phenelzine
- May cause muscle spasm, pain, and paresthesia.
- May result in peripheral neuropathy.
- Additional signs and symptoms:
  - √ Stomatitis
  - √ Anemia
  - √ Ataxia
  - √ Hyperreflexia
  - √ Seizure/coma (rarely)
  - √ Hyperacusis
  - √ Hyperirritability
  - √ Depression
  - √ Carpal tunnel pain
- Management
  - √ Treat with pyridoxine 100 mg daily.
  - √ Expect response in 2–10 weeks.
  - √ Avoid excessive pyridoxine dosing.

Word-finding difficulty
- Lower or stop MAO inhibitor.

ENDOCRINE EFFECTS

Hypoglycemia and carbohydrate craving
- Management: May require MAO inhibitor discontinuation.

EYES, EARS, NOSE, AND THROAT

- Dry eyes, blurred vision, and narrow-angle glaucoma
- Nasal congestion
- Vertigo, tinnitus, nystagmus

GASTROINTESTINAL EFFECTS

Hepatotoxicity
- Rare but potentially severe
- Complaints of weakness, malaise, nausea, anorexia
- Accompanied by signs of jaundice and skin rash
- Laboratory evidence of eosinophilia and elevated liver enzymes
- Management: drug discontinuation.

Weight gain
- Most common with phenelzine, least with tranylcypromine.
- May relate to fluid retention or increased appetite.

SEXUAL EFFECTS

- Decreased sexual interest (libido), arousal, and orgasm/ejaculation are common across MAO inhibitors (20–70%) and have previously been underreported.

ANTIDEPRESSANTS

• Management
  √ Dose reduction/switch to another MAO inhibitor.
  √ Sildenafil may be helpful in both men and women without heart disease.
  √ Other agents, such as cyprohepatidine and bethanechol, are alternatives.

Drug and Food Interactions

DRUG–DRUG INTERACTIONS

Drugs to Avoid During MAO Inhibitor Therapy

Drugs (X) Interact with:	MAO Inhibitors (M)[a]	Comments
Antidepressant		
MAO inhibitor	M↓	Hypertensive crisis
SSRI	X↑	Serotonergic crisis; death reported.
TCA	M↑	*Do not add TCA to MAO inhibitor*; risk of noradrenergic or serotonergic crisis.
Antihypertensive	X↑	Hypotension
Antipsychotics	X↑ M↑	Hypotension; may increase EPS, particularly in FGAs and in risperidone at higher doses (> 5 mg).
Bronchodilators (e.g., albuterol, theophylline)	X↑	Palpitations, tachycardia, anxiety, increased BP
Insulin	X↑	May lower blood sugar.
Narcotic (e.g., meperidine, pentazocine, dextromethorphan)	M↑	Serotonergic crisis, increased reslessness, potentiation of analgesic effect
Stimulants/ sympathomimetics (e.g., ephedrine, amphetamine, methylphenidate, levodopa)	M↑	Increased blood pressure and hypertensive crisis, specially at high doses

[a]↑ = increases; ↓ = decreases.

Combining MAO inhibitors and TCAs, SSRIs, or SNRIs can generate two major problems:

• *Serotonergic crisis (hyperthermic reaction)*
  √ Avoid MAO inhibitors with SSRI, venalfaxine, mirtazapine, imipramine, or clomipramine.
• *Noradrengergic crisis (hypertensive reaction)*
  √ Avoid MAO inhibitors with other TCAs, venlafaxine, bupropion, or mirtazapine.
• However, nonserotonergic TCAs can be combined with MAO inhibitors under carfully supervised conditions in treatment-refractory depression. However, both agents should be started together or MAO inhibitor added to TCA.

Symptoms of Serotonergic or Noradrenergic Crisis Due to MAO Combination

Serotonergic Crisis	Noradrenergic Crisis
Elevated temperature, fever, shivering	Hypertension (BP increases 30–60 points)
Abnormal muscle movements, such as	Occipital headaches
fasciculations, twitches, myoclonic jerking	Stiff or sore neck
Hyperreflexia	Retroorbital pain
Hypotension, shock	Flushing, sweating, cold and clammy skin
Anxiety, agitation	Tachycardia > bradycardia
Enhanced startle response	Nausea, vomiting
Insomnia	Sudden unexplained nosebleeds
Confusion, delirium	Dilated pupils, visual disturbances
Seizures, death	Photophobia
	Constricting chest pains
	Stroke or coma, death

DRUG–FOOD INTERACTIONS

Severity of reaction is directly proportional to the quantity of tyramine in the food portion.

Food and Beverages to Avoid During MAO Inhibitor Therapy

Food Type	Foods To Be Avoided	Foods Allowed (in moderate quantities)
Cheese	All matured or aged cheese (cheese should be considered aged unless known safe)	Fresh cottage cheese, cream cheese, ricotta cheese, and processed cheese slices
	Casseroles made with these cheeses (e.g., lasagna)	Fresh milk products (e.g., sour cream, yogurt, ice cream)
Meat	Fermented/dry sausage (e.g., pepperoni, salami, mortadella, summer sausage)	All fresh packaged or processed meat, such as hot dogs, fish, or poultry: Store in refrigerator immediately and eat as soon as possible.
	Improperly stored meat, fish, or poultry	
	Improperly stored pickled herring	
Fruits and vegetables	Fava or broad bean pods (not beans)	Banana pulp
	Banana peels	All other fruits and vegetables
Beverages	All tap (draft) beer	Alcohol: no more than two bottled or canned beers or two 4-ounce glasses of wine per day
	Red wine	Spirits in limited quantities
Miscellaneous	Marmite concentrated yeast extract	Other yeast extract (e.g., Brewer's yeast)
	Sauerkraut	Pizzas without aged cheeses
	Soy sauce or other soybean condiments	Soybean milk, tofu

- With MAO inhibition, there is an inability to deaminate tyramine in the gut, resulting in displacement of intracellular stores of norepinephrine.
- Wide interindividual variations in susceptibility to tyramine reactions exist.
  √ For most people, at least 6–8 mg of tyramine in a meal is required to precipitate a hypertensive crisis.
  √ The risk of a hypertensive crisis is greater with tranylcypromine ($\geq$ 5 mg tyramine may be risky).

ANTIDEPRESSANTS

Special Populations

CHILDREN AND ADOLESCENTS

- MAO inhibitors are generally not recommended due to concerns about dietary and drug interactions.
- Limited evidence from case series suggests beneficial effects.

WOMEN: PREGNANCY AND POSTPARTUM

- Not recommended during pregnancy.

Pregnancy Rating	• Category C
Teratogenicity (1st trimester)	• Increased congenital malformations have been reported with phenelzine and tranyl-cypromine.
Direct Effect on Newborn (3rd trimester)	• Most severe risk is hypertensive crisis during pregnancy—an unacceptable risk to fetus.
Lactation	• In breast milk; potential risk of interaction with soybean milk or other food ingested by infant.

LATE LIFE

Advantages
- Less anticholinergic side effects
- Demonstrated clinical efficacy
- May limit age-related increase in MAO-B activity.

Disadvantages
- Increased risk of falls due to orthostatic hypotension
- Concerns about drug interactions with polypharmacy

Effects on Laboratory Tests

Effects of Monoamine Inhibitors on Blood/Serum and Urine Tests

	Blood/Serum Tests		Urine Tests	
Generic Name	Marker	Results[a]	Marker[a]	Results
Isocarboxazid	LFT	↑		
Moclobemide	Prolactin	↑		
Phenelzine	Glucose	↓	5-HIAA, VMA	
	LFT	↑		
Selegiline	None			
Tranylcypromine	Glucose	↓	5-HIAA, VMA	

[a]↑ = increases; ↓ = decreases.
LFT = liver function tests (AST/SGOT, ALT/SGPT, alkaline phosphatase, bilirubin, and LDH).

Discontinuation

- Abrupt discontinuation is not recommended.
- Discontinuation emergent symptoms include:
  √ Agitation
  √ Headache
  √ Tremulousness, muscle weakness
  √ Confusion, delirium, mania
  √ Hallucinations, psychosis
  √ Sleep disturbance/vivid dreams associated with REM rebound
- Residual effects of MAO inhibitors may exist after discontinuation of the therapy.
- MAO inhibitor diet and concomitant drug restriction should persist for at least 2 weeks after phenelzine, tranylcypromine, isocarboxazid.
- Moclobemide washout of 3–5 days is adequate.
- Initiation of SSRI or SNRI therapy before drug washout has resulted in death.

Overdose: Toxicity, Suicide, and Treatment

A 10-day supply of an MAO inhibitor can be lethal in overdose.

Overdose symptoms

- May develop in 4–12 h.
- Maximal at 24–48 h.
- Usually resolve in 3–4 days.
- May persist for 12–14 days.

Toxic effects can be divided into four phases:

- Phase I: asymptomatic or latent period
- Phase II: neuromuscular excitation
- Phase III: central nervous system depression, cardiovascular collapse
- Phase IV: secondary complications

Management of MAO-inhibitor overdose

- Remember that diet and drug interactions may also occur during overdose.
- If suspect overdose of MAO inhibitor, collect specimens for a toxicology screen, electrolytes, CBC, and blood glucose.
- Renal function, including BUN and creatinine should be monitored.
- For hepatoxtocity, evaluate liver function tests about 2 weeks and again 4–6 weeks after MAO-inhibitor overdose.
- Hypotension
  √ May evolve into shock, coma, cardiovascular insufficiency, myocardial infarction, or arrhythmias.
  √ Pressor amines (e.g., norepinephrine) should be used with extreme caution and the dose carefully titrated to response.
  √ Avoid CNS stimulants and contraindicated drugs.

- Seizures can be managed with conventional anticonvulsant therapy.
- For increased temperature, apply external cooling.
- Carefully observe patient for at least 1 week after the overdose.

Precautions

Contraindicated in presence of:

- Cerebrovascular disease and congestive heart failure
- Pheochromocytoma
- Foods with large amounts of tyramine and dopamine
- Medications previously listed (*see* p. 70).
- Recurrent or severe headache, unless good home BP monitoring
- Hypersensitivity to MAO inhibitors
- Myelography
  √ Stop MAO inhibitor at least 48 h before myelography.
  √ Resume MAO inhibitor at least 24 h after myelography.
- Liver disease or abnormal liver function
- Children under 16 y.o.

Use with *caution* in presence of:

- Hyperthyroidism
- Diabetes mellitus
- Renal impairment
- Epilepsy
- Recurrent or severe headaches (requires good home BP monitoring)
- Hypertension
  √ Monitor for spontaneous BP increase (seen more with tranylcypromine).
  √ Lower the antihypertensive dose if common MAO-inhibitor hypotensive effect is seen.
- Anginal pain
  √ Patients with coronary heart disease should be warned about overexertion, as MAO inhibitors may suppress pain.
- Parkinson's disease
  √ Symptoms may be increased, but more often are decreased, as seen with selegiline.
- Asthma
  √ Okay if patient managed well with nonsystemic steroids and/or cromolyn.
  √ Acute crisis will require epinephrine, not indirect pressors.
- Severe allergic reactions
  √ Epinephrine probably okay, but test dose with BP monitoring required.

Key Points to Communicate to Patients and Families

- Provide a wallet card describing the MAO inhibitor regimen and nifedepine 10 mg capsule for emergency use.

- Ensure that up-to-date diet and drug interaction information has been provided.
- Encourage self-monitoring of blood pressure for hypotensive and hypertensive changes.
- Managing hypotension
  √ Dosage decrease, diuretic, support stockings may all help.
- Managing hypertension
  √ Advise emergency room visit if diastolic blood pressure > 120 mm Hg or systolic blood pressure >175 mm Hg.
  √ Nifedipine 10 mg is indicated for rapid treatment of hypertensive crisis.
  √ Phentolamine 5–10 mg IV is an alternative.

TRANSPORTER INHIBITORS

Dosing, Dose Form, and Color

Profile of Transporter Inhibitors

Generic Names	Therapeutic Dose Range (mg/day)	Geriatric Dose (mg/day)	Dose Form (mg)[a]	Color
TRICYCLIC ANTIDEPRESSANTS (TCAs)				
Amitriptyline	100–300	25–100	t: 10/25/50/75/ 100/150 p: 10 mg/ml	t: blue/yellow/beige/orange/ mauve/blue
Amoxapine	200–400	100–150	t: 25/50/100/150	t: white/orange/blue/peach
Clomipramine	125–300	50–150	c: 25/50/75	c: ivory–melon yellow/ ivory–aqua-blue/ivory– yellow
Desipramine	150–300	20–100	t: 10/25/50/75/ 100/150	t: blue/yellow/ green/orange/ peach/white
Doxepin	150–300	30–150	c: 10/25/50/75/ 100/150 o: 10 mg/ml	c: red–pink/blue–pink/ peach–off-white/pale pink–light pink/blue– white/blue
Imipramine	150–300	30–100	t: 10/25/50 p: 25 mg/2 ml	t: All coral t: oval orange/round
Maprotiline	150–225	50–75	t: 25/50/75	orange/oval white
Nortriptyline	75–150	10–75	c: 10/25/50/75 o: 10 mg/5 ml	c: orange–white/orange– white/white/orange
Protriptyline	30–60	10–30	t: 5/10 c: 10/25	t: orange/yellow c: cream/gold
Trimipramine	150–300	25–150	c: 25/50/100	c: blue–yellow/blue–orange/ blue–white
SELECTIVE SEROTONIN REUPTAKE INHIBITORS (SSRIs)				
Citalopram	20–40	10–20	t: 20/40	t: pink/white
Escitalopram	10–20	10	t: 5/10/20 o: 5 mg/5 ml	t: all white to off-white
Fluoxetine	20–60	5–40	c: 10/20 o: 20 mg/5 ml	c: green–gray/off-white
Fluvoxamine	100–300	50–200	t: 50/100	t: yellow/beige
Paroxetine	20–60	10–40	t: 20/30	t: pink/blue
Sertraline	50–200	25–150	t: 50/100	t: light blue/light yellow

Generic Names	Therapeutic Dose Range (mg/day)	Geriatric Dose (mg/day)	Dose Form (mg)[a]	Color
SEROTONIN AND NOREPINEPHRINE REUPTAKE INHIBITORS (SNRIs)				
Desvenlafaxine	100–200			
Duloxetine	30–90	30–60	c: 20/30/60	c: green/blue–white/ green–blue
Milnacipran[b]	50–150	25–100	c: 25/50	c: pink/red–pink
Venlafaxine	75–375	37.5–225	t: 25/37.5/50/ 75/100	t: all peach
NOREPINEPHRINE AND DOPAMINE REUPTAKE INHIBITOR (NDRI)				
Bupropion	150–450	75–150	t: 100/150	t: blue/purple

[a]c = capsule; o = oral concentrate; p = parenteral concentrate; t = tablets.
[b]Not available in United States.

Pharmacology

PHARMACOKINETICS

- TCAs
  - √ Divided into tertiary and secondary amines.
    - □ Tertiary amines amitriptyline and imipramine are respectively metabolized to the secondary amines nortriptyline and desipramine.
  - √ Primarily absorbed in the small intestine
  - √ Absorption can be affected by changes in the gut motility.
  - √ Lipophilic and extensively metabolized in the liver on first pass
  - √ Highly protein bound (85–95%)
  - √ Relatively narrow therapeutic index (based on cardiotoxicity)
  - √ Evidence for dose–response relationships, particularly desipramine and nortriptyline, supported the use of plasma monitoring for safety and effectiveness.
- SSRIs
  - √ Well absorbed and not generally affected by food administration
    - □ Sertraline is an exception to this rule—plasma level may be increased by food.
  - √ Metabolized by hepatic microsomal enzymes and are potent inhibitors of these enzymes with different agents impacting on different subsets of enzymes.
  - √ Varying half-lives ranging from 15 hours to several days
  - √ Fluoxetine is the only SSRI with an active metabolite (norfluoxetine: half-life of 7–15 days).
    - □ Thus, it may take several weeks to achieve steady sate with this agent.
  - √ Highly protein bound
  - √ Eliminated in the urine as inactive metabolites
  - √ Fluoxetine and paroxetine are capable of inhibiting their own clearance at clinically relevant doses.
  - √ Minimal support for plasma monitoring due to lack of relationship between plasma levels and safety or effectiveness

- SNRIs
  √ Well absorbed from the gastrointestinal tract
  √ There is a 3-hour delay in absorption and a 30% increase in clearance with an evening dose of duloxetine as compared to a morning dose.
  √ Low protein binding with milnacipran, venlafaxine, desvenlafaxine
  √ Metabolized predominately by the liver
  √ Limited role for plasma monitoring
- NDRI (bupropion)
  √ Rapid absorption with peak concentration occurring within 3 h
  √ Highly protein bound
  √ Metabolized predominately by the liver
  √ Weak inducer of its own metabolism, as well as of other drugs
  √ Use cautiously in patients with hepatic impairment—reduce dose or frequency of administration.

Pharmacokinetic Properties of Transporter Inhibitors

Generic Names	Bioavailability (%)	Protein Binding (%)	Half-Life (h)	P450 Systems Substrate	P450 Systems Inhibitor	Excretion (%)[a]
Amitriptyline	48 ± 11	94	21	2D6, 2C, 1A2, 3A4	2D6	98 R
Amoxapine		90	8			69 R 18 F
Bupropion	> 80		9.8	2B6	2D6	87 R 10 F
Citalopram	80	80	35	2C19, 3A4, 2D6	2D6	85 R 10 F
Clomipramine	50	97	32	2D6, 1A2, 2C19	2D6	51–60 R 24–32 F
Desipramine	33–51	87 ± 3	22	2D6	2D6	70 R
Desvenlafaxine		Low	9–11			
Doxepin	27 ± 10	90	17		2D6	98 R
Duloxetine	50	> 90	12	2D6, 1A2	2D6	70 R 20 F
Escitalopram	80	56	35		2D6	
Fluoxetine	72	94 ± 1	60	2D6, 2C9	2D6, 2C9, 2C19	60 R 30 F
Fluvoxamine	53	80	15.6	2D6, 2C9	2D6, 1A2, 2C19, 3A4	90 R
Imipramine	50	93 ± 1.5	25	2D6, 2C19, 3A4	2D6	80 R 20 F
Maprotiline		88	40			60 R 30 F
Milnacipran[b]	85	13	8			
Nortriptyline	51 ± 5	92 ± 2	32	2D6		67 R 10 F
Paroxetine	50	94 + 1	26	2D6	2D6	64 R 36 F
Protriptyline	77–93	92	78	2D6		50 R
Sertraline	44	98	26	3A4	2D6, 2C9	45 R 45 F
Trimipramine	40	95	10	2D6		80 R 10 F
Venlafaxine	92	30 ± 2	5 ± 1	2D6, 3A3/4		87 R

[a]F = fecal; R = renal.
[b]Not available in United States.

PHARMACODYNAMICS

- TCAs
  - √ Most act as inhibitors of norepinephrine transporter, although several have equal or greater affinity for serotonin transporter.
  - √ Tertiary TCAs tend to be more anticholinergic, antihistaminic, and anti-alpha-adrenergic than secondary TCAs.
    - □ These receptor-blocking actions result in a wide range of side effects.
- SSRIs
  - √ Selective for reuptake inhibition of serotonin, with few effects on the adrenergic, histaminergic, and cholinergic systems.
- SNRIs
  - √ Affinity for both norepinephrine and serotonin transporters.
  - √ Absence of additional receptor effects results in fewer side effects compared to TCAs.
- NDRI (Bupropion)
  - √ Inhibits reuptake of norepinephrine and into presynaptic neurons.
  - √ Antidepressant activity is mediated primarily through noradrenergic and/or dopaminergic pathways.

Antidepressant Postsynaptic Receptor and Reuptake Blockade of Neurotransmitters

Generic Names	Postsynaptic Receptor Blockade[a]					Reuptake Blockade[a]	
	H_1	DA	ACH	α_1	α_2	NE	5-HT
Amitriptyline	3	1	4	4	3	2	2
Amoxapine	2	2	1	3	2	3	+/−
Bupropion	+/−	+/−	0	+/−	0	+/−	0
Citalopram	2	1	3	1	0	1	3
Clomipramine	3	1	3	4	2	2	3
Desipramine	1	1	2	2	1	4	+/−
Desvenlafaxine	0	+/−	0	0	0	1	1
Doxepin	4	1	3	4	3	2	1
Duloxetine	0	1	0	0	0	3	4
Escitalopram	0	0	0	0	0	1	3
Fluoxetine	+/−	1	+/−	+/−	0	1	3
Fluvoxamine	0	0	0	+/−	0	1	4
Imipramine	2	1	3	3	2	2	2
Maprotiline	3	1	1	3	1	3	0
Nortriptyline	2	1	2	3	2	3	+/−
Paroxetine	0	0	2	+/−	0	+/−	4
Protriptyline	2	1	4	2	1	4	+/−
Sertraline	0	3[b]	+/−	1	0	1	4
Trimipramine	4	2	3	4	4	1	0
Venlafaxine	0	+/−	0	0	0	1	1

[a]4 = most potent; +/− = weak affect; 0 = no effect.
[b]This primarily represents *pre*synaptic uptake blockade rather than *post*synaptic blockade.

Clinical Indications

GENERAL INFORMATION

- Antidepressants typically require 7–21 days at a therapeutic dose to start working.

- In the majority of responders improvement will be apparent after 4 weeks.
- Response may be delayed up to 12 weeks in some patients.
- Too low dosing and/or too short duration are frequent reasons for treatment failures.
- Remission may take significantly longer than response.
- Remission results in reduced rate of relapse and better quality of life.

MAJOR DEPRESSION

- The presence of external stressors does not preclude antidepressant therapy. Stressful events add to genetic and other biological vulnerability factors, thus increasing the risk of depression and influencing therapeutic response, and even adverse event propensity.
- 50–70% of moderately to severely depressed patients respond to antidepressant therapy.
- SSRIs and SNRIs are first choice for most depressed patients based on superior tolerability and comparable efficacy to TCAs.
- Some evidence that TCAs may have slight superiority in severe inpatient or melancholic depression.
- Remission rates (35–50%) are generally lower than response rates (60–70%) with first antidepressant.

BIPOLAR DEPRESSION

In known bipolar patients

- An antidepressant alone is not the first-line treatment.
- TCAs, venlafaxine, and MAO inhibitors are more likely to induce mania or hypomania (about 15% of patients).
- Bupropion, paroxetine, and sertraline (and probably other SSRIs) induce mania less often (2–3%) than TCAs or venlafaxine.
- Bupropion has a lower risk of inducing mania.

OBSESSIVE–COMPULSIVE DISORDER (OCD)

- Clomipramine, fluvoxamine, fluoxetine, paroxetine, and sertraline are approved for use in treating OCD.
- Other SSRIs and venlafaxine are also effective.
- Although these agents are significantly better than placebo, in practice, they may only reduce symptoms by 30–50%.
- OCD patients often need higher mean doses of antidepressants compared to depressed patients, and time to improvement can be significantly longer (3–6 months).

PANIC DISORDER

- SSRIs (citalopram, escitalopram, paroxetine, or sertraline) and venlafaxine are considered the first-line treatment for anxiety disorders, with good evidence of efficacy in panic disorder.

ANTIDEPRESSANTS

- Other SSRIs as well as TCAs are also effective.
- Start at low doses (e.g., 5 mg of fluoxetine) and increase slowly to an effective dose to minimize potential side effects.

GENERALIZED ANXIETY DISORDER (GAD)

- Good evidence exists for the use of SSRIs and SNRIs.
- TCAs have also shown moderate effectiveness but more side effects.

OTHER INDICATIONS

These agents are also approved for use in

- Social anxiety disorder (paroxetine, sertraline, venlafaxine)
- Nocturnal enuresis (imipramine)
- Bulimia nervosa (fluoxetine)
- Neuropathic pain (duloxetine, milnacipran under investigation)

Side Effects

ANTICHOLINERGIC EFFECTS

The use of TCAs is markedly limited by their effects on the cholinergic system, including

- √ Confusion, memory impairment
- √ Dry mouth
- √ Constipation, paralytic ileus
- √ Urinary hesitancy or retention
- √ Blurred vision, dry eyes, narrow-angle glaucoma, photophobia
- √ Nasal congestion

CARDIOVASCULAR/HEMATOLOGIC EFFECTS

Bleeding
- Bleeding complications have been reported with use of SSRIs, including melena, rectal bleeding, menorrhagia, nose bleeding, and bruising.
  √ A result of inhibitory action on serotonin uptake by platelets.
- There is also an increased risk of peri-operative bleeding in patients undergoing surgery.
  √ It is recommended to discontinue the drug before elective surgery.

Blood pressure
- *Hypertension*
  √ Venlafaxine may elevate BP, particularly at higher doses.
    □ Treatment-emergent hypertension: 375 mg/day, 4.5%; 225 mg/day, 2.2%; 75 mg/day, 1.1%; placebo, 1.1%.
    □ Sustained hypertension (defined as supine diastolic blood pressure > 90 mm Hg and > 10 mm Hg above baseline for 3 consecutive visits):

300 mg/day, 13%; 201–300 mg/day, 7%; 101–200 mg/day, 5%; < 100 mg/day, 3%; placebo, 2%.
- *Hypotension with dizziness*
  √ Most common form is orthostatic hypotension.
  √ TCAs generate considerable hypotension (least with secondary amines).
  √ SSRIs and SNRIs cause almost no hypotension.
  √ Hypotension more common in
     □ Cardiac patients (14–24%) than in medically well patients (0–7%)
     □ Older adults report a 4% injury rate due to falls (e.g., fractures, lacerations).
  √ Measure BPs reclining, sitting, and standing, before and during the first few weeks of TCA treatment, and with every dose increase.
  √ Management (*see* p. 67)

Heart rate fluctuations
- *Arrhythmias*
  √ TCAs are Type IA antiarrhythmic drugs, a class that has been associated with increased risk of mortality in postmyocardial infarction patients
  √ Occur unexpectedly
  √ About 0.4%, more common after TCA overdose (e.g., > 500 ng/ml imipramine and desipramine)
     □ Desipramine is most likely to cause this fatality in O.D.
- *Bradycardia*
  √ Occasional reports of significant bradycardia with fluoxetine.
     □ May occur with other SSRIs.
- *Tachycardia*
  √ Occasionally seen with noradrenergic TCAs (e.g., desipramine, protriptyline)
  √ May be more pronounced in younger patients

Cardiac conduction
- *ECG changes* with TCAs include:
  √ Nonspecific ST and T wave changes
  √ Prolongation of PR interval
  √ Widening of QRS complex
  √ Prolongation of QTc interval
- TCA doses, and not cardiac disease, incite these ECG alterations.
- TCAs can increase cardiac risk with certain types of heart block.
  √ Some risk with bundle-branch or bifasicular block
  √ Little risk in first-degree atrioventricular or hemiblock
  √ Can produce fatalities in patients with second- and third-degree heart block
- In patients with cardiac conduction disease
  √ Start with SSRI or SNRI.
  √ Restrict use of TCA to treatment-resistant depression and with close monitoring.
  √ Monitor using ECG and plasma levels if TCA used.

Heart failure
- *Myocardial depression, decreased cardiac output, congestive heart failure*
- *Pedal edema* frequently induced by amitriptyline.

CENTRAL NERVOUS SYSTEM EFFECTS

Agitation
- Most common with bupropion and SSRIs, especially fluoxetine.
- May resolve after 2–4 weeks.
- Management
   √ Gradual increase in dose
   √ Short-term use of benzodiazepines

Confusion, disturbed concentration, disorientation, delirium, memory impairment
- Most with TCAs.
- Greater risks of confusional states in elderly than in younger adults using TCAs (40–50% in age 60 and older).
- Management
   √ Discontinue TCA and switch to SSRI.
      □ Start with SSRI if > 40 y.o.
   √ If TCA needed, consider secondary amines.
- *Delirium*
   √ Most commonly seen with TCAs and when using multiple agents
   √ Dose-dependent; in 6% of tertiary TCA-treated patients
   √ Increased risk with high plasma levels
   √ May be superimposed on current depression or psychosis and may be difficult to diagnose.
      □ Increased TCA dose or adding antipsychotic may worsen toxicity.
- *Memory impairment*
   √ Especially in older adults treated with TCAs, with high anticholinergic effects.
   √ If there is memory impairment, consider
      □ Depression
      □ CNS illness
      □ Endocrine (e.g., hypothyroidism) or infectious (e.g., pneumonia) basis
      □ Medication-induced toxicity
- Difficulties in word finding and name recall have been reported with all antidepressants (ADs).
   √ Frequency and mechanism unknown

Perceptual abnormalities (e.g., visual or auditory hallucinations)
- Case reports of visual hallucinations with fluoxetine, fluvoxamine, paroxetine, and sertraline
- May occur with concurrent use of SSRI and MAO inhibitor (except selegiline or moclobemide)
   √ Beware long half-life of fluoxetine, requiring a 5-week washout before initiating MAO inhibitor therapy.

- May occur in "serotonin syndrome"
- Management
  √ Reduce/discontinue agent and substitute another novel agent.

For serotonin syndrome, serotonin antagonist cyproheptadine 4–12 mg is useful with discontinuation of SSRI, and hospitalization is indicated.

Depersonalization, "spaciness"
- May occur with TCAs, SSRIs, or SNRIs
- Management
  √ Limit dose or escalate more slowly.
  √ If side effect persists, switch to another AD.

Extrapyramidal side effects
- Rare with novel antidepressants
- Most often seen with amoxapine, a derivative of the antipsychotic loxapine.
  √ Presents with parkinsonian symptoms: dyskinesia and akathesia and tardive dyskinesia in the long term.
  √ Not always dose-related.
  √ Neuroleptic malignant syndrome (*see* pp. 10–12)

Headache
- Common with all ADs, most with SSRIs and venlafaxine
- Dose-dependent
- Worsening of migraine
- Management
  √ Gradual increase in dose
  √ Analgesic prn

Insomnia
- Most common with SSRIs, bupropion, venlafaxine, and protriptyline
- Management
  √ Use A.M. dosing.
  √ Add trazodone 25–100 mg qhs, zolpidem 10–20 mg po qhs, or standard hypnotic.

Muscle tremors, twitches, jitters (occasional)

Panic attack or anxiety
- If h/o panic disorder, start with very low dose.
  √ Imipramine 10 mg or citalopram 10 mg
  √ Avoid exciting antidepressants (e.g., fluoxetine).
- Without h/o panic disorder, try another antidepressant.
  √ Reaction may have been idiosyncratic.
  √ Less activating drug should be considered (e.g., stop fluoxetine and try paroxetine).

A
N
T
I
D
E
P
R
E
S
S
A
N
T
S

Paresthesias (infrequent)

Sedation
- Often seen at higher doses: $>$ 45 mg fluoxetine and $>$ 225 mg venlafaxine
- Occurs during first 2 weeks of therapy.
- Management
  √ Give all ADs in single hs dose except those requiring divided dosing, including:
    □ Bupropion SR
    □ Fluvoxamine
    □ Venlafaxine
  √ Switch to less sedating AD, in particular fluoxetine, sertraline, or bupropion.

Seizures
- Primarily reported in patients with underlying seizure disorder.
  √ Afflicts 0.1% of SSRI patients.
    □ Similar risk estimated with new formulations of bupropion.
  √ Afflicts 0.2% of patients on TCA or venlafaxine.
- With TCAs, seizures can occur following
  √ Abrupt drug increase
  √ Drug withdrawal
  √ Overdose (most with blood level $>$ 1000 ng/ml).
- Higher TCA plasma levels ($>$ 450 ng/ml) increase risk of seizures.

Suicidal ideation
- ADs can cause restlessness or agitation before improving core symptoms of depression.
- This agitation may worsen, with suicidal thoughts and behavior associated with the depressive disorder.
- Risk for suicide should be closely monitored during the first few weeks of AD therapy and when dose is adjusted.
- An FDA warning statement recommends close observation of worsening depression or the emergence of suicidality in adult and pediatric patients treated with AD agents.
- Some evidence that adolescents and young adults may be more vulnerable.
  √ Fluoxetine may be the preferred agent in this population.

Tremor
- Fine tremor seen with TCAs, SSRIs, venlafaxine, and bupropion.
- Management
  √ Dose reduction
  √ Low doses of benzodiazepines (clonazepam or alprazolam)
  √ Add propranolol 10–20 mg bid–qid, if severe.

Vivid dreaming, nightmares
- Can occur with any AD.
- Management

√ Change AD.
√ Spread dose throughout day.

Yawning without sedation
• Occasionally seen with serotonergic drugs (SSRIs and clomipramine).

ENDOCRINE EFFECTS

• Syndrome of inappropriate antidiuretic hormone (SIADH)
  √ Cases of hyponatremia have been reported with SSRIs and venlafaxine.
    □ Usually in volume-depleted or dehydrated patients, including those taking diuretics
    □ Symptoms include nausea, dizziness, fatigue, and cognitive impairment.
  √ Risk factors include age, female gender, and polypharmacy.
  √ Reversal of hyponatremia when AD was discontinued.

EYES, EARS, NOSE, AND THROAT

• Dry eyes, blurred vision, and narrow-angle glaucoma.
• Dry mucous membrane
• Nasal congestion

All side effects (except nasal congestion) due to anticholinergic blockade (*see* pp. 52–54).

• All rare with fluoxetine and sertraline.

GASTROINTESTINAL EFFECTS

Anorexia, nausea, vomiting, dyspepsia
• Common (21–35%) with SSRIs and SNRIs.
• Tolerance usually develops over 10–14 days.
• If TCA, reduce dose.
• If SSRI or SNRI, take with meals or switch to controlled-release preaparations.
  √ May add antacid (e.g., bismuth salicylate).

Constipation
• Generally correlated with cholinergic blockade.
• Lowest with bupropion, citalopram, fluoxetine, fluvoxamine, sertraline, and desipramine.

Diarrhea
• Common (11–16%) with SSRIs.
• Usually transient and dose-related.
• Tolerance may develop.
• If without tolerance, loperamide (Imodium) usually works.

Dry mouth
- Occurs as noradrenergic and anticholinergic effects.
- *See* page 18.

Paralytic ileus
- Commonest with TCAs.
- Rare but potentially fatal.
- Discontinue TCAs.

Peculiar taste, "black tongue" glossitis

Weight gain, appetite stimulation, carbohydrate craving
- Weight gain develops over time with all TCAs, paroxetine, venlafaxine, and fluvoxamine, and to a lesser extent with other SSRIs.
- TCAs increase appetite and food intake; correlated with H_1 blockade (*see* p. 78).
- Management
  - √ Nutritional counseling
  - √ Exercise
  - √ Dose reduction
  - √ Changing AD (e.g., bupropion)

RENAL EFFECTS

- Urinary hesitancy or retention
  - √ Correlated with cholinergic blockade (*see* p. 20).

SEXUAL EFFECTS

Deceased libido, erectile dysfunction, diminished arousal, impaired orgasm
- Highest with SSRIs, clomipramine, and venlafaxine
- The effect is dose-related.
- Erectile dysfunction more common with TCAs.
  - √ Often secondary to anticholinergic effects
- Management
  - √ Although approved for erectile dysfunction, sildenafil (25–100 mg), tadalafil (5–10 mg), or vardenafil (5–20 mg) on a prn basis about 30 minutes before sexual activity may be helpful for other aspects of sexual dysfunction in men and women.
  - √ Bupropion (100–300 mg) or buspirone (15–60 mg) prescribed on a regular basis may improve SSRI-related sexual dysfunction.
  - √ Other agents that have been evaluated are:
    - □ Amantadine 100–400 mg/day (not used prn)
    - □ Bethanechol 10 mg tid or yohimbine 5 mg tid may reduce erectile dysfunction.
    - □ Cyproheptadine 2–6 mg prn 2 h before intercourse or tid
    - □ Ginkgo biloba 120–240 mg/day may improve SSRI-related sexual side effects after daily use for several weeks.

Testicular swelling (rare)

• Reported from desipramine
  √ Discontinue drug.

SKIN, ALLERGIES, AND TEMPERATURE

Allergic reactions are rare but may develop within 2-3 weeks of starting AD.

• Symptoms and signs include
  √ Rash, urticaria, pruritus, photosensitivity
  √ Arthralgia, fever, and lip swelling
  √ Jaundice, hepatitis
• Management
  √ In most cases, medication should be discontinued.
  √ Substitution of AD from a different class is preferred.
  √ Gradual reintroduction of original AD may be an option.

Sweating
• SSRIs and SNRIs increase sweating (7–12%)
• Management
  √ Concentrate on increased personal hygiene.
  √ Antiperspirant agents

Drug and Food Interactions

Drug Interactions with Transporter Inhibitors

Drug (X) Interacts with:	Antidepressants (A)[a]	Comments
Alcohol	X↑ A↑	CNS depression with TCA; not seen with SSRIs and SNRIs
Antidepressant MAO inhibitor	X↑ A↑	Avoid adding TCAs to MAO inhibitors. If TCAs are to be used, first taper MAO inhibitor, then keep patient off MAO inhibitor for 10–14 days. Combining SSRI or SNRI with MAO inhibitor may result in hypertensive crisis and serotonergic reaction.
SSRI (fluoxetine, fluvoxamine, paroxetine, sertraline)	A↑	Elevated TCA/SNRI plasma level; monitor plasma level and for signs of toxicity.
Antihypertensive (e.g., clonidine, guanethidine, methyldopa)	X↓	Decreased antihypertensive effect with norepinephrine uptake blockers.
Antipsychotic	X↑ A↑	Potentiate each other; toxicity; more anticholinergic TCAs may diminsh EPS; SSRIs may increase EPS and akathisia.
Estrogen	A↑	Increased TCA level, effect, toxcity; inhibits TCA metabolism; higher estrogen doses may decrease TCA effect.
Stimulant	X↑ A↑	Potentiated effect in the treatment of depression and ADHD.
Sympathomimetic	X↑	Avoid TCAs with direct-acting sympathomimetics. Increased arrhythmias, hypertension, and tachycardia.

[a]↑ = increases; ↓ = decreases.

Special Populations

CHILDREN AND ADOLESCENTS

- Regulatory agencies have imposed the requirement of a "black box" warning about the potential increased risk of suicidality (suicidal thinking and behavior) in children and adolescents who are being treated with antidepressants.
- TCAs are not useful in treating prepubertal children, and are of moderate benefit for adolescents.
- TCAs are associated with clinically important adverse effects, and most are toxic in overdose.
- SSRIs and SNRIs have generally been considered the first-choice medication.
- Clinical trials suggest that a combination of medication and psychotherapy is the most effective treatment for adolescents with depression.

WOMEN: PREGNANCY AND POSTPARTUM

Pregnancy Rating	• Bupropion: Category B
	• Imipramine, nortriptyline, paroxetine: Category D
	• Others: Category C
Teratogenicity (1st trimester)	• Little evidence of teratogenicity
	• Associated with increased miscarriage rate.
Direct Effect on Newborn (3rd trimester)	• Irritability, feeding difficulties, changes in muscle tone, respiratory distress, temperature instability, and seizures occurred in infants upon delivery when mothers are exposed to SSRIs or SNRIs.
	• Urinary retention has been associated with TCA use.
	• TCAs and SSRIs have produced neonatal withdrawal syndrome that includes irritability, convulsions, and anticholinergic symptoms in the newborn.
Lactation	• Secreted into breast milk to varying extents.
	• TCAs are reported to have low transfer into breast milk.
	• Fluoxetine transfers to a greater extent (up to 17% of maternal dose).

LATE LIFE

- Precautious with TCAs due to altered pharmacokinetics and drug interactions.
  - √ Postural hypotension is a common side effect, leading to increased risk of falls.
- Most drug interactions with TCA, fluoxetine, and paroxetine.

Effects on Laboratory Tests

Effects of Transporter Inhibitors on Blood/Serum and Urine Tests

	Blood/Serum Tests		Urine Tests	
Generic Name	**Marker**	**Results[a]**	**Marker**	**Results**
Amoxapine	WBC, LFT[b]	↑↓	None	
Desipramine	Glucose	↑↓	None	
Doxepin	Glucose	↑↓	None	
Duloxetine	LFT	↑		
	Sodium	↓		
Fluoxetine	ESR	↑↑	Albuminuria	
	Bleeding time	↓		
	Glucose	↓		
	Cholesterol, lipids	↑↑		
	Potassium Sodium	↓↓		
	Iron	↓		
	LFT	↑↓		
Imipramine	Glucose	↑↓	None	
Maprotiline	Glucose	↑↓	None	
Nortriptyline	Glucose	↑↓	None	
Paroxetine	Sodium	↑		
	Cholesterol	↑		
Sertraline	Bleeding time	↑		
	ALT	↑		
	Cholesterol	↑		
	Triglycerides	↑		
	Uric acid	↓		
Venlafaxine	Cholesterol	↑		

[a] ↑ = increases; ↓ = decreases; ↑↓ = increases and decreases.
[b] LFT = liver function tests (AST/SGOT, ALT/SGPT, alkaline phosphatase, bilirubin, and LDH) WBC = white blood cell; ESR = erthrocyte sedimentation rate.

Discontinuation

Antidepressants do not cause

- Dependence
- Tolerance
- Addiction
- But are associated with discontinuation emergent symptoms and sometimes loss of efficiency over time in some patients ("poop out").

TCAS

Abrupt discontinuation from high doses of TCAs may cause cholinergic rebound, resulting in

A
N
T
I
D
E
P
R
E
S
S
A
N
T
S

- Flu-like syndrome without fever
  - √ Anorexia, nausea, vomiting, diarrhea
  - √ Increased salivation
  - √ Anxiety, agiation, irritability
  - √ Cold sweat
  - √ Tachycardia
  - √ Tension headache, neck pains,
  - √ Chills, coryza, malaise, rhinorrhea, and dizziness
- Sleep disturbances
  - √ Insomnia
  - √ Hypersomnia
  - √ Excessive dreaming
  - √ Nightmates (due to REM rebound)
- Hypomanic or manic symptoms (rare).

These withdrawal-like symptoms

- Begin 2–4 days after discontinuation.
- Occasionally are seen as an interdose phenomenon while patient is still on TCA.
  - √ More likely on once-daily dosing
  - √ Symptoms occur several hours before next dose.
    - □ Change to bid dosing.
- May persist for 1–2 weeks
- Are not life-threatening
- Can be treated or prevented by gradually tapering AD (e.g., imipramine 25 mg q 2–3 days)
  - √ Titrate dose according to symptoms.

SSRIS AND SNRIS

Sudden discontinuation of SSRIs (except fluoxetine) or SNRIs can result in a discontinuation syndrome with features that are similar to TCA discontinuation, plus

- Serotonergic "pre-migraine" features
  - √ Vertigo often with emesis
- Visual and/or auditory hallucinations
- Headache, often migraine-like

Most commonly seen after abrupt discontinuation of paroxetine or venlafaxine. Best prevented by gradual tapering of AD or with a stat dose of fluoxetine.

Overdose: Toxicity, Suicide, and Treatment

TCAS

TCAs have a narrow therapeutic index. Symptoms of toxicity are extensions of the common side effects, and cardiotoxicity is often the cause of death.

- 10–20 mg/kg of a TCA may result in moderate to severe toxicity.
- 30–40 mg/kg of a TCA is often fatal for adults.

Deaths associated with overdoses of bupropion alone have been reported rarely in patients ingesting massive doses of the drug. Multiple uncontrolled seizures, bradycardia, cardiac failure, and cardiac arrest prior to death were reported in these patients.

Management of TCA overdose

- Establish and maintain airway, ensure adequate oxygenation and ventilation.
- Gastric lavage and use of activated charcoal should be considered.
  - √ Induced vomiting by syrup of ipecac is contraindicated (except following overdose with bupropion).
- Monitor cardiac vital signs.
- If seizure occurs, consider IM or IV diazepam.
- For cardiorespiratory problems
  - √ Cardiac arrhythmias
    - □ When QRS interval is < 0.10, ventricular arrhythmias are less frequent.
    - □ Treat ventricular arrhythmias with phenytoin, lidocaine, or propranolol.
    - □ Phenytoin often preferred because it also treats seizures.
  - √ Cardiac conduction problems
    - □ Give IV sodium bicarbonate to achieve pH of 7.4–7.5.
    - □ Quinidine, procainamide, and disopyramide should be avoided in managing conduction problems and arrhythmia, because they further depress cardiac function.
  - √ Cardiac failure: Use digoxin.

SSRIS AND SNRIS

- These agents are relatively safe with overdose when taken alone.
- No predictable dose–toxicity relationship established.
- Symptoms of SSRI overdose include
  - √ Nausea and vomiting
  - √ Agitation
  - √ Tremor
  - √ Myoclonus
- Symptoms of SNRI overdose include
  - √ Dizziness
  - √ Hypotension
  - √ Tachycardia
  - √ Arrhythmias
- Details of serotonergic (serotonin syndrome) and noradrenergic crises are highlighted in the table on page 70.

ANTIDEPRESSANTS

Precautions

TCAs are *contraindicated* in patients with

- Cardiovascular disease, including hypertension and recent myocardial infarction
  √ Hyperthyroidism may foster cardiovascular toxicity, including arrhythmias.
- Current or recent (within past 14 days) MAO inhibitor use
- Known hypersensitivity to TCAs
- Narrow-angle glaucoma
- Increased intraocular pressure

Use with *caution* in presence of

- Seizures
  √ Avoid bupropion, maprotiline, or clomipramine in patients who have an increased risk of developing seizures due to head injury, neurologic disease, active alcohol or drug abuse, or h/o anorexia nervosa or bulimia nervosa.
  √ SSRIs are preferred.
  √ Secondary amine TCAs do not appreciably lower the seizure threshold.
- Bipolar disorder
  √ ADs (especially TCAs and venlafaxine) can precipitate mania (12–50%) and increase the chance of rapid cycling.
  √ It is common for patients recovering from depression to undergo a "switch phase" into a "high" before returning to normality.
  √ This "high" might last only a day and should not be overtreated. Yet if a true switch has uncovered a manic process, it is best to treat by
    □ Reducing or discontinuing dose of AD,
    □ Initiating second-generation antipsychotic, or
    □ Adding lithium or alternative mood stabilizer.
- Abuse and dependence
  √ Although rare, misuse of amitriptyline in doses up to 2000 mg/day has been reported. This causes intoxication followed by prolonged sleep and retrograde amnesia. Discontinuing amitriptyline can be difficult; closely monitored tapering is required.
  √ Occasionally fluoxetine is abused to achieve transient stimulating effects.

Key Points to Communicate to Patients and Families

- Antidepressants are neither "happy pills" nor are they addictive.
  √ They have relatively little or no effect as euphoriants or stimulants in most mentally healthy persons.
  √ They only work in depressed individuals.
- All medications have side effects. For example, most people experience GI upset, including nausea and diarrhea, in the first few days after starting an SSRI.
  √ Some patients also report a transient increase in anxiety and "inner restlessness" with SSRIs.
  √ Most of these side effects resolve within 1–2 weeks.

- If side effects persist or are intolerable, another antidepressant from a different class can be prescribed instead.
- Antidepressant treatment should be maintained for at least 1 year after the first episode and 2 years or more after subsequent episodes.
  √ Missed doses can cause problems.
  √ At the termination of antidepressant therapy, the medication should be tapered gradually over several weeks.
- Physical symptoms of depression (e.g., disturbed sleep and appetite, agitation, and fatigue) are first to improve on AD medication.
- Psychological symptoms of depression usually take a few weeks longer to improve (e.g., poor concentration, apathy, sadness, hopelessness, low self-esteem, and suicidal ideation).
- Alcohol consumption should be reduced substantially during AD therapy.
- Keep medication away from bedside or any readily accessible place for safety reasons.

RECEPTOR ANTAGONISTS/AGONISTS

Dosing, Dose Form, and Color

Profile of Receptor Antagonists/Agonists

Generic Names	Total Daily Dose Range (mg/day)	Geriatric Dose (mg/day)	Dose Form (mg)[a]	Color
Agomelatine	25–50	25	t: 25	t: orange-yellow
Mirtazapine	15–45	7.5–30	t: 15/30/45	t: yellow/red–brown/white
Trazodone	200–600	50–200	t: 50/100/150/300	t: orange/white/orange/yellow

[a]t = tablets.

Pharmacology

PHARMACOKINETICS

Agomelatine

- Absorbed rapidly by the oral route, with peak plasma concentration occurring 1–2 hours after administration.
- Metabolized by the liver with metabolites predominately excreted in the urine.
- Hepatic impairment significantly increases plasma level.

Mirtazapine

- Bioavailability is low due to gut wall and hepatic first-pass metabolism; food slightly decreases absorption rate.
- Highly protein bound.
- Has long half-life allowing once-a-day dosing.
- Females and older adults show higher plasma concentrations than males and young adults.

ANTIDEPRESSANTS

- Hepatic clearance is decreased by 40% in patients with cirrhosis.
- Clearance is reduced by 30–50% in patients with renal impairment.

Trazodone

- Completely absorbed from the GI tract; food significantly delays and decreases peak plasma effect.
- Highly bound to plasma protein
- Metabolized primarily by the liver

Pharmacokinetic Properties of Receptor Antagonists/Agonists

Generic Names	Bioavailability (%)	Protein Binding (%)	Half-Life (h)	P450 Systems		Excretion (%)[a]
				Substrate	Inhibitor	
Agomelatine	Low	> 95	2.3	1A2, 2C9		
Mirtazapine	50	85	31	2D6, 1A2, 3A4		75 R 15 F
Trazodone	81	93 ± 2	5	3A4		70–75 R 20–25 F

[a]F = fecal; R = renal

PHARMACODYNAMICS

- Agomelatine has a novel mechanism of action: It is a potent agonist of melatonin MT_1 and MT_2 receptors, and an antagonist of 5-HT_{2C} receptors.
- Trazodone and mirtazapine equilibrate the effects of biogenic amines.
  - √ Trazodone is a serotonin reuptake inhibitor and also a 5-HT_2 and α_1 receptor antagonist.
  - √ Mirtazapine has dual enhancement of central noradrenergic and serotonergic neurotransmission by blockade of both α_2 (presynaptic) and $5\text{-HT}_{2/3}$ receptors.

Clinical Indications

MAJOR DEPRESSION

- Mirtazapine and agomelatine are effective and well tolerated for the treatment of moderate to severe major depression.
- Trazodone is rarely used alone to treat depression because of excessive sedation at therapeutic doses.
  - √ It is used more often at low doses (50–100 mg) as an adjunctive hypnotic in depressed patients.

Side Effects

Early in the drug development phase of agomelatine few side effects (e.g., dizziness) have been reported with frequency exceeding placebo. Sedation and weight gain are common with mirtazapine. All three drugs have favorable sexual side effect profiles because of their ability to block 5-HT_2 receptors.

ANTICHOLINERGIC EFFECTS

- Occur occasionally with trazodone and mirtazapine
  √ Include dry mouth, constipation, and blurred vision (*see* pp. 17–18).

CARDIOVASCULAR EFFECTS

Arrhythmias
- Reported with trazodone at doses > 200 mg/day
  √ Of most concern is ventricular fibrillation.

Hypotension with dizziness
- Most common form is orthostatic hypotension
- Measure BPs reclining, sitting, and standing, before and during the first few days of treatment.
- Management (*see* p. 67)

Tachycardia
- Rarely occurs with mirtazapine

CENTRAL NERVOUS SYSTEM EFFECTS

Confusion, disturbed concentration, or disorientation
- Mainly seen with trazodone
- Management
  √ Escalate dose more slowly.
  √ If side effect persists, switch to another AD.

Precipitation of hypomania or mania in bipolar patients
- Lower rates compared to TCAs and venlafaxine.
- Increased risk for bipolar patients with comorbid substance abuse.

Sedation, drowsiness
- Agomelatine restores circadian rhythms and should only be prescribed as bedtime medication.
- Most common (20–50%) adverse effect of trazodone and mirtazapine
- Sedation with mirtazapine may decrease at higher doses due to increased release of norepinephrine.
- Management
  √ Prescribe mirtazapine or trazodone at bedtime only.

ENDOCRINE EFFECTS

Hypercholesterolemia and hypertriglyceridemia
- Mirtazapine may increase blood levels of cholesterol and triglycerides through its effect of weight gain.
  √ Increase in serum cholesterol levels (> 20% above upper normal levels) was reported in 15% of patients following therapeutic use.
  √ Triglyceride increases of greater than 500 mg/dL were seen in 6% of patients.

Syndrome of inappropriate antidiuretic hormone (SIADH)
• Rarely, trazodone can induce SIADH with hyponatremia.
• Risk increases with age.

Weight gain
• Common with mirtazapine
   √ Increased appetite and weight gain (of over 4 kg) reported in approximately 16% of patients.
   √ Occurs primarily in the first month of treatment and may be dose-related.
   √ May be beneficial in emaciated, depressed patients.

GASTROINTESTINAL EFFECTS

Nausea and vomiting
• Relatively common with trazodone.
• Infrequent (1%) with mirtazapine due to 5-HT$_3$ blockade.

Peculiar taste, "black tongue," glossitis

SEXUAL EFFECTS

Agomelatine and mirtazapine have favorable sexual side effect profiles. Rare sexual side effects have been reported with trazodone, including the following:

Spontaneous orgasm
• Usually associated with yawning
• More common in females

Priapism
• Occurs primarily during first month of treatment; non-dose-related.
• Due to unopposed α-adrenergic blockade.
• If untreated, condition may be irreversible, resulting in permanent erectile dysfunction.
• Management
   √ Discontinue drug.
   √ Administer α-adrenergic stimulants.
      ▢ Neosynephrine (10 mg/30 cc) injected intracorporally (6 cc every 10–15 min) until response is seen or maximum of three doses is reached
      ▢ Metaraminal 10 mg intracavernosal injection into penis
   √ May require surgery.

Testicular swelling, painful ejaculation, retrograde ejacuation
• Rarely occurs.
• Discontinue drug.

SKIN, ALLERGIES, AND TEMPERATURE

Allergies are rare, and may result in

- Rashes
- Edema
- Jaundice, hepatitis

In all cases, medication should be discontinued and an unrelated antidepressant tired.

Drug and Food Interactions

Drug Interactions with Receptor Antagonists/Agonists

Drugs (X) Interacts with:	Antidepressants (A)[a]	Comments
Alcohol	X↑ A↑	Trazodone may cause enhanced sedation when used with alcohol.
Anticoagulant (e.g., warfarin)	X↑	Case reports of decreased prothrombin time and INR with trazodone
Anticonvulsants	X↑ A↓	Carbamazepine and phenytoin, CYP3A4 inducers, increased mirtazapine clearance about 2-fold, resulting in a 45–60% decrease in plasma mirtazapine concentrations. Plasma level of phenytoin increased due to inhibition of metabolism with trazodone.
Antiemetics	A↑	Case reports of serotonin syndrome with mirtazapine
Antidepressent MAO inhibitor	X↑ A↑	Possible serotonergic reaction with mirtazapine; do not combine. Trazodone only antidepressant consistently safe with MAO inhibitor, but may increase hypotension.
SSRI (fluoxetine, fluvoxamine, paroxetine, setraline)	A↑	Increased risk of serotonin syndrome; may inhibit the metabolism of trazodone via CYP2D6, resulting in elevated plasma levels. Fluvoxamine may inhibit the metabolism of agomelatine via CYP1A2.
CNS depressants (e.g., antihistamines, benzodiazepines, hypnotics, alcohol)	X↑ A↑	Increased sedation; CNS depression
Digoxin	X↑	Increased digoixin plasma level with trazodone may lead to toxicity.
Ginkgo biloba	X↑ A↓	Case report of coma with low-dose trazodone (suggested to be due to excess stimulation of GABA receptors).
St. John's wort	A↑	Trazodone increased serotonergic effects.

[a]↑ = increases; ↓ = decreases; INR = international normalized ratio.

Lack of clinical experience with agomelatine limits information about food or drug interactions.

Special Populations

CHILDREN AND ADOLESCENTS

- The safety and effectiveness in children have *not* been established.

WOMEN: PREGNANCY AND POSTPARTUM

Pregnancy Rating	• Category C
Teratogenicity (1st trimester)	• Trazodone in high doses was found to increase risk of major malformations; should be avoided if possible.
	• Insufficient data from the use of agomelatine or mirtazapine
Direct Effect on Newborn (3rd trimester)	• No available data
Lactation	• Trazodone is secreted into breast milk.

LATE LIFE

• The use of trazodone in elderly patients should be restricted due to risk of side effects (daytime sleepiness, dizziness) and drug interactions.
• Mirtazapine appears to have a faster onset of action and better tolerability profile in elderly patients compared to other antidepressants.
• Due to reduced clearance, elderly patients should be started at low doses.
   √ Adjustments should be made gradually, depending on tolerance and response.

Effects on Laboratory Tests

Effects of Receptor Antagonists/Agonists on Blood/Serum and Urine Tests

	Blood/Serum Tests		Urine Tests	
Generic Names	Marker	Results[a]	Marker	Results
Agomelatine				
Mirtazapine	Cholesterol	↑	None	
	Glucose	↑		
	Triglycerides	↑		
Trazodone	WBC, LFT[b]	↑↓	None	

[a]↑ = increases; ↓ = decreases; ↑↓ = increases and decreases.
[b]LFT = liver function tests (AST/SGOT, ALT/SGPT, alkaline phosphatase, bilirubin, and LDH).

Discontinuation

Abrupt cessation of agomelatine is not associated with discontinuation symptoms. Abrupt cessation of mirtazapine may result in dizziness, nausea, anxiety, insomnia, and paresthesia.

• Generally these events are mild to moderate and are self-limiting.

Abrupt discontinuation of high doses of trazodone may result in cholinergic rebound leading to:

• Flue-like syndrome without fever
   √ Anorexia, nausea, vomiting, diarrhea

√ Increased salivation
√ Anxiety, agiation, irritability
√ Cold sweat
√ Tachycardia
√ Tension heachage, neck pains,
√ Chills, coryza, malaise, rhinorrhea, and dizziness
• Most likely to occur 1–2 days after discontinuation, or after a large dosage decrease.
• Rebound depression can also occur.

Overdose: Toxicity, Suicide, and Treatment

Death due to overdose of trazodone administered alone is rare. Symptoms of overdose may include:

• Painful/prolonged erection
• Irregular heartbeat
• Difficulty breathing
• Drowsiness
• Vomiting
• Seizures

No reports of lethality following overdose of mirtazapine or agomelatine.

MANAGEMENT

• Treatment should be symptomatic and supportive.
• Ensure an adequate airway, oxygenation, and ventilation.
• Monitor cardiac rhythm and vital signs.
• Induction of emesis is not recommended.
• Gastric lavage should be performed soon after ingestion or in symptomatic patients.
• Forced diuresis may be useful in facilitating elimination of trazodone.

Precautions

TRAZODONE

• Contraindicated for
  √ Those in recovery period after myocardial infarction
  √ Those with hypersensitivity to trazodone
• Give cautiously in patients with
  √ Cardiovascular disease
  √ Suicidal behavior

MIRTAZAPINE

• Contraindicated with:
  √ Concurrent MAO inhibitor therapy
  √ Hypersensitivity to mirtazapine

A
N
T
I
D
E
P
R
E
S
S
A
N
T
S

- Give cautiously in patients with
  - √ History of seizures
  - √ History of suicide attempt
    - □ May increase risk of suicide attempt/ideation, especially during early treatment or dose adjustment; risk may be greater in children or adolescents.
  - √ History of mania/hypomania
  - √ Obese patients/abnormal lipid profile
  - √ Hepatic or renal insufficiency

AGOMELATINE

- No data on absolute or relative contraindications available yet.

Key Points to Communicate to Patients and Families

- Agomelatine, mirtazapine, and trazodone should be taken only as nighttime medication.
- Advise patient to avoid concurrent use of alcohol or other CNS-depressant drugs.
- Trazodone and mirtazapine may cause drowsiness and blurred vision. Caution patient to avoid driving and other activities requiring alertness if these side effects occur.
- Advise patient not to stop any drugs suddenly, as this may result in an unpleasant discontinuation syndrome lasting days and occasionally weeks.

THERAPEUTIC APPLICATION

Initiation of Treatment

SSRIs and various dual-action agents have superior side effect and safety profiles and generally comparable efficacy to TCAs and MAO inhibitors. Those benefits have resulted in their adoption as first-choice antidepressants for the treatment of major depressive disorder. Recent evidence has been presented to support higher rates of remission for some dual-action agents compared with SSRIs.

- Side effects on the initiation of antidepressants may be minimized by starting at a low dose and increasing the dose slowly, until a satisfactory therapeutic response is achieved.
- Increased risk of "suicidality," which includes suicidal thoughts as well as acts, has been reported during treatment with various antidepressants, particularly in the first few weeks of treatment.
- If there is no improvement after a 12-week course, an antidepressant from an alternative class or another treatment strategy should be considered.

Treatment-Resistant Depression

- Evidence-based sequences for antidepressant interventions are limited, but some guidelines are available.

√ There is agreement that several strategies should be considered, including optimization, switching, augmentation, and combination strategies.

√ Until recently, no single large trial had been carried out to compare many of these options.

• The Sequenced Treatment Alternatives to Relieve Depression (STAR*D) study, sponsored by the National Institute of Mental Health, was a nationwide public health clinical trial designed to determine the effectiveness of successive treatments for people with major depressive disorder who failed to achieve remission with previous intervention.

• The study employed four sequential steps that included antidepressants, cognitive therapy, and combination strategies for patients who did not achieve remission.

√ Level 1: The first treatment level consisted of citalopram at maximally tolerated doses, titrated as quickly as could be achieved.

√ Level 2: Nonremitters were randomized, depending on their preference, to switch to a different medication (bupropion SR, sertraline, or venlafaxine XR) or augment citalopram with another medication (bupropion SR or buspirone). Cognitive therapy was also an option for both groups.

√ Level 3: Nonremitters were randomized to switch to mirtazapine or nortriptyline or augment level 2 treatment with lithium or thyroid medication.

√ Level 4: Nonremitters were required to switch to tranylcypromine or to a combination of venlafaxine XR and mirtazapine.

Augmentation and Combination Therapies

• There is most evidence to support antidepressant augmentation with lithium and olanzapine.

• However, the comparable outcomes with lithium and T_3 augmentation as level 3 interventions in STAR*D support renewed interest in thyroid augmentations.

• Lithium-induced side effects are dose-related and were more burdensome in STAR*D than side effects with T_3.

Recommendations for Augmentation Strategies in Treatment-Resistant Depression

Therapeutic Choice	Recommendations	Dose
First	Lithium	600–900[a] mg
	Quetiapine	150–300 mg
	Olanzapine	5–15 mg
	Triiodothyronine (T_3)	25–50 mg
Second	Risperidone	0.5–2 mg
	Buspirone	30–60 mg
	Psychostimulants[b]	usual doses
	Pramipexole	1–5 mg
Third	Lamotrigine	100–200 mg
	Trazodone	100–200 mg
	Tryptophan[c]	2–4 g
Not recommended	Pindolol	7.5–1.5 mg

[a]Aim for 0.5–0.8 MEqIL serum level.
[b]Enhances motivation and energy.
[c]Limited availability.

ANTIDEPRESSANTS

- Several combination antidepressant strategies have been advocated, but few have been studied in a controlled design.
- Two antidepressants with different monoaminergic actions are often prescribed in treatment-resistant depression.
  - √ For example, combining desipramine and an SSRI provides both norepinephrine and serotonin (5HT) transporter inhibition.
  - √ Unfortunately, the combination of fluoxetine and desipramine has potentially dangerous kinetic interactions that may result in high plasma desipramine levels and cardiac death.
- In other cases the combination may allow one agent to offset the adverse effects of the other in addition to enhancing antidepressant outcomes.
  - √ This has been the rationale for bupropion combinations with an SSRI or venlafaxine to increase remission rates and improve sexual dysfunction.
- Generally, adding two antidepressants in combination is well tolerated, but drug–drug interactions must be considered. Pharmacokinetic and pharmacodynamic interactions occur with a combination of an SSRI and a TCA.
- The drawbacks to combination antidepressant use include the possibility that a patient might simply have responded to monotherapy with the second agent alone, yet he or she is exposed to additional side effects and the extra cost of a second medication.

Recommendations for Combination Strategies in Treatment-Resistant Depression

Therapeutic Choice	Recommendations[a]
First	SSRI/venlafaxine + mirtazapine/mianserin
Second	SSRI/SNRI + bupropion SR
Third	SSRI + TCA (caution for increased serum TCA levels with SSRI)
	SSRI + RIMA[b]

[a]RIMA = reversible inhibitor of monoamine = a; SNRI = serotonin and norepinephrine reuptake inhibitor; SSRI = selective serotonin reuptake inhibitor; TCA = tricyclic antidepressant.
[b]Caution for serotonin syndrome.

4. Dementia-Treating Agents

INTRODUCTION TO DRUG CLASS

The dementias are progressive, deteriorating illnesses with different treatment requirements at different stages of disease progression. Alzheimer's disease, vascular dementia, Lewy body dementia, and frontotemporal dementia are the most common types. Patients with dementia display a broad range of cognitive impairments, mood and behavioral symptoms, and functional decline.

Nonpharmacological strategies are generally recommended as first-line approaches during the early stages of dementia. Theses include safety modifications to the home environment, prevention of high-risk activities such as driving, and education for caregivers. Psychotropic medications (e.g., antidepressant, antipsychotic, or antianxiety agents) are frequently prescribed for behavioral control, but may also be required in the management of comorbid psychiatric syndromes associated with neuropathological changes.

Herein, the emphasis is on medications that reduce and/or delay the rate of deterioration in cognitive symptoms of dementia, delay the emergence of challenging behaviors, and slow the loss of activities of daily living. Deterioration of cognitive abilities is related to reduction in cholinergic function in the basal forebrain and the appearance of neurofibrillatory tangles and plaques containing β-amyloid. The reversible cholinesterase inhibitors—donepezil, galantamine, rivastigmine, and tacrine—represent the available "cognitive enhancers." The NMDA antagonist memantine represents an additional option for cognitive symptoms.

Cognitive Enhancers by Chemical Class

Chemical Class	Generic Name	Trade Name
CHOLINESTERASE INHIBITOR		
Acridine	Tacrine	Cognex
Carbamate	Rivastigmine	Exelon
Piperidine	Donepezil	Aricept
Phenentrine alkaloid	Galantamine	Razadyne
NMDA antagonist	Memantine	Namenda

CHOLINESTERASE INHIBITORS

Dosing, Dose Form, and Color

Profile of Cholinesterase Inhibitors

Generic Names	Therapeutic Dose Range (mg/day)	Dose Form (mg)[a]	Color
Donepezil	5–10 (qd)	t: 5/10 o: 1 mg/ml	t: white/yellow
Galantamine ER	16–24(qd)	er: 8/16/24 1: 4 mg/ml	er: white/pink/caramel
Rivastigmine	6–12 (bid)	c: 1.5/3/4.5/6 o: 2 mg/ml ts: 4.6/9.5	c: yellow/orange/red/ red–orange
Tacrine	80–160 (qid)[b]	c: 10/20/30/40	c: yellow–dark green/ yellow–light blue/yellow– orange/yellow–lavender

[a]c = capsule; er = extended-release capsules; l = liquid; o = oral solution; t = tablets; ts = transdermal system.
[b]For adult patients who have elevations in serum ALT/SGPT concentration, see table on p. 114.

Pharmacology

PHARMACOKINETICS

Donepezil
- Rapidly and completely absorbed from the GI tract following oral administration.
  - √ Bioavailability is independent of food and time of administration (morning vs. evening dose).
  - √ Also available in rapidly dissolving tablet.
- Extensively metabolized by the liver to four major metabolites, two of which are pharmacologically active.
  - √ Clearance decreased by 20% in patients with liver cirrhosis.
- Metabolites (40%) and unchanged drug (17%) are excreted in the urine.

Galantamine
- Rapidly absorbed from the GI tract following oral administration.
  - √ Food may delay the rate but not the extent of absorption.
- Primarily metabolized by the liver, with 20% of the parent compound being excreted unchanged in the urine.

- Clearance is decreased in
  √ Female gender (by 20%)
  √ Presence of hepatic and/or renal insufficiency

Rivastigmine
- Well absorbed from the GI tract following oral administration.
  √ Food may delay the rate but increase the extent of absorption.
- Extensively metabolized via hydrolysis in the liver.
  √ The decarbamylated phenolic metabolite is pharmacologically active; it accounts for 10% of the activity of the parent compound.
  √ Minimal metabolism occurs via the cytochrome P450 isoenzymes, resulting in a low potential for drug–drug interactions.
- Renal excretion is the major route of elimination of the metabolites.
- Clearance is decreased in patients with hepatic and/or renal insufficiency.
- In addition to oral administration, rivastigmine is also available as a transdermal patch.
  √ The transdermal system allows sustained plasma levels, longer duration of action, reduced side effects, and improved patient compliance.

Tacrine
- Rapidly but poorly absorbed from the GI tract following oral administration.
  √ Food reduces bioavailability by 30–40%.
- Extensively metabolized by the liver and excreted in the urine.
- Clearance is decreased in
  √ Females (by 50%)
  √ Patients with hepatic insufficiency

Pharmacokinetic Properties of Cholinesterase Inhibitors

Generic Names	Bioavailability (%)	Protein Binding (%)	Plasma Half-Life (h)	Metabolism	Excretion[a] (%)
Donepezil	100	96	70–80	CYP2D6, 3A4	57 R/15 F
Galantamine	90	18	5–7	CYP2D6, 3A4, glucuronidation	95 R/5 F
Rivastigmine	36	40	1–2	Esterase enzymes	90–97 R/ < 1 F
Tacrine	17–33	55–75	2–4	CYP1A2, 2D6	< 1 R (unchanged)

[a]F = fecal; R = renal.

PHARMACODYNAMICS

- Elevates acetylcholine concentrations in the brain via reversible inhibition of enzyme cholinesterases.
  √ There are two main types of central cholinesterase: acetylcholinesterase (AChE) and butyrylcholinesterase (BuChE).
    □ Tacrine and rivastigmine are dual inhibitors of AChE and BuChE.
    □ Donepezil and galantamine are selective inhibitors of AChE.

- Galantamine is also an allosteric modulator of presynaptic nicotinic receptors.
  √ This may cause an increased release of acetylcholine.

Clinical Indications

DEMENTIA OF THE ALZHEIMER'S TYPE

- The cholinesterase inhibitors have demonstrated efficacy in the treatment of mild to moderate Alzheimer's disease (AD). Donepezil has demonstrated efficacy in severe AD
- There is no real difference in the effectiveness among donepezil, galantamine, and rivastigmine.
  √ Tacrine is rarely used due to hepatotoxicity.
- Although consistent gains on cognitive and global scores compared to placebo have been demonstrated, there is considerable debate on the cost-effectiveness of these agents.

LEWY BODY DEMENTIA

- The cholinergic deficit is thought to be greater in Lewy body dementia (LBD) then in Alzheimer's disease.
- For this reason, the cholinesterase inhibitors are effective as first-line agents to provide improvements in apathy, delusions, and hallucinations. Rivastigmine is the only Cholinesterase inhibitor with positive randomized controlled trials (RCTs) in both LBD and Parkinson's disease-associated dementia (PDD).

VASCULAR DEMENTIA

- Although cholinesterase inhibitors have been shown to enhance cognitive and global function, they are not licensed for the treatment of vascular dementia.
- The main treatment focus is on primary and secondary prevention to reduce vascular events.
  √ Early identification and treatment of hypertension (e.g., ACE inhibitors)
  √ Use of lipid-lowering agents and anticoagulants to minimize risk of stroke.
  √ Tight control of glucose levels in diabetics
  √ Life-style changes, including weight reduction, smoking cessation, and nutritional education, are recommended.

Side Effects

CARDIOVASCULAR EFFECTS

Dizziness
- Usually mild and transient.
- Syncope (1–3%) reported with donepezil, rivastigmine, and galantamine.
- Management
  √ If dizziness is associated with a bradycardia (pulse rate < 60) or with falls, withhold the drug until etiology is identified.
  √ Baseline ECG is recommended to exclude problems with cardiac conduction.

CENTRAL NERVOUS SYSTEM EFFECTS

Aggression, irritability, or nervousness
- Occurs early in treatment; tends to resolve with time.
- Management: Prescribe medication earlier in the day.

Headache
- Mild
- Management: Take pain medication (aspirin, acetaminophen) when required.

Sleep disturbances
- Insomnia and abnormal dreams (e.g., nightmares or vivid dreams) have been reported.
- Occur more frequently with donepezil.
- Management
  √ Reduce dose, or
  √ Switch to morning dosing.

EYES, EARS, NOSE, AND THROAT EFFECTS

Blurred vision
- *See* page 17.

Dry eyes
- *See* page 17.

Nasal congestion

Tinnitus
- Reported with rivastigmine.

GASTROINTESTINAL EFFECTS

Nausea, vomiting, diarrhea, anorexia
- Due to cholinomimetic activity
- Occur early in treatment; tend to resolve with time.
- More frequently during rapid dose titration
- Management: Take medication with food or milk.

HEPATIC EFFECTS

Elevated liver enzymes
- Liver transaminase (ALT/SGPT) levels increase in up to 50% of patients who are receiving tacrine 160 mg/day.
- Seen within the first 12 weeks of treatment.
- Management
  √ Discontinue drug if serum ALT/SGPT concentration is more than 5 times greater than the upper limit of normal.
  √ ALT/SGPT concentration usually returns to normal 4–6 weeks after the drug is discontinued.
  √ Once the ALT/SGPT level is normalized, a recallenege with the usual initial dosage of tacrine can be considered.

A
G
E
N
T
S

F
O
R

D
E
M
E
N
T
I
A

RENAL EFFECTS

Urinary tract infection

Frequent urination, incontinence

SKIN, ALLERGIES, AND TEMPERATURE

Flushing

Rash

Sweating

Drug–Drug Interactions

Drug Interactions with Cholinesterase Inhibitors

Drugs (X) Interact with:	Cholinesterase Inhibitor (C)[a]	Comments
Antiarrhythmic (e.g., quinidine)	C↑	Inhibited metabolism of donepezil and galantamine via CYP2D6
Antibiotic (e.g., erythromycin)	C↑	Increased systemic exposure of galantamine (by 10–30%) due to inhibited metabolism via CYP3A4
Anticholinergic (e.g., benztropine)	X↓C↓	Antagonism of effects
Anticonvulsant (e.g., carbamazepine, phenobarbital, phenytoin)	C↓	Increased metabolism of donepezil via enzyme induction
Antidepressants	C↑	*Donepezil*: Paroxetine may increase plasma level of donepezil by inhibiting metabolism via CYP2D6. *Galantamine*: Amitriptyline, fluoxetine, and fluvoxamine may decrease clearance of galantamine (by 25–30%) due to inhibited metabolism via CYP2D6. Paroxetine may increase system exposure (by 40%) of galantamine due to inhibited metabolism via CYP2D6. *Tacrine*: Fluvoxamine may increase plasma level of tacrine (by 5-fold) due to inhibited metabolism via CYP1A2.
Antifungal (e.g., ketoconazole)	C↑	Inhibited metabolism of donepezil and galantamine via CYP3A4
Antipsychotic (e.g., risperidone, haloperidol)	X↑	Cases of EPS exacerbation when used concurrently with donepezil or tacrine
Antitubercular drug (e.g., rifampin)	C↓	Increased metabolism of donepezil via enzyme induction
Antiulcer agent (e.g., cimetidine)	C↑	Increased systemic exposure of galantamine (by 16%) due to inhibited metabolism via CYP3A4
β-blocker (e.g., propranolol)	X↑C↑	Increased risk of bradycardia
Cholinergic agents (e.g., bethanechol)	X↑C↑	Combination may lead to synergistic effects and increased toxicity.
Neuromuscular blocker (e.g., succinylcholine)	X↑	Prolonged neuromuscular blockade
NSAID	X?C?	Cholinesterase inhibitors may increase gastric acid secretion, which may contribute to GI irritation. Patient should be monitored for occult gastrointestinal bleeding.
Smoking	C↓	Decreased half-life and plasma level of tacrine due to induction of metabolism via CYP1A2

[a]↑ = increases; ↓ = decreases.

Special Populations

CHILDREN AND ADOLESCENTS

• Not appropriate for use in children.

WOMEN: PREGNANCY AND POSTPARTUM

• Pregnancy rating
  √ Donepezil, tacrine: Category C
  √ Galantamine, rivastigmine: Category B
• No adequate and well-controlled studies have been done in humans.
• Unknown if these agents are excreted in human milk.

LATE LIFE

• Dose escalation should proceed with caution in patients with comorbid disease.
• Female elderly patients (> 85 years old) with low body weight are at high risk for adverse events.
• Galantamine has been associated with an unexpected increase in mortality among patients with mild cognitive impairment.
  √ Treatment outside the approved indication is not advised.

Effects on Laboratory Tests

Effects of Cholinesterase Inhibitor on Blood/Serum and Urine Tests

Generic Name	Blood/Serum Tests		Urine Tests	
	Marker	Results[a]	Marker	Results
Tacrine	ALT/SGPT	↑	None	

[a]↑ = increases.

Discontinuation

• Abrupt discontinuation can cause a sudden decline in cognitive function or increase in behavioral disturbances.
• Discontinue via a gradual 1- or 2-week reduction in dosage.

Overdose: Toxicity, Suicide, and Treatment

• Overdose can result in cholinergic crisis characterized by
  √ Nausea, vomiting
  √ Salivation (excessive), sweating

A G E N T S F O R D E M E N T I A

√ Bradycardia, hypotension
√ Increasing muscle weakness (may lead to respiratory failure)
√ Convulsions
• Management
  √ General supportive measures should be employed (*see* p. 24).
  √ In asymptomatic rivastigmine overdose, no further dose should be given for the next 24 hours.
  √ The immediate use of atropine may abolish or obtund GI side effects or other muscarinic reactions.
    □ Administer IV atropine sulfate 1–2 mg, with subsequent doses based upon clinical response.
  √ The value of dialysis in treatment of cholinergic crisis in unknown.

Precautions

• *Contraindications*
  √ Known hypersensitivity to these agents
  √ Galantamine: patients with severe hepatic and/or renal impairment (creatinine clearance < 9 ml/min)
  √ Rivastigmine: Patients with severe hepatic impairment
  √ Tracrine: Patients previously treated with the agent who developed treatment-associated jaundice (serum bilirubin > 3 mg/dL)

• Use with *caution* in patients with
  √ A history of
    □ Bradycardia, sick sinus syndrome, cardiac conduction disturbances, coronary artery disease, congestive heart failure
    □ Ulcer disease, GI bleeding, urinary obstruction
    □ Asthma, chronic obstructive pulmonary disease (COPD)
    □ Seizure
  √ Concurrent use of NSAIDs
  √ Concurrent use of anesthetic
  √ Low body weight, over 85 years of age, and/or female

Key Points to Communicate to Patients and Families

• These medications are not a cure for dementia.
• They do not work for everyone.
• Ask your doctor for alternative suggestions if there is no benefit after 2–4 months.
• Report any changes in sleeping, eating habits, mood, or behavior to your doctor.
• If a dose is missed by 6 h, skip the dose and resume medication at the next regularly scheduled time.
  √ Do *not* double the dose.
• Place medications away from bedside or any readily accessible area due to safety concerns. Keep out of reach of children.

NMDA ANTAGONIST

Dosing, Dose Form, and Color

Profile of NMDA Antagonist

Generic Name	Therapeutic Dose Range (mg/day)	Dose Form (mg)[a]	Color
Memantine	5–20 (bid)	t: 5/10 o: 2 mg/ml	t: tan/gray o: clear

[a]o = oral solution; t = tablet.

Pharmacology

PHARMACOKINETICS

- Well absorbed after oral administration.
  √ Food has no effect on absorption.
- Undergoes partial hepatic metabolism with minimal involvement of the microsomal CYP450 enzyme system.
- Approximately 48% of administered drug is excreted unchanged in urine.
  √ Renal elimination rate decreases upon alkalinization of the urine.

Pharmacokinetic Properties of NMDA Antagonist

Generic Name	Bioavailability (%)	Protein Binding (%)	Plasma Half-Life (h)	Metabolism	Excretion (%)[a]
Memantine	100	45	60–100	Glucuronidation, hydroxylation, N-oxidation	75–90 R

[a]R = renal.

PHARMACODYNAMICS

- An uncompetitive NMDA antagonist, binding near the Mg^{2+} site within the ion channel
  √ This property is postulated to protect the brain from glutamate-related excitotoxicity by preventing prolonged influx of Ca^{2+} ions through the NMDA channel.
- Stimulates dopamine release with consequent antiparkinsonian effects.

Clinical Indications

DEMENTIA OF ALZHEIMER'S TYPE

- Memantine is indicated for the treatment of moderate to severe dementia of the Alzheimer's type with a small beneficial effect on cognitive function and functional decline.

- Several studies support the use of memantine as monotherapy or as an adjunct to cholinesterase inhibitors for moderate to severe Alzheimer's disease.

VASCULAR DEMENTIA

- Memantine has demonstrated modest benefit on cognitive function in patients with mild to moderate vascular dementia.

Side Effects

CARDIOVASCULAR EFFECTS

Dizziness
- Common (2–10%)
- Mild to moderate

CENTRAL NERVOUS SYSTEM EFFECTS

Agitation, confusion
- Confusion occurs most commonly 1 month after starting memantine; improves within 2 weeks.

Insomnia
- Management: Prescribe medication earlier in the day.

Headache
- Mild
- Management: Take pain medication (aspirin, acetaminophen) when required.

GASTROINTESTINAL EFFECTS

Constipation
- Relieve by increasing the amount of fiber and water intake in diet.

RENAL EFFECTS

Urinary tract infection

Incontinence

Drug–Drug Interactions

Drug Interactions with NMDA Antagonist

Drugs (X) Interact with:	Memantine (M)[a]	Comments
Alkaline agents (e.g., antacids, sodium bicarbonate, carbonate anhydrase inhibitors)	M↑	Reduced clearance of memantine by 80% in alkaline urine (pH > 8). May lead to an accumulation of the drug with a possible increase in adverse events.
Aminoadamantanes (e.g., amantadine, rimantadine)	X↑M↑	Adverse events may be enhanced due to additive effects on NMDA receptors. *DO NOT COMBINE.*

Drugs (X) Interact with:	Memantine (M)[a]	Comments
Anesthetic (e.g., ketamine)	X↑M↑	Adverse events may be enhanced due to additive effects on NMDA receptors. *DO NOT COMBINE.*
Anticonvulsant (e.g., valproate)	X↑M↑	Synergistic effect in seizure suppression reported in animal studies.
Hydrochlorothiazide	X↑↓	May reduce renal excretion of hydrochlorothiazide. Bioavailability of hydrochlorothiazide reduced by 20%.
L-dopa	X↑M↑	Synergistic effect reported in animal studies.

[a]↑ = increases; ↓ = decreases; ↑↓ = increases and decreases.

Special Populations

CHILDREN AND ADOLESCENTS

• Not appropriate for use in children.

WOMEN: PREGNANCY AND POSTPARTUM

• Pregnancy Category B; no adequate control studies have been performed in humans.
• Unknown if memantine is excreted in human milk.

LATE LIFE

• There are no differences in pharmacokinetics between younger and older adults.
• Use with caution in patients with renal insufficiency.

Effects on Laboratory Tests

• Memantine is not known to interact with commonly used clinical laboratory tests.

Discontinuation

• No evidence of dependence, addiction, or withdrawal symptoms upon discontinuation of therapeutic doses.

Overdose: Toxicity, Suicide, and Treatment

• Overdose (up to 400 mg) resulted in restlessness, psychosis, visual hallucinations, somnolence, stupor, and loss of consciousness.
• Management
  √ General supportive measures should be utilized.
  √ Elimination of memantine can be enhanced by acidification of urine.

Precautions

• *Contraindicated* in patients with known hypersensitivity to the agent.
• Use with *caution* in patients with renal impairment.

AGENTS FOR DEMENTIA

Key Points to Communicate to Patients and Families

- It may take several weeks before memantine appears to take effect. You should not stop taking your medication unless directed by your doctor.
- The most common side effects are agitation, confusion, insomnia, constipation, headache, and dizziness.
- Changes in diet (particularly a change from a mixed diet that includes meat and vegetables to a vegetarian diet) may increase blood levels of memantine.
  √ Talk to your doctor before you make any major changes to your diet.
- If a dose is missed by 6 h, skip the dose and resume medication at the next regularly scheduled time.
  √ Do *not* double the dose.
- Place medications away from bedside or any readily accessible area due to safety concerns. Keep out of reach of children.

THERAPEUTIC APPLICATION

Initiation of Treatment

- The typical candidate for cholinesterase inhibitors:
  √ Outpatients with mild to moderate dementia of the Alzheimer's type
- Treatment should be initiated at a low dose and, depending on tolerability, titrated to a target dose. Always titrate cholinesterase inhibitors at 4-week intervals.
  √ Donepezil: Start at 5 mg/day.
  √ Galantamine ER: Start at 8 mg/day.
  √ Rivastigmine: Start at 1.5 mg bid.
  √ Tacrine: Start at 10 mg qid.
    □ Tacrine dose escalation is guided by transaminase (ALT/SGPT) levels expressed as multiples of ULN (upper limit of normal) and measured biweekly for 16 weeks (*see* next table).

Monitoring Regimen for Tacrine

ALT/SGPT Serum Concentrations	Tacrine Dosage Adjustment
≤ 3 × ULN	No dosage adjustment is necessary. If the ALT serum concentration is > 2 times the ULN, monitor ALT weekly until concentration returns to normal.
> 3 to ≤ 5 × ULN	Reduce the daily dose by 40 mg/day and monitor ALT/SGPT concentrations weekly. Dosage may be resumed at the initial dose after ALT concentrations have returned to normal levels.
> 5 to ≤ 10 × ULN	Withhold tacrine and closely monitor the patient for signs and symptoms of tacrine-induced hepatitis. A rechallenge with the usual initial dose of tacrine may be considered upon return to normal limits.
≥ 10 × ULN	Clinical experience is limited. These patients may be subjected to risk for serious or fatal liver damage. A rechallenge is *not recommended*.

Note: ALT/SGPT = alkaline phosphatase; ULN = upper limit of normal.

- The typical candidates for memantine:
  √ Patients who have failed treatment with, or failed to tolerate, cholinesterase inhibitors.
  √ Outpatients with moderate to severe dementia of the Alzheimer's type.
- Memantine can be titrated at 1-week intervals.
  √ Start at 5 mg/day; doses greater than 5 mg/day should be divided into two and given in the morning and evening.

Treatment Resistance

When a patient who has only recently started treatment does not appear to be responding to a cholinesterase inhibitor, there are four options:

- Optimize the dose.
- Switch to another cholinesterase inhibitor.
- Discontinue the drug and consider memantine.
- Combine current cholinesterase inhibitor with memantine.

Maintenance

- The patient should be assessed 2–4 months after a maintenance dose is established. Treatment should continue only if cognitive function has improved or not changed and if behavioral or functional assessment shows improvement.
- The patient should be assessed every 6 months thereafter.

5. Mood Stabilizers

INTRODUCTION TO DRUG CLASS

During the past decade, there has been substantial progress in the development of treatments that possess mood-stabilizing properties. We have taken a pragmatic, albeit broad, approach to defining mood stabilizers to include agents with antimanic and/or recurrence-prevention properties in bipolar disorder. A further criterion for mood stabilizer is that the agent does not induce an affective switch and/or destabilize the longitudinal course of bipolar disorder. Mood stabilizers encompass disparate classes of psychotropic agents, including lithium, anticonvulsant drugs, and antipsychotics. Information regarding the efficacy, safety, and tolerability of antipsychotic drugs is detailed in Chapter 1. Although lithium is prescribed less frequently for mood disorders, the empirical evidence supporting its efficacy, as well as emerging evidence describing the anti-suicidal properties of lithium, have provided the impetus for a resurgence of usage. Several novel anticonvulsant agents have been introduced for the treatment of various phases of bipolar disorder, and their broad spectrum of effectiveness and acceptability to patients has provided the basis for their popularity in treating mood syndromes. This chapter details practical tactics and strategies to facilitate the safe clinical use of mood stabilizers in psychiatric populations.

Mood Stabilizers by Chemical Class

Chemical Class	Generic Name	Trade Name
Lithium	Lithium carbonate	Eskalith
		Lithobid
		Lithonate
		Lithotab
	Lithium citrate	Cibalith-S
Anticonvulsant	Carbamazepine	Tegretol,
		Equetro,
		Carbatrol

Chemical Class	Generic Name	Trade Name
	Clonazepam	Klonopin
	Divalproex sodium	Depakote
	Lamotrigine	Lamictal
	Oxcarbazepine	Trileptal
	Valproic acid	Depakene
Antipsychotic		
First generation	Chlorpromazine	Thorazine
	Haloperidol	Haldol
Second generation	Aripiprazole	Abilify
	Olanzapine	Zyprexa
	Paliperidone	Invega
	Quetiapine	Seroquel
	Risperidone	Risperdal
	Ziprasidone	Geodon

LITHIUM

Dosing, Dose Form, and Color

Profile of Lithium

Generic Name	Therapeutic Dose Range (mg/day)	Geriatric Dose (mg/day)[a]	Dose Form (mg)[b]	Color
Lithium carbonate	600–1800	150–1200	t: 300 c: 300 sr: 300/450	t: gray c: gray–yellow sr: pink–yellow
Lithium citrate	600–1800	150–1200	s: 8 mEq/5 ml	s: raspberry

[a]Dosing to therapeutic level 0.8–1.2 mEq/l for acute mania and 0.6–1.0 mEq/l for antidepressant effect and relapse prevention.
[b]c = capsules; s = syrup; t = tablets; sr = sustained release tablets.

Pharmacology

PHARMACOKINETICS

- Readily absorbed from the GI tract.
- Not hepatically metabolized.
- Predominately excreted by kidneys.
  - √ Freely filtered by the glomerulus; 80% of the filtered lithium is reabsorbed.
- Adequate renal function and salt intake are essential to avoid lithium retention and toxicity.
- Prolonged elimination half-life (up to 58 h) occurs in elderly individuals or patients taking lithium chronically.
- Once-daily dosing is preferred due to improved adherence and decreased risk of tubular dysfunction.

Pharmacokinetic Properties of Lithium

Generic Name	Bioavailability (%)	Protein Binding (%)	Half-Life (h)	Excretion (%)[a]
Lithium	60–100	0	8–35	95 R 4–5 S 1 F

[a]F = fecal; R = renal; S = sweat.

PHARMACODYNAMICS

- Exact mechanism of action unknown.
- Postulated that lithium may modulate intracellular calcium homeostasis and engage pleiotropic neurochemical systems.
- Alters the activities of cellular signal transduction systems (e.g., cyclic AMP and phosphoinositide second-messenger systems).
- Chronic lithium use attenuates programmed cell death (apoptosis), exerting neuroprotective effects.

Clinical Indications

BIPOLAR DISORDER: MANIA

- Considered first-line option as monotherapy or in combination with antipsychotics for the treatment of acute mania.
- "Classic" euphoric mania preceded by well interval exhibits highest response rate.
- Less response noted in patients with
  √ Dysphoric/psychotic mania or in mixed states (30–40%)
  √ Rapid-cycling bipolar disorder (20–30%)
  √ Multiple prior episodes
  √ Comorbid medical conditions or substance abuse
  √ Depression–mania interval pattern (the clinical presentation of depressed episodes preceding periods of mania, which are then followed by intervals of recovery)
- Administration of lithium requires 10–14 days before the optimal therapeutic effect is observed.

Side Effects

CARDIOVASCULAR EFFECTS

At therapeutic lithium levels, the most common ECG changes are

- T-wave flattening or inversion and
- Widening of QRS complex

MOOD STABILIZERS

Lithium-related ECG changes are typically

- Benign.
- Reversed by discontinuing lithium.
- Should not be confused with more serious problems (e.g., hypokalemia).
- May persist or disappear spontaneously during treatment.

Arrhythmias
- Use lithium cautiously in patients with preexisting cardiac disease.
- Sinoatrial node dysfunction with fainting, dizziness, palpitations, or without symptoms is commonly seen.
- Reversed by discontinuing lithium.
- Ventricular arrhythmias rarely reported.
- Bradyarrhythmia and/or conduction defects seen in $\geq$ 50% of bipolar patients with lithium-induced hypocalcaemia and seen in $\leq$ 25% of bipolar patients without hypercalcaemia.

Sudden deaths
- Have occurred on lithium, usually in patients with preexisting heart disease.
- Consider obtaining a cardiologist's consultation before placing a cardiac patient on lithium or if patient has significant risk factors (e.g., severe hypertension).

CENTRAL NERVOUS SYSTEM EFFECTS

Cognitive blunting, memory difficulties
- Word-recall memory impaired in normal volunteers.
  - √ Occurs with lithium levels $\geq$ 0.8 mmol/l.
  - √ Often described as "cognitive blunting."
  - √ Younger patients more likely to complain of memory problems.
- Management
  - √ Assess lithium plasma level and thyroid function.
  - √ Use slow-release preparations.
  - √ Consolidate dosing to once-a-day at night.
  - √ Liothyronine may improve cognitive function.

Neuromuscular dysfunction
- Lithium tremor
  - √ More likely in those with a preexisting tremor or a family h/o essential tremor.
  - √ Tremors may disappear after the first 2–3 weeks of constant lithium dose.
  - √ Present at rest and increases with voluntary movement or with efforts to maintain posture.
  - √ Usually confined to fingers but
    - □ If severe, may involve hands and wrists.
  - √ Irregular in amplitude and rhythm.
- Lithium tremor can be distinguished from parkinsonian and pseudoparkinsonian tremor by

√ Its association with voluntary movement
√ Its lack of response to antiparkinsonian medications
• Management
√ Reduce lithium dose while maintaining serum levels within the therapeutic range.
√ Eliminate caffeine intake.
√ β-blocker (e.g., propranolol or atenolol) may be of benefit.
• A coarse tremor may be a sign of lithium toxicity.
• Cogwheel rigidity and choreoathetosis reported.

Pseudotumor cerebri
• Uncommonly reported adverse event
• Blurred vision often first complaint.
√ Headache not always present.
• Papilledema seen.
√ Usually resolves after a few months off lithium.
• Elevated lumbar puncture pressure
√ Does not always completely resolve.
√ Shunt sometimes needed.

Seizures
• Tonic–clonic (rarely).
• Although lithium has been safely used in bipolar individuals with comorbid epilepsy, treatment with another anticonvulsant mood stabilizer is preferred.

ENDOCRINE EFFECTS

Euthyroid goiter, hypothyroidism
• Clinical hypothyroidism occurs in up to 30–40% of patients.
√ Often within the first year
√ Risk greater in women over age 40 and in individuals with rapid cycling course.
√ May be more common in regions of high dietary iodine.
• Subclinical hypothyroidism (high TSH and normal T_4) documented in up to 25% of patients prescribed lithium.
• Goiter (not necessarily associated with hypothyroidism) may be more common in regions of iodine deficiency.
• Management
√ Monitor TSH level.
√ May require levothyroxine therapy.

Hyperparathyroidism
• Abnormally high serum calcium and parathyroid hormone levels in 10–40% of patients on maintenance therapy
• May predispose to decreased bone density or to cardiac conduction disturbances.
• Occasional reports of parathyroid adenoma and hyperplasia

M
O
O
D

S
T
A
B
I
L
I
Z
E
R
S

GASTROINTESTINAL EFFECTS

Diarrhea
- Up to 20% incidence
- Slow-release preparation may worsen this side effect in some patients.
- Management
  √ If on a slow-release product, change to a regular lithium preparation.
  √ Less problems noted with lithium citrate preparations.

Nausea
- Up to 50% incidence; may arise from normal serum lithium levels.
- Often occurs early in treatment, especially when titrating doses and with fluctuating plasma levels.
- Accompanied by other GI symptoms.
- Management
  √ Administer with food.
  √ Use slow-release preparations.
  √ Replace with lithium citrate syrup.

Vomiting
- 20% incidence; higher with increased plasma level.
- Management
  √ Use multiple daily dosing
  √ Change to slow-release preparation.
  √ Lower the dose.

Weight gain
- Up to 60% incidence (25% patients gain excessive weight)
- May be related to increased appetite, fluid retention, altered carbohydrate and fat metabolism, or to hypothyroidism.
- Mean gain is 7.5 kg (range 3–28 kg) on lithium alone (may be higher with drug combinations).
- Variable effect on insulin sensitivity
- Management
  √ Reduce caloric intake.

HEMATOLOGIC EFFECTS

Leukocytosis
- Mainly mature neutrophils are increased, yielding average 35% transient increase in neutrophil count after 3–10 days of lithium administration.
- Normalization of blood count may take up to 6 months after the initiation of lithium.
- Reversible, benign, and not indicative of disease
- WBC count approximately 12,000–15,000/mm^3
- Rarely need to stop lithium.

RENAL EFFECTS

Polyuria and polydipsia
- Up to 60% risk (dose-related)
- Usually reversible if lithium stopped.
- Cases of persistent diabetes insipidus reported > 5 years after lithium discontinuation.
- Management
  √ Monitor for fluid and electrolyte imbalance.
  √ Lithium once a day is preferred as initial approach.
    □ Sustained-release lithium is associated with increased renal concentrating impairment.
  √ Potassium-sparing diuretic (amiloride 10–20 mg/day) or desmopressin (10 mg nasal spray or tablets 0.2 mg) may be useful.

Tubulo-interstitial nephritis/renal insufficiency
- 10–20% of patients on long-term (≤ 10 years) lithium have kidney changes.
  √ Interstitial nephrosis
  √ Tubular atrophy
  √ Sometimes glomerular atrophy
- More often seen with long-term lithium therapy.
- Gradual rise in serum creatinine and decline of creatinine clearance.
  √ An initial serum creatinine of > 2.5 mg/dl identifies high-risk group for subsequent progression to end-stage renal disease, requiring dialysis.
  √ Consider discontinuing lithium while problem is potentially reversible.

SKIN, ALLERGIES, AND TEMPERATURE EFFECTS

Acne
- Engendered and exacerbated by lithium treatment.
- May respond to
  √ Pyridoxine 50 mg bid
  √ Zinc sulfate 110 mg bid
  √ β-carotene 25,000 IU daily

Dryness and thinning of hair
- May be related to hypothyroidism.
- Alopecia reported in 12–19% of patients on chronic therapy.
- Changes in color and texture also reported.

Psoriasis
- Aggravation of preexisting or dormant psoriasis.
- Dry noninflamed papular eruption is common.
- Management
  √ First try lowering lithium dose.
  √ If this fails, may respond to inositol up to 6 g/day.

Drug–Drug Interactions

Drug Interactions with Lithium

Drugs (X) Interact with:	Lithium (L)[a]	Comments
Alcohol	L↑	Increased tremor/shakiness wtih chronic alcohol use
Anesthetic (e.g., ketamine)	L↑	Increased lithium toxicity due to sodium depletion
Angiotensin-converting enzyme (ACE) inhibitors	L↑	Increased serum lithium—lithium toxicity and impaired kidney function may occur; may need to stop lithium or ACE inhibitor.
Antibiotics (e.g., ampicillin, metronidazole, spectinomycin, tetracycline)	L↑	Increased lithium effect and toxicity due to decreased renal clearnace of lithium. Monitor lithium level if combination used.
Anticonvulsants (e.g., carbamazepine, phenytoin, valproate)	X↑ L↑	Increased neurotoxicity of both drugs at therapeutic doses; synergistic mood-stabilizing effect with carbamazepine and valproate. Valproate may aggravate action tremor.
Antidepressants (e.g., MAO inhibitors, TCAs, SSRIs)	L↑	Elevated lithium serum level, with possible neurotixicity and increased serotonergic effects. May increase lithium tremor. Synergistic antidepressant effect in treatment-resistant patients.
Antihypertensives	L↑↓	May increase or decrease lithium effects due to alteration in renal clearance of lithium.
Caffeine	L↓	Increased renal excretion of lithium resulting in decreased plasma level. May increase lithium tremor.
NSAIDs (e.g., diclofenac, ibuprofen, indomethacin)	L↑	Increased lithium level and possible toxicity due to decreased renal clearance of lithium. Serum creatinine increased in several reports. Use with caution and monitor lithium level every 4–5 days until stable. Acetaminophen does not appear to change levels.
Neuromuscular blockers (e.g., succinylcholine, pancuronium)	X↑	Potentiation of muscle relaxation
Sodium salt	L↑↓	Decreased intake causes increased lithium plasma level; increased intake results in decreased lithium plasma level.
Urinary alkalizers (e.g., potassium citrate, sodium bicarbonate)	L↓	Enhanced renal lithium clearance and reduced plasma level

[a]↑ = increases; ↓ = decreases; ↑↓ = increases and decreases.

Special Populations

CHILDREN AND ADOLESCENTS

- Lithium has been used successfully in children with
  √ Bipolar disorder
  √ Chronic aggressive conduct disorders
  √ Periodic mood and behavior disorders
  √ Pervasive developmental disorder (e.g., autism)
- Shorter half-life and increased clearance when compared to adults

WOMEN: PREGNANCY AND POSTPARTUM

Pregnancy Rating	• Category D
Teratogenicity (1st trimester)	• Avoid in pregnancy.
	• Overall risk of fetal malformations is 4–12%.

• Cardiovascular malformations can occur (e.g., tricuspid valve malformations; 0.05–0.1% risk of Ebstein's anomaly).
√ Can be detected by fetal echocardiography and high-resolution ultrasound at 16–18 weeks gestation.

• If necessary, use lithium at the lowest possible divided daily dose to avoid peak concentrations.

• Monitor drug levels during pregnancy monthly, especially first two trimesters, as well as postdelivery.

Direct Effect on Newborn (3rd trimester)

• A significant association noted between higher doses of lithium in the first trimester and premature deliveries; a higher rate of macrosomia reported in these premature infants.

• Use of lithium near term may produce severe toxicity in the newborn, which is usually reversible. Effects include nontoxic goiter, atrial flutter, T-wave inversion, nephrogenic diabetes insipidus, floppy baby syndrome, cyanosis, and seizures.
√ If lithium is used, despite advice to the contrary, dose should be decreased or drug discontinued 2–3 days prior to delivery.

Lactation

• Present in breast milk at a concentration of 30–100% of mother's serum.

• Monitor infant lithium levels.

• Infant has decreased renal clearance.

• Avoid until infant is at least 5 months of age.
√ If breastfeeding is undertaken against medical advice, the mother should be educated about signs and symptoms of lithium toxicity and risk of infant dehydration.

MOOD STABILIZERS

LATE LIFE

• Good kidney function and adequate salt and fluid intake are essential.
• Ability to eliminate lithium decreases with age, resulting in a longer elimination half-life.
• Start therapy at lower doses and monitor serum level.
• Incidence of side effects may be greater and occur at lower plasma level, including tremor, GI disturbances, polyuria, ataxia, myoclonus, and EPS.
• Elderly are at increased risk for
  √ Hyponatremia after an acute illness or if fluid intake is restricted
  √ Neurotoxicity and cognitive impairment, even at therapeutic plasma levels
• Slow-release preparations may decrease side effects that occur as a result of peak plasma levels.

Effects on Laboratory Tests

Effects of Lithium on Blood/Serum and Urine Tests

Generic Name	Blood/Serum Tests		Urine Tests	
	Marker	Results[a]	Marker	Results[a]
Lithium	T_3, T_4	↓	Glycosuria	↑
	Leukocytes	↑	Albuminuria	↑
	Eosinophils	↑	VMA[b]	↑
	Platelets	↑	Renal concentrating ability	↓
	Lymphocytes	↓	Electrolytes	↑↓
	Na^+, K^+	↑↓		
	Ca^{++}, Mg^{++}	↑↑		
	Serum phosphate	↓		
	Parathyroid hormone	↑		
	Glucose tolerance	↑↓		

[a]↑ = increases; ↓ = decreases; ↑↓ = Increases and decreases.
[b]VMA=vanillylmandelic acid.

Discontinuation

• Rarely anxiety, instability, and emotional lability reported following abrupt withdrawal.
• Rapid discontinuation of lithium (i.e., over a period of $\leq$ 2 weeks) may increase the risk of relapse.
• 50% rate of manic or depressive recurrence within 3–5 months among previously stable patients reported with abrupt withdrawal.

Overdose: Toxicity, Suicide, and Treatment

At toxic levels lithium may inhibit its own excretion, as can

• Renal dysfunction
• Sodium depletion
• Certain drugs (e.g., NSAIDs)

Lithium toxicity usually correlates with elevated serum levels, and patients often have CNS signs and symptoms. However, not all patients with high lithium levels have advanced symptoms, at least during the initial phase of intoxication. This discrepancy between serum levels and clinical toxicity reflects delayed distribution of the drug into susceptible tissues.

Mild toxicity

- At lithium levels of 1.5–2 mmol/l
- Occasionally occurs in patients receiving long-term lithium therapy.
- Side effects such as
  √ Fine resting tremor, generalized weakness
  √ Mild confusion, drowsiness
  √ Diarrhea

Moderate–severe toxicity

- Progressive intoxication (levels > 2 mmol/l) may be manifested by
  √ Worsening of tremor, stupor, confusion
  √ Muscle fasciculation, hyperreflexia, clonus
  √ Nystagmus
  √ ECG changes such as flat or inverted T waves
  √ Epileptic seizures
- Deaths have been reported; when serum lithium level exceeds 4 mmol/l the prognosis is poor.

The general management of lithium overdoses includes

- Induce emesis in the alert patient or use gastric lavage and ion exchange resin to bind lithium.
- Restore fluid and electrolyte balance; correct sodium depletion.
- Get a baseline ECG (to determine arrhythmia, sinus node dysfunction).
- Blood lithium concentration may be reduced by forced alkaline diuresis or by prolonged dialysis or hemodialysis.
- Excretion may be facilitated by IV urea, sodium bicarbonate, acetazolamide, or aminophylline.
- Convulsions may be controlled by a short-acting barbiturate (e.g., thiopental sodium).

Precautions

Contraindications

- Hypersensitivity to lithium
- Renal tubular disease
- Cardiovascular disease
- Myasthenia gravis
- Severe debilitation
- Pregnancy (first trimester), breastfeeding

MOOD STABILIZERS

Cautionary concerns

- Excessive loss of sodium (e.g., due to vomiting, diarrhea, use of diuretics) causes increased lithium retention, possibly leading to toxicity.
  √ Lower doses of lithium are necessary if the patient is taking a salt-restricted diet (which includes most low-calorie diets).
- Profuse sweating may lead to changes in plasma level of lithium.
- Concurrent ECT may increase the possibility of developing cerebral toxicity to lithium.
  √ Discontinue during courses of ECT if possible.
- Do not rapidly increase lithium and antipsychotic dosage at the same time, due to risk of neurotoxicity.

Key Points to Communicate to Patients and Families

- Carry a Medic Alert wallet card or bracelet indicating lithium use.
- Remind physicians and surgeons, especially primary care providers, cardiologists, and GI specialists, about taking lithium when they wish to introduce another new drug.
- Some of the most common side effects when starting on lithium are upset stomach, diarrhea, and frequent urination.
  √ These side effects are not necessarily signs of toxicity early in treatment. However, after a steady state is achieved, diarrhea or a coarse tremor may be early signs of toxicity.
  √ Tolerance to GI and GU side effects may occur with gradual dosage adjustment.
- Ingest lithium at regular times each day, as decided with physician.
  √ Ingest with meals, snack, or milk to diminish GI irritation.
- If a dose is missed by 3 h, skip the dose and resume medication at the next regularly scheduled time. Do *not* double the dose.
  √ Lithium level should be checked 12 hours after the last dose.
- To prevent accidents, do not place lithium at bedside or any other quickly accessible place. Keep away from children.

ANTICONVULSANTS

Dosing, Dose Form, and Color

Profile of Anticonvulsants

Generic Names	Therapeutic Dose Range (mg/day)	Geriatric Dose (mg/day)	Dose Form (mg)[a]	Color
Carbamazepine	300–1600	200–1000	t: 100/200 su: 100 mg/5 ml er-c: 100/200/300	t: red-spackled/pink su: yellow–orange er-c: blue/blue–gray/ blue–black
Clonazepam	0.5–3		t: 0.5/1/2	t: orange/blue/white

Generic Names	Therapeutic Dose Range (mg/day)	Geriatric Dose (mg/day)	Dose Form (mg)[a]	Color
Divalproex sodium	750–3000		dr-t: 125/250/500	dr-t: salmon–pink/ peach/lavender
			er-t: 250/500	er-t: white/gray
			c: 125	c: white–blue
Lamotrigine	100–500	25–200	t: 25/100/150/200	t: white/peach/cream/ blue
Oxcarbazepine	600–1200	300–600	t: 150/300/600	t: green–gray/yellow/light pink
			su: 300 mg/5 ml	su: off-white
Valproic acid	1000–2500	250–2000	c: 250/500	c: orange/pale yellow
			s: 250 mg/5 ml	s: red

[a]c = capsules; dr = delayed-release; er = extended-release; s = syrup; su = suspension; t = tablets.

Pharmacology

PHARMACOKINETICS

Carbamazepine
- Absorbed slowly; ingestion of food has no significant influence on the rate and extent of absorption.
- Primarily metabolized in the liver.
  √ Because carbamazepine induces its own liver metabolism, level of carbamazepine must be monitored and its dose often must be raised during the early phase of treatment.
- Plasma concentration of the principal active metabolite, 10,11-epoxide, varies between 10–50% of that of the parent drug.
  √ The epoxide metabolite is the primary mediator of carbamazepine toxicity.
- Extended-release capsule formulation offers several advantages to immediate-release formulations, such as
  √ Decreased dosing frequency
  √ Lowered plasma fluctuations

Oxcarbazepine
- Completely absorbed following oral administration; food has no effect on the rate and extent of absorption.
- Extensively metabolized by the liver to its pharmacologically active 10-monohydroxy metabolite (MHD).
- Elimination half-life of MHD is prolonged in renally-impaired patients.

Lamotrigine
- Rapidly and completely absorbed following oral administration.
- Metabolized predominantly in the liver by glucuronic acid conjugation.
  √ Half-life is prolonged in hepatic dysfunction.
- Large interindividual variation seen in plasma concentration in patients with renal impairment.

MOOD STABILIZERS

Valproate
- Rapidly absorped after oral administration.
  - √ Valproic acid and divalproex sodium (a combination of valproic acid and valproate) dissociate to the valproate ion in the GI tract.
- Bioavailability unaffected by food, though absorption may be delayed.
- Exhibits concentration-dependent protein binding.
  - √ At high doses and high plasma concentration a larger proportion may exist in unbound (free) form.
- Pharmacokinetics show significant variation with changes in body weight.

Pharmacokinetic Properties of Anticonvulsants

Generic Names	Bioavailability (%)	Protein Binding (%)	Half-Life (h)	P450 Systems		Excretion Unchanged (%)[a]
				Substrate	Inhibitor/ Induction	
Carbamazepine	75–85	75–90	25–65 (acute use) 10–20 (chronic use)	1A3, 3A4, 2C8, 2C9	Induces 3A4, 1A2, 2C9, 2B6	15–25 F
Divalproex sodium	100	90	6–16	2C9, UGT[b]	2C9, 2C19, UGT	< 3 R or F
Lamotrigine	98	55	25–33	Glucuronic acid conjugation, UGT		10 R
Oxcarbazepine	> 95	40	2	Conjugation	Inhibits 2C19 Induces 3A4	< 1 R/ 4 F
Valproic acid	78	60–95	5–20	2C9, UGT	Inhibits 2D6, 2C9, 2C19, UGT	

[a]UGT = uridine diphosphate-glucuronosyl transferase.
[b]F = fecal; R = renal.

PHARMACODYNAMICS

Carbamazepine
- Has anticonvulsant and GABAergic effects.
- Inhibits kindling, a process that increases behavioral and convulsive responses to a repetition of the identical stimulus.
- Blocks voltage-dependent sodium channels that initiate neuronal action potentials.

Lamotrigine
- Has anticonvulsant and GABAergic effects.
- Blocks voltage-dependent sodium channels and calcium channels.
- Inhibits the release of excitatory neurotransmitters (glutamate).

Valproate
- Has anticonvulsant, antikindling, and GABAergic effects.
- Blocks voltage-dependent sodium channels and calcium channels.
- Increases serotonergic activity.
- Enhances neuropeptide Y expression.

Clinical Indications

BIPOLAR DISORDER: MANIA AND RECURRENCE PREVENTION

- Divalproex is indicated in the treatment of manic episodes associated with bipolar disorder.
  √ It is equally effective in both euphoric and mixed manic episodes.
  √ It is also effective in rapid-cycling bipolar disorder and for individuals whose illness is complicated by substance abuse or anxiety disorders.
- Carbamazepine is considered a second-line treatment for acute mania or maintenance therapy.
  √ It is less effective than lithium but may sometimes be employed as monotherapy if lithium is ineffective and especially in patients who do not show "classic" mania.
  √ Oxcarbazepine can be considered due to its lower potential for pharmacokinetic interactions.
- Lamotrigine is approved for maintenance treatment of bipolar I disorder.
  √ It has demonstrated evidence of antidepressant activity compared to placebo in the acute and prophylactic treatment of major depressive episodes in patients with bipolar I disorder.
  √ Clinical improvement became evident as early as the third week of treatment.
- Clonazepam has demonstrated effectiveness as adjunctive treatment in acute mania.
  √ Prescribed for short-term use to restore sleep and modulate irritability or agitation.
  √ Recommend to gradually taper and discontinue clonazepam within 2–3 weeks of achieving adequate symptom control in mania.
- Newer anticonvulsant medications, including gabapentin, topiramate, and oxcarbazepine, are being studied to determine their efficacy as mood stabilizers in bipolar disorder.
  √ Some studies suggest that different combinations of lithium and anticonvulsants may be helpful.

NON-BIPOLAR INDICATIONS

Migraine headaches

- Valproate is effective for the prophylactic treatment of migraine headache.
  √ It may reduce frequency and intensity of attacks.

Paroxysmal pain syndromes

- Carbamazepine is considered as a first-line treatment for trigeminal neuralgia.
  √ Although it provides relief during the first few years of treatment, longer-term efficacy does not tend to be maintained in most people.

Side Effects

CARDIOVASCULAR EFFECTS

Atrioventricular block and sinus node dysfunction
- AV conduction delay and bradyarrhythmias can occur at therapeutic doses of carbamazepine.
- Use with caution when combining with TCA or other quinidine-like drugs.
- Avoid carbamazepine in patients with heart block or at high risk for cardiac conduction abnormalities (e.g., myotonic dystrophy).
  √ Consider divalproex as an alternative.

Dizziness
- Frequent with lamotrigine (38%)

CENTRAL NERVOUS SYSTEM EFFECTS

Confusion
- Occurs with carbamazepine at higher doses.
- May be secondary to
  √ Use of lithium
  √ Hyponatremia
  √ Water intoxication

Sedation
- Dose-related; administer bedtime dosing.

Tremor
- Common with valproate at high doses and levels (10%).
- Tends to be fine, rapid, and most prominent in the upper extremeities.
- Management
  √ Reduce dose.
  √ Add propranolol (10–60 mg).

ENDOCRINE AND SEXUAL EFFECTS

Hyperinsulinemia, dyslipidemia
- Reported with valproate.
  √ More common in obese patients.
  √ Dyslipidemia characterized by low high-density lipoprotein levels and high serum triglycerides.

Hyponatremia and water intoxication
- Occur with carbamazepine (5–15%) and oxcarbazepine (30%)
- Higher risk in the elderly
- Management
  √ Demeclocycline 300–600 bid

Menstrual disturbances, hyperandrogenism, polycystic ovaries
- Reported in women receiving valproate (up to 60%) or carbamazepine (up to 25%) monotherapy.
- Management
  √ Discontinue drug.
  √ Switch to lamotrigine.
  √ Regular monitoring of reproductive function is recommended.

EYES, EARS, NOSE, AND THROAT

Blurred vision
- *See* page 17.

GASTROINTESTINAL AND HEPATIC EFFECTS

Hepatitis, hepatotoxicity
- Valproate and carbamazepine raise LFTs slightly during the first 3 months of therapy.
  √ Valproate may induce hyperammonemia, often with confusion and lethargy.
  √ High LFTs do not predict liver damage.
    □ Bilirubin may be better indicator.
- Valproate generates (very rarely) potentially fatal hepatotoxicity, especially in patients
  √ Under 2 years old
  √ Taking other anticonvulsants
  √ With severe neurological disease, mental retardation, or inborn error of metabolism
- Hepatotoxicity is rarely seen in adults on anticonvulsant monotherapy; it is preceded by malaise, weakness, lethargy, anorexia, vomiting, and seizures.

Nausea, vomiting, anorexia, indigestion
- Usually transient; typically occur on empty stomach or if initial dose is too high or increased too rapidly.
  √ Poor appetite and/or nausea are most common GI side effects.
- Management
  √ If started on valproic acid, switch to divalproex sodium or divalproex sodium extended-release.
  √ If this fails, try divalproex sodium-coated particles.
  √ Take with meals.

Pancreatitis
- Observed with acute and chronic valproate administration in pediatric and adult populations.

- Fatality has been observed (1 in 10,000).
- Abdominal pain, nausea, vomiting, and/or anorexia require prompt medical evaluations.

Weight change
- Valproate increases appetite and weight.
  √ Weight gain increases as a function of treatment duration with variable plateau.
  √ More common in females and with high plasma levels.
  √ May be associated with features of insulin resistance.
- Carbamazepine is associated with minimal weight gain; may be secondary to peripheral edema.

HEMATOLOGIC EFFECTS

Anemia (aplastic), agranulocytosis
- Severe and potentially fatal.
- Carbamazepine produces aplastic anemia in < 0.002% of patients.

Leukopenia
- Carbamazepine may mildly lower WBC by up to 25% initially, but this decrease is usually transitory without adverse events.
  √ Women at higher risk than men.
- In 2% of patients, carbamazepine induces a persistent leukopenia.
  √ With carbamazepine-induced leukopenia 76% is moderate (3000–4000 WBC/mm^3) and 24% is severe (< 3000 WBC/mm^3).
    □ 50% develop leukopenia within 16 days.
    □ Recovery usually occurs within 6 days after discontinuing carbamazepine.
- Management
  √ If WBC count drops to $4000/mm^3$ during carbamazepine therapy
    □ Obtain another WBC count in 2 weeks.
    □ If WBC count does not return to normal in 2 weeks, reduce carbamazepine dose.
  √ Discontinue carbamazepine immediately with any of these symptoms:
    □ WBC count below $3000/mm^3$
    □ Neutrophil count below $1500/mm^3$
    □ LFTs increased 3-fold or bilirubin elevated
    □ Fever
    □ Infection, sore throat
    □ Petechiae, bruising
    □ Weakness
    □ Pallor
  √ Coadministration of lithium, which stimulates white cell production, may reverse the leukopenic effects of carbamazepine.

Thrombocytopenia
- < $100,000/mm^3$ platelets
- Petechiae, bruising, hemorrhage, nose bleeds, and anemia have been reported with divalproex.

• More likely with $\geq$ 2000 mg qd divalproex.
√ If mild thrombocytopenia, reduce dose.

SKIN, ALLERGIES, AND TEMPERATURE

Alopecia
• Reported with valproate (12–28%) and carbamazepine (6%).
• Tends to be transient.
• Supplementation with zinc and/or selenium is recommended (case reports).

Fever, chills, sweating, lymphadenopathy, muscle cramps,
and joint aches
• May arise from carbamazepine.

Pulmonary hypersensitivity
• Arises from carbamazepine, with symptoms of hay fever, dyspnea, pneumonitis, or pneumonia.

Rash
• Allergic rash is a common side effect of carbamazepine (10–15%).
• Usually arises between 9 and 23 days after starting carbamazepine.
• Stop carbamazepine if
  √ Exfoliative reaction
  √ Urticaria reaction, or
  √ Steven–Johnson syndrome (acute inflammatory skin disorder with "iris" target lesions).
• Management
  √ Avoid sunlight; may be a photosensitivity reaction.
  √ Treat minor rashes with antihistamines.
    □ Some patients may desensitize over 1–3 weeks.
  √ May be allergic to binder in pill, not carbamazepine.
    □ Try different form (e.g., 100 mg chewable, different brand).
• Lamotrigine also risks serious and possibly fatal rash.
  √ 10% risk of mild to serious rash
  √ 1.1% serious in pediatric population
  √ 0.3% serious in adult population
  √ Valproate may increase lamotrigine blood levels and significantly risks more rashes that may become serious.
  √ Severe rashes include
    □ Stevens–Johnson syndrome[a]
    □ Toxic epidermal necrolysis
    □ Lennox–Gastaut syndrome
  √ Severe skin reactions suggest impending blood dyscrasia.
  √ Rash incidence reduces with lower initiation dose and gradual titration (particularly when coprescribed with divalproex).

[a]In Asian populations, HLA genotyping can predict risk.

Drug–Drug Interactions

Drug Interactions with Anticonvulsants

Drugs (X) Interact with:	Carbamazepine (C)[a]	Comments
Acetazolamide	C↑	Decreased metabolism leading to increased level and toxicity.
Anthelminthic Mebendazole	X↓	Decreased plasma mebendazole concentration by induction of hepatic microsomal enzymes; may impair therapeutic response.
Antibiotics Doxycycline	X↓	Decreased plasma concentration and half-life of doxycycline due to induction of hepatic microsomal enzyme activity.
Clarithromycin, erythromycin, troleandomycin	C↑	Increased carbamazepine level and toxicity (1–2 ×); may subside in 2–3 days after discontinuation of antibiotics. Spiramycin probably safe alternative.
Antidepressants SSRIs	X↓C↑	Decreased plasma sertraline concentration due to induction of CYP3A4 (case report). Increased plasma concentration of carbamazepine with fluoxetine and fluvoxamine.
TCAs	X↓	Reduced TCA level; may require higher doses of TCA if not responding.
Antipsychotics	X↓C↓	Decreased effect of both antipsychotic and carbamazepine.
Antitubercular drug Isoniazid (INH)	C↑	Increased plasma level and toxicity of carbamazepine; frequently occurs on INH doses > 200 mg/day. Symptoms may disappear 2 days after INH is discontinued.
Benzodiazepines	X↓	Decreased alprazolam and clonazepam plasma levels (20–50%) due to enzyme induction.
Cimetidine	C↑	Transient increase in carbamazepine level due to inhibited metabolism; risk of toxicity. Chronically taking both drugs poses no particular risk. When cimetidine discontinued, carbamazepine toxicity dissipates in about 1 week. Ranitidine may substuitue for cimetidine.
Corticosteroids (e.g., dexamethasone, methylprednisone, prednisolone)	X↓	Carbamazepine may chronically reduce levels and actions of most corticosteroids; may need to increase steroid dose.
Danazol	C↑	Plasma levels of carbamazepine increased by 50–100%; may lead to toxicity. If used together, closely monitor carbamazepine level and adjust dose of one or both drugs.
Lithium	X↑C↑	Increased neurotoxicity of both drugs.
Muscle relaxant Gallamine, pancuronium	X↓	Carbamazepine antagonizes the effects of nondepolarizing muscle relaxants.
Narcotic Methadone	X↓	Increased metabolism of methadone resulting in discontinuation symptoms.
Oral contraceptives	X↓	Diminished oral contraceptive levels; risk of unwanted pregnancy.

Drugs (X) Interact with:	Oxcarbazepine (O)	Comments
Other anticonvulsants (e.g., carbamazepine, phenobarbital, phenytoin, valproate)	X↑O↓	Decreased plasma concentrations of oxcarbazepine and its 10-monohydroxy metabolite. Increased concentrations of phenobarbital (by 14%) and phenytoin (by 40%).
CNS depressants (e.g., alcohol, hypnotics, narcotics)	X↑O↓	Increased sedation.
Dihydropyridine calcium channel antagonists (e.g., felodipine, verapamil)	X↓	Decreased plasma concentrations of dihydropyridine calcium channel blockers via induction of CYP3A4 and CYP3A5.
Oral contraceptives	X↓	Decreased plasma concentrations and effectiveness of oral contraceptives.

Drugs (X) Interact with:	Lamotrigine (L)	Comments
Other anticonvulsants Carbamazepine, phenobarbital, phenytoin, primidone	X↑L↓	Decreased lamotrigine plasma concentration by 40% due to increased metabolism. Lamotrigine may enhance the toxicity of carbamazepine by increasing the concentration of the active epoxide metabolite.
Valproate	L↑	Increased half-life and plasma concentration of lamotrigine due to competition for hepatic glucuronidation; may increase the risk of severe skin rash.
Antipsychotics (e.g., olanzapine)	L↓	Reduced AUC (24%) and Cmax (20%) of lamotrigine
CNS depressants (e.g., alcohol, hypnotics)	X↑L↑	Increased sedation
Protease inhibitor (e.g., lopinavir/ritonavir)	L↓	Decreased plasma level of lamotrigine by induction of glucuronidation
Oral contraceptives	L↓	Decreased plasma level of lamotrigine by 50%; breakthrough seizures, unexpected pregnancies and menstrual bleeding disorders have been reported. Maintenance dose of lamotrigine may need to be increased by as much as 2-fold in women starting or currently taking oral contraceptives.

Drugs (X) Interact with:	Valproate (V)	Comments
Antibiotic (e.g., erythromycin)	V↑	Increased valproate plasma level and toxicity; may occur with other macrolide antibiotics.
Anticoagulant (e.g., warfarin)	X↑	Displacement of warfarin from protein binding site, leading to a transient increase in INR.
Other anticonvulsants Carbamazepine, phenobarbital, primidone	X↑V↓	Valproate inhibits the metabolism and increases the plasma levels of anticonvulsants (by 30–50%). Decreased valproate levels due to increased clearance.
Phenytoin	X↑V↓	Increased phenytoin toxicity at therapeutic levels due to displacement from binding protein (free fraction increased by 60%) and inhibited metabolism. Vaproate level may decrease.
Felbamate	V↑	Increased level and toxicity of valproate. Monitor levels; decrease in valproate dosage may be necessary.
Ethosuximide	X↑	Increased half-life of ethosuximide (by 25%) due to decreased clearance.

MOOD STABILIZERS

Drugs (X) Interact with:	Valproate (V)	Comments
Lamotrigine	X↑	Increased half-life and plasma concentration of lamotrigine due to competition for hepatic glucuronidation.
Antidepressants		
TCAs	X↑	Decreased clearance of nortriptyline (by 35%) and amitriptyline (by 20%).
SSRI	V↑	Increased plasma level of valproate (case reports).
Cimetidine	V↑	Increased half-life of valproate; monitor level or switch to ranitidine.
Salicylates	X↑ V↑	Elevation in plasma-unbound fraction of valproate due to displacement from protein binding sites. Symptoms resolve when salicylate discontinued.

^a↑ = increases; ↓ = decreases.

Special Populations

CHILDREN AND ADOLESCENTS

Carbamazepine
• Children eliminate carbamazepine more rapidly than adults and thus require comparatively higher doses (relative to weight) to achieve effective concentrations in serum.
• Children may be at risk for neurotoxicities due to accumulation of active metabolite carbamazepine-10,11-epoxide.

Oxcarbazepine
• Indicated for use as monotherapy or adjunctive therapy in the treatment of children with partial seizures.
• May emerge as treatment for bipolar disorder.

Lamotrigine
• Demonstrated to be well tolerated in pediatric patients.
• Common adverse events include infection, benign rash, headache, pharyngitis, and fever.
• The events are normally mild to moderate in intensity and do not usually necessitate discontinuation of the drug.

Valproate
• Use with caution, preferably as monotherapy, in children under 2 years of age due to increased risk for fatal hepatotoxicity.
• Long-term use in female children and adolescents is associated with
  √ Hyperinsulinemia and dyslipidemia
  √ Excessive weight gain
  √ Polycystic ovaries and hyperandrogenism

WOMEN: PREGNANCY AND POSTPARTUM

Pregnancy Rating	• Lamotrigine, oxcarbazepine: Category C
	• Others: Category D

Teratogenicity
(1st trimester)

- Avoid carbamazepine. Overall incidence of fetal malformation is 5.7%. Risk of spina bifida (1%) and congenital heart defects (2.9%).
  √ If necessary, use lowest amount possible in divided doses.

- AVOID valproate throughout pregnancy; incidence of malformations is 11.1% (dose-related). Risk of spina bifida (1–2%), neural tube defects (5%), neurological dysfunction and developmental deficits (71%).
  √ If necessary use < 1000 mg/day in three or more divided doses.

- Monitor carbamazepine and valproate levels throughout pregnancy, maternal alpha fetoprotein around week 16, and do fetal ultrasound around week 20.

- Lamotrigine is associated with a 3.2% risk of malformation (e.g., cleft lip and/or cleft palate).

- Risks to humans are currently unknown for oxcarbazepine.

- Vitamin K supplementation suggested to reduce bleeding.

- If a woman taking antiepileptics becomes pregnant, discontinuing the drug abruptly can cause rebound seizures.

Direct Effect on Newborn
(3rd trimester)

- Infants exposed in utero to valproate have a significantly higher risk of hypoglycemia and hepatotoxicity.

Lactation

- Carbamazepine concentrations range from 7 to 95% in breast milk.
  √ Metabolized rapidly in newborns, resulting in a relatively low risk of adverse effects; compatible with breastfeeding.

- Oxcarbazepine is excreted in breast milk at about 50% of maternal plasma concentration.

- Valproate is excreted in breast milk in low levels; compatible with breastfeeding.

M O O D   S T A B I L I Z E R S

- Lamotrigine is excreted in breast milk.
  √ Mean milk–plasma ratio is 0.6; drug levels in infant serum range from 23 to 33% of maternal levels.
  √ Due to slow elimination in the infant, concentrations may reach therapeutic range.

LATE LIFE

- Lower initial doses and more gradual adjustments are recommended.
- Elderly patients are more vulnerable to adverse CNS events; these effects may occur at lower blood levels.
- Due to decreased protein binding, elderly may have a higher free fraction of valproate.
  √ This may contribute to dose-dependent toxicity and will not be apparent from the total serum measurements.
- Higher risk of hyponatremia and osteoporosis with carbamazepine and oxcarbazepine.
  √ Avoid in patients taking sodium-depleting agents (e.g., diuretics).

Effects on Laboratory Tests

Effects of Anticonvulsants on Blood/Serum and Urine Tests

	Blood/Serum Tests		Urine Tests	
Generic Names	**Marker**	**Results[a]**	**Marker**	**Results[a]**
Carbamazepine	Calcium	↓	Albuminuria	↑
	BUN	↑	Glycosuria	↑
	Thyroid function	↓		
	LFT[b]	↑		
	WBC, platelets	↓		
	RBC	↓		
	Sodium	↓		
	TCA[c]	↑		
Clonazepam	LFT[c]	↑		
Valproic acid	LFT[c] (mainly AST [SGOT], ALT [SGPT], LDH)	↑	Ketone tests	False ↑
	WBC, platelets	↓		
	Thyroid function	↓		
	Lymphocytes, macrocytes	↑		
	Ammonia	↑		

[a]↑ = increases; ↓ = decreases.
[b]LFT = liver function tests (AST/SGOT, ALT/SGPT, alkaline phosphatase, bilirubin, and LDH. Increases in transaminases [SGOT, SGPT, and LDH] are usually benign; increases in bilirubin and other tests suggest hepatotoxicity).
[c]False positive for TCA when Abbot TCA immunoassay used.

Discontinuation

In nonepileptic patients, anticonvulsants do not produce

- Psychological dependence
- Tolerance
- Addiction

No specific symptoms have been described following the abrupt discontinuation of anticonvulsants. However, since withdrawal seizures may occur in non-epileptic patients, it is safest to gradually taper by 10% qod.

Overdose: Toxicity, Suicide, and Treatment

CARBAMAZEPINE

- Onset of symptoms begins 1–3 h after acute overdose (above 50 mmol/l).
- In overdoses, AV block is common; respiratory depression, stupor, and coma are also not infrequent.
- Other signs and symptoms include
  √ Nausea, vomiting, decreased intestinal motility, urinary retention
  √ Agitation, restlessness, irritability
  √ Mydriasis, nystagmus, blurred vision, transient diplopia
  √ Tremor, twitching, involuntary movements, abnormal reflexes, opisthotonos, athetoid movements, ataxia
  √ Dizziness, blood pressure changes
  √ Flushing, cyanosis
- Management: no known antidote; treat symptomatically.

OXCARBAZEPINE

- Lethal overdose has not been reported; the maximum dose taken was approximately 24,000 mg.
- Management: no known antidote; treat symptomatically.

LAMOTRIGINE

- Overdose can result in
  √ Ataxia, drowsiness, lethargy
  √ Intraventricular conduction delay
  √ Respiratory depression
  √ Seizures, coma
- Management: no known antidote; treat symptomatically.

VALPROATE

- Toxic effects are associated with daily doses above 1800 mg and blood levels above 100 g/ml.
- Children younger than 2 years are at significant risk of developing potentially fatal hepatotoxic syndrome.
  √ Signs and symptoms
    □ Somnolence, ataxia, tremor
    □ Heart block
    □ Cerebral edema
    □ Coma
- Management
  √ Naloxone may reverse the CNS depressant and antiepileptic effects.
  √ L-carnitine is reportedly helpful in treating hyperammonemia, hepatotoxicity, and coma associated with valproate overdose.

M
O
O
D

S
T
A
B
I
L
I
Z
E
R
S

Precautions

Avoid or *monitor closely* in patients with
• History of hepatic disease
  √ Valproate-induced hepatic toxicity may show no relation to hepatic enzyme levels.
  √ Monitor liver function prior to therapy.
  √ In high-risk patients, monitor serum fibrinogen and albumin for decreases in concentration, and ammonia for increases secondary to decrease in carnitine levels.
  √ Discontinue drug if hepatic transaminase is 2–3 times the upper limit of normal.
• History of cardiovascular disease
• Bone-marrow depression, leukopenia, thrombocytopenia
• Known hypersensitive to anticonvulsants
• Current clozapine use
  √ Combining clozapine with certain anticonvulsants (especially carbamazepine) may increase the risk of agranulocytosis.
• Intraocular pressure or urinary retention (carbamazepine)

Key Points to Communicate to Patients and Families

• Do not change dose or stop the drug without first discussing with your physician; abrupt discontinuation of drug can cause an uncontrollable seizure.
• If a dose is missed by 4 h, skip the dose and resume medication at the next regularly scheduled time.
  √ Do *not* double the dose.
• To reduce GI irritation, take medication with food or by slowly raising the dose.
• Capsules or tablets should be swallowed whole; do not crush or chew them.
• If on valproate, avoid aspirin unless approved by physician.
  √ Bleeding, bruises, and petechiae may arise.
• These drugs may impair mental and physical abilities. Avoid activity that requires alertness, such as driving a car or operating potentially dangerous equipment.
• Avoid during pregnancy, but if pregnancy suspected
  √ Do *not* immediately stop drug.
  √ Consult with doctor.
• Place anticonvulsants away from bedside or any readily accessible area due to safety concerns. Keep out of reach of children.

THERAPEUTIC APPLICATION

Treatment Initiation

MANIA

• Lithium, divalproex, and several second-generation antipsychotics (olanzapine, risperidone, quetiapine, ziprasidone, and aripiprazole) are first-line antimanic agents.

• The decision to treat with monotherapy or a combination of these medications is influenced by
  √ Current medication and previous response.
  √ Patient preference and history of adherence.
  √ Physical risk factors, particularly renal disease, obesity and diabetes.
• Benzodiazepines are useful adjuncts to provide sedation but should not be used alone.

Lithium monotherapy
• Recommended for classic bipolar mania (65–70% full initial response)
• Obtain blood tests prior to initiating lithium (*see* table below).
• Be aware that the therapeutic index is narrow.
• Start lithium at 300 mg bid and increase dose by 300 mg q 3–4 days.
  √ Divided dosing can reduce early nausea, but
  √ If nausea is posing no problem, qd dosing can be used.
• Raise dose until clear therapeutic results, or plasma level reaches 1.2 mEq/l.
  √ If no therapeutic effect after 10 days and no significant side effects, raise dose further to 1.5 mEq/l.
• Measure initial lithium level around days 4–7 after starting the drug to determine plasma level.
  √ Draw lithium serum concentrations 12 h post-dose.
  √ If at appropriate level, get further lithium levels in 2 weeks or 3–4 days after last lithium increase.
  √ Obtain levels every month for the next 6 months, and then
    ▫ Every 2–3 months, or
    ▫ If two or three consecutive lithium levels are stable, can wait 3 months and then 6 months.
• Onset of action 7–10 days (if therapeutic levels for acute mania are rapidly achieved) but may require up to 3–5 weeks.
• Reduce above doses by 50% in patients over 60 or in patients with a renal disorder.

Schedule of Laboratory Tests Recommended for Lithium Treatment

	Before Starting Lithium	Every 6 Months	Every 12 Months
ECG[a]	Yes		Yes
Electrolytes[a]	Yes		
CBC, differential[b]	Yes		
BUN, creatinine (creatinine clearance if risk of renal impairment suspected)	Yes	Yes[c]	
Urinalysis	Yes		
Fasting blood sugar (optional)[d]	Yes		
T_3RU, T_4RIA, T_4I[e]	Yes		
TSH	Yes	Yes[f]	Yes[f]
Antithyroid antibodies (optional)[g]	Yes		
Calcium[h]	Yes		Yes

MOOD STABILIZERS

	Before Starting Lithium	Every 6 Months	Every 12 Months
Pregnancy test (women at risk)	Yes	Optional	Optional
Side effect checklist	Yes	Yes	
Physical exam and general medical history[i]		Yes	Yes

[a]For patients over 40 or with h/o cardiac disease; these patients should also have another ECG 1 month after obtaining steady-state plasma level.
[b]Obtain new baselines WBC with expected leukocytosis 4–6 weeks after lithium begins; neutrophils most increased.
[c]Check renal function q 2–3 months during the first 6 months of treatment.
[d]Helps establish baseline to determine later if lithium significantly alters glucose tolerance. Hypoglycemia greater risk from lithium.
[e]Can help detect those who are mostly likely to become hypothyroid.
[f]Many women who develop hypothyroidism do so within 2 years; 6-month monitoring recommended. After 2 years male and female euthyroid can be monitored yearly.
[g]RU = resin uptake; RIA = radio immunoassay; I = free thyroxin index.
[h]Obtain serum calcium 2–6 weeks after lithium begins. Further assay should be done if clinical symptoms of hypercalcemia are seen: neuromuscular signs, ataxia, apathy, dysphoria, depression. Levels approaching 11 mg/dl should be followed closely.
[i]Special emphasis on cardiac, renal, thyroid, and dermatologic systems and risk of pregnancy.

Divalproex monotherapy
- Recommended for mania with atypical features, frequent episodes, or mixed manic–depressive symptoms.
- Patients improve 4–14 days after reaching a therapeutic plasma level.
- Divalproex can often be started at target dose.
- If severe acute mania and nongeriatric, start at 20 mg/kg in divided doses with meals. With divalproex ER, may only need medication qd.
- If rapid treatment not needed, start at 10–15 mg/kg.
  √ To minimize GI and neurologic toxicity, start at 250 mg tid.
  √ Can increase 250–500 mg q 3 days, depending on response and side effects.
  √ Start lower and go slower with euthymic, hypomanic, depressed, or elderly patients.
  √ Give tid doses until stabilized.
  √ Dosing bid is effective for maintenance treatment.
- Check serum levels in 3–4 days.
  √ Goal is 50–100 μg/ml.

Second-generation antipsychotic monotherapy
- Shown to be equally effective in patients with or without psychotic symptoms.
- Evidence to suggest that olanzapine may be effective in patients with rapid cycling as well as those with mixed states.
- Optimize antipsychotic dose
  √ Olanzapine: Start at 10–15 mg qd.
    □ Increase by 5 mg/day at intervals of not less than 24 hours.
    □ Maximum dose 20 mg/day
  √ Risperidone: Start at 2–3 mg qd.
    □ If needed, adjust dose by 1 mg/day in intervals of at least 24 hours.
  √ Paliperidone: Start at 6 mg/day.
    □ Dosing range 3–9 mg/day.
  √ Quetiapine: Start at 50 mg bid.
    □ Titrate to 400 mg/day by day 4.

□ Titrate to 800 mg/day by day 6 (if clinically indicated).

√ Quetiapine SR: Start at 300 mg/day.

□ Titrate to 600 mg/day within 3 days, as tolerated.

√ Ziprasidone: Start at 40 mg bid (with food).

□ May increase to 60–80 mg bid by day 2.

√ Aripiprazole: Start at 30 mg qd.

□ May require a decrease to 15 mg qd based on tolerability.

• Monitor for symptoms of hyperglycemia (polydipsia, polyuria, polyphagia, and weakness).

• Get fasting blood glucose in patients who develop symptoms of diabetes mellitus.

Combination therapy

• Synergistic therapeutic and toxic effects are often seen.

√ Toxic effects can be seen when each drug is in the "normal" serum level range.

• Often low-normal plasma levels of both agents are preferred to maximize synergistic therapeutic effects and minimize toxicity.

• Initiate a benzodiazepine if patient is agitated but not psychotic, or still agitated on adequate antipsychotic dose, or if TD risk makes an antipsychotic a poor choice.

BIPOLAR DEPRESSION

Although monotherapy is the preferred initial regimen, combination therapy is often required to control the symptoms of both depression and mania that are characteristic of bipolar disorder. Several first-line options can be considered:

• Lithium monotherapy

√ Yields a 60–75% response in bipolar depression.

• Lamotrigine monotherapy

√ Yields a 40–50% response in bipolar depression.

√ Low risk of manic switch in bipolar depressed patients.

√ Start at 25 mg/day during weeks 1 and 2; titrate to 200 mg/day by week 6.

• Lithium or divalproex plus SSRI or bupropion

√ If patient is currently on lithium or divalproex, the dosage should be adjusted to achieve a target 12-hour trough serum concentration of 0.8–1.2 mEq/l or 45–120 mcg/ml, respectively.

√ Adding an SSRI or bupropion may enhance and accelerate antidepressant effectiveness and reduce the likelihood of switching moods.

• Olanzapine plus fluoxetine

• Lithium plus divalproex

• Quetiapine monotherapy

RAPID CYCLING

• Four or more recurrences in a single year

• Divalproex has superior efficacy compared to lithium in this population in the treatment of mania.

• Second-generation antipsychotic agents are highly effective and have the largest evidence base.

If rapid cycling occurs

- Check (and treat) for hypothyroidism.
- Reduce or stop antidepressants with gradual taper.
- Avoid caffeine, nicotine, alcohol, and illicit drugs.
- T_4 supplementation (0.075–4 mg/day) can be considered for patients with mildly elevated TSH level associated with lithium treatment.
  √ T_4 dosage increases should occur about q 3–5 weeks.
    □ It takes about 4–6 weeks for thyroid axis to equilibrate after each change in dosage.
    □ Suprametabolic doses risk tachycardia, tremor, anxiety, agitation, congestive heart failure, osteoporosis, and atrial fibrillation.
- Prescribe two mood stabilizers (e.g., lithium + divalproex; lithium + carbamazepine) if still cycling after 2–4 months.
  √ The chief problem with lithium plus carbamazepine is acute confusion.
    □ Repeat mental status testing.
  √ Lithium plus divalproex is less likely to cause confusion.
- Several second-generation antipsychotics (e.g., clozapine, olanzapine, quetiapine, risperidone) have also demonstrated significant symptom relief in patients with rapid cycling.

Treatment Resistance

- Before adding or switching therapies
  √ Optimize the dose of current medication.
    □ If therapy with one of the first-line agents at optimal doses is inadequate or not tolerated, the next step should involve switching to, or adding, an alternate first-line agent.
  √ Identify nonadherence.
    □ Nonadherence to treatment (30–50%) is often associated with adverse effects, particularly in the early stages of therapy.

Maintenance

- Maintenance therapy with a mood stabilizer is recommended for any patient with
  √ At least two major episodes or
  √ After a particularly severe episode of bipolar illness.
- The therapeutic goals of maintenance therapy are to
  √ Prevent relapse and recurrence.
  √ Reduce risk of morbidity and mortality.
  √ Allow patient to resume lifestyle.
- Lithium, divalproex, lamotrigine, olanzapine, and aripiprazole have best empirical evidence to support use in maintenance treatment.
- Lithium maintenance considerations include:
  √ Achieve serum concentrations between 0.6–0.8 mEq/l.
  √ Patient should be informed about risks of
    □ Weight gain
    □ Edema

□ Toxicity; characterized by new-onset diarrhea, tremors, confused thinking

□ Cognitive impairment

√ Before stopping lithium

□ Identify in detail the first signs of mania and depression.

□ Taper lithium gradually (e.g., 300 mg/month) rather than abruptly; abrupt discontinuation carries high risk of early relapse.

√ If patient stops but then must return to lithium, and if he or she has previously tolerated a particular lithium dose well, restart on this full dose without titrating upward if no side effects are noted when first started.

□ Have patient report side effects immediately.

□ Get lithium level in 3–4 days after achieving steady state.

• Divalproex maintenance considerations include:

√ Serum drug levels q 3–6 months.

√ Aim for levels 300–700 umol/l.

√ Obtain repeat LFTs at 3–4 month intervals or if symptoms of liver disease appear.

□ Mild SGPT elevations are usually benign but should be monitored for significant changes.

□ Elevations of bilirubin are clinically more important and warrant a consultation from a specialist and possible discontinuation of drug.

√ Patient should report increased bruising or bleeding in case thrombocytopenia develops.

√ Disturbing maintenance side effects include:

□ Hair loss (alopecia) in about 8%; twice or more common in females than males

□ Increased appetite and weight gain

□ Polycystic ovaries, amenorrhea, androgenism; highest risks in teenage girls.

√ Patient should be informed about risks in pregnancy.

• Lamotrigine maintenance considerations include:

√ Recommended to those with recurrent bipolar illness.

√ Routine monitoring of blood levels is not needed.

√ Benign skin rashes in about 10% of patients, serious skin rashes in about 0.03%.

□ Highest risk if dosing rate exceeds recommendations.

□ The drug should be stopped unless it is clear that the rash is not related to the use of lamotrigine.

□ Use dose titration to avoid rash.

• Olanzapine maintenance considerations include:

√ Routine monitoring of blood levels is not needed.

√ Can cause significant weight gain and metabolic abnormalities.

□ Monitor blood glucose and lipids regularly.

• Aripiprazole maintenance considerations include:

√ Patient should be informed about the common adverse effects, which include tremor, akathisia, vaginitis.

√ Monitor physical parameters such as weight, fasting blood sugar, and full lipid screen when necessary.

6. Antianxiety Agents

Psychotropic agents with an anxiolytic profile are often used in the treatment of anxiety disorders and in the relief of anxiety symptoms in other patient populations. Most patients experience a rapid relief of anxiety symptoms during short-term benzodiazepine use; nevertheless, concerns about tolerance and dependence have limited the prescription of this class of agents by psychiatrists. Several azapirones were evaluated for anxiolytic properties; however, only buspirone has been approved for the treatment of generalized anxiety disorder. Barbiturates and carbamates are now rarely prescribed, although these agents were used extensively prior to the benzodiazepine era.

Beta-blockers such as propranolol are often prescribed off-label for the relief of somatic anxiety symptoms. The antihistamines (e.g., hydroxyzine) have also been employed frequently for the management of somatic and psychological anxiety symptoms. Virtually every psychotropic drug class has some anxiolytic effects, so it is not surprising that SSRI and SNRI antidepressants, first-generation and second-generation antipsychotics, as well as anticonvulsants have shown effectiveness and/or efficacy in the treatment of anxiety.

Although anxiety relief and sedation are largely a function of dose, some of these medications (e.g., SSRIs) are indicated only to treat anxiety *disorders* rather than anxiety symptoms, and some benzodiazepines are indicated only for hypnotic use. This chapter discusses the pharmacological treatment of anxiety, and Chapter 7 deals with the hypnotics.

The main anxiety disorders listed in DSM-IV that require pharmacotherapy are:

- Generalized anxiety disorder
- Panic disorder (with and without agoraphobia)
- Social anxiety disorder
- Posttraumatic stress disorder
- Obsessive–compulsive disorder

ANTIANXIETY AGENTS

149

The main therapeutic agents for relief of anxiety can be subdivided into benzo-diazepine and nonbenzodiazepine agents.

Antianxiety Agents by Chemical Class

Chemical Class	Generic Name	Trade Name
Benzodiazepine	Alprazolam	Xanax
	Chlordiazepoxide	Librium
	Clonazepam	Klonopin
	Clorazepate	Tranxene
	Diazepam	Valium
	Lorazepam	Ativan
	Oxazepam	Serax
Nonbenzodiazepine		
Adrenergic agent	Propranolol	Inderal
Anticonvulsant	Divalproex sodium	Depakote
	Gabapentin	Neurontin
	Pregabalin	Lyrica
	Tiagabine	Gabitril
	Valproic acid	Depakene
Antidepressant		
TCA	Clomipramine	Anafranil
SSRI	Citalopram	Celexa
	Escitalopram	Lexapro
	Fluvoxamine	Luvox
	Paroxetine	Paxil
	Sertraline	Zoloft
SNRI	Venlafaxine	Effexor
Antihistamine	Hydroxyzine	Atarax, Vistaril
Azapirone	Buspirone	Buspar

BENZODIAZEPINES

Dosing, Dose Form, and Color

Profile of Benzodiazepines

Generic Names	Therapeutic Dose Range (mg/day)	Geriatric Dose (mg/day)	Dose Form (mg)[a]	Color
Alprazolam	1.0–2.0	0.25–0.5	t: 0.25/0.5/1/1	t: white (oval)/peach/blue/white (oblong)
			er: 0.5/1/2/3	er: white/yellow/blue/green
Chlordiazepoxide	15–75	5–30[b]	c: 5/10/25 p: 20 mg/ml	c: green–yellow/green–black/green–white
Clonazepam	0.5–1.5	0.25–1.0	t: 0.5/1/2	t: orange/blue/white
Clorazepate	15–67.5	15–60[b]	t: 3.75/7.5/15 t: 11.25/22.5	t: blue/peach/lavender t: blue/tan
Diazepam	4–30	1–10	t: 2/5/10 p: 5 mg/ml	t: white/yellow/blue
Lorazepam	2–6	0.5–1.5	t: 0.5/1/2 p: 2/4 mg/ml	t: all white
Oxazepam	30–60	10–30	t: 15 c:10/15/30	t: yellow c: white–pink/white–red/white–maroon

[a]c = capsules; er = extended release; p = parenteral; t = tablets.
[b]Due to exceedingly long half-lives, not generally recommended for more than 1 week in elderly or with impaired hepatic function. Use lorazepam instead.

Pharmacology

PHARMACOKINETICS

Absorption
- Well absorbed from GI tract after oral administration.
- Food can delay the rate, but not the extent, of absorption.

Half-lives
- The longer the half-life of a benzodiazepine, the greater the likelihood that the compound will have an adverse effect on daytime functioning (e.g., impaired concentration, daytime sleepiness).
- With shorter half-life benzodiazepines, greater withdrawal and anxiety symptoms are seen between doses (i.e., interdose rebound).

Lipophilic and hydrophilic properties
- Single doses of highly lipophilic benzodiazepines (e.g., diazepam, clorazepate)
  √ Enter the brain rapidly.
  √ Have a rapid onset of action.
  √ Wear off quickly.
  √ Redistribute into adipose tissue.
- Single doses of less lipophilic benzodiazepines (e.g., lorazepam)
  √ Produce clinical effects more slowly, but
  √ Provide more sustained effect.

Duration of effects
- With acute doses, rates of absorption and distribution half-life are critical.
- With repeated doses, distribution is complete; the elimination half-life, which determines the drug's steady-state levels, becomes critical.

Metabolism
- Benzodiazepines can be subclassified according to routes of metabolism (*see* figure on p. 152):
  √ 2-keto compounds (clorazepate, chlordiazepoxide, diazepam, flurazepam)
    □ Slowly oxidized in the liver, resulting in longer half-lives
    □ Clorazepate is a prodrug.
  √ 3-hydroxy compounds (lorazepam, oxazepam, temazepam)
    □ Direct conjugation to more water-soluble glucuronide derivatives
    □ More rapid than oxidation, resulting in shorter half-lives
    □ May be preferred in conditions characterized by diminished hepatic function.
  √ Triazolo compounds (alprazolam, triazolam, estazolam)
    □ Oxidized, limited active metabolites
    □ Relatively short half-lives
  √ 7-nitro compounds (clonazepam)
    □ Metabolized by nitroreduction (some by oxidation)
    □ Long half-life
- Biotransformation by oxidation can be impaired by disease states (e.g., hepatic cirrhosis), by age, or by drugs that impair the metabolism.
  √ Drugs undergoing conjugation only (e.g., oxazepam) are not so affected.

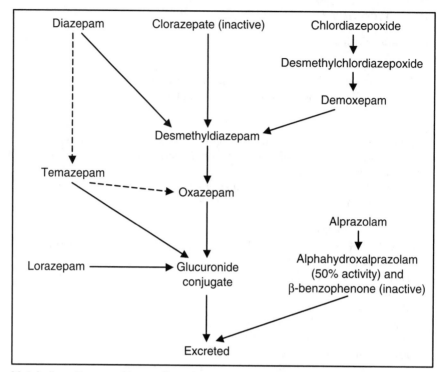

Metabolic pathways of benzodiazepines: —— indicates major pathway; – – indicates minor pathway.

Pharmacokinetic Properties of Benzodiazepines

Generic Names	Time to Peak Concentration (h)	Lipid Solubility	Half-Life (h)[a]	Major Active Metabolite	P450 Substrate
Alprazolam	1–2	Moderate	6–27	α-hydroxy-alprazolam	3A4, 1A2
Chlordiazepoxide	1–4	Moderate	4–29 (parent drug); 28–100 (metabolites)	Desmethylchlordiazepoxide	Oxidation
Clonazepam	1–4	Low	19–60	None	2B4, 2E1, 3A4
Clorazepate	1–2	High	1.3–120 (metabolites)	N-desmethyl-diazepam	Oxidation
Diazepam	0.5–2	High	14–80 (parent drug); 30–200 (metabolites)	N-desmethyl-diazepam	3A4, 2C9, 2C19, 2B6
Lorazepam	1–6	Moderate	8–24	None	Conjugation
Oxazepam	1–4	Low	3–25	None	Conjugation

[a]Longer in elderly; more important in chronic administration.

PHARMACODYNAMICS

- Benzodiazepines enhance the actions of GABA, the brain's major inhibitory neurotransmitter.
  - √ GABA inhibits the firing of neurons by opening chloride channels in a GABA–benzodiazepine receptor complex located on the neuronal membrane.
  - √ This influx of negative charge causes a hyperpolarization of the cell membrane and therefore inhibits depolarization.
- Alprazolam also acts on the noradrenergic system.
  - √ This may distinguish it from other benzodiazepines and supports its antipanic effect.
- The potency of a benzodiazepine for the GABA–benzodiazepine–chloride receptor complex is correlated with the affinity of the parent drug or its active metabolites.
  - √ Lorazepam and alprazolam are high-potency agents and are most likely to be associated with significant discontinuation symptoms.

Clinical Indications

GENERAL INFORMATION

- Benzodiazepines are frequently prescribed in primary care for adjustment disorders, particularly those with anxiety or mixed anxiety and depression.
- Rapid symptom relief is a significant advantage of benzodiazepines over other anxiolytic agents with delayed onset of action.
- These benefits must be weighed against the limited role of benzodiazepines in treating comorbid depressive symptoms and their potential risk for tolerance and dependence.
- Benzodiazepines are also commonly prescribed as short-term adjuncts to other psychotropic medications.
- Benzodiazepines may be used in the treatment of adjustment disorder with anxious mood, generalized anxiety disorder, panic disorder or specific phobia, but are not generally helpful in treating obsessive–compulsive disorder.

ADJUSTMENT DISORDER WITH ANXIOUS MOOD

- When possible avoid pharmacotherapy, particularly for mild-to-moderate severity of symptoms.
- If symptoms are severe, consider longer-acting benzodiazepines (e.g., clonazepam) for less than 1 month.
  - √ If stressor onset is predictable, take 1–2 h in advance.

GENERALIZED ANXIETY DISORDER (GAD)

- Benzodiazepines are no longer the first-line treatment for GAD.
- When used, long-acting low-potency benzodiazepines (e.g., chlordiazepoxide 25–75 mg/day) are preferred for GAD.
  - √ They are less likely to result in interdose anxiety.

ANTIANXIETY AGENTS

- Benzodiazepines may be more effective in treating specific GAD symptoms, particularly somatic autonomic symptoms, in contrast to the psychological symptoms.
- Tolerance to sedation, impaired concentration, and amnesia may develop within several weeks, but tolerance to the anxiolytic effect has not been observed.
- Duration of use should be limited to acute treatment (2–4 weeks) to minimize dependency.
- Long-term use is reserved for patients who have failed to respond to SSRIs, venlafaxine, buspirone, or other antidepressants or are intolerant to their side effects.

PANIC DISORDER

- Benzodiazepines (e.g., alprazolam, clonazepam) may be used to treat panic disorder if:
  √ SSRI/SNRI agents are not effective or their side effects are not well tolerated.
  √ Medication is needed for immediate relief of severe symptoms of panic disorder, anxiety about having a panic attack, or agoraphobia.
- Alprazolam has been shown to provide rapid relief due to its fast-acting nature, but may be associated with tolerance and dependency.
  √ Start at 0.25 mg tid and increase by 0.25 mg q 3 days.
  √ Usually effective at 3–5 mg/day; doses of 4–6 mg/day may be required to achieve remission of panic disorder.
  √ Frequent dosing limits usefulness; increased risk of discontinuation effects with missed doses.
    □ This may be alleviated by use of the extended-release form.
- Clonazepam has a longer half-life than alprazolam.
  √ This requires less frequent dosing and is less problematic during discontinuation.
  √ Start at 0.25 mg bid and increase by 0.25 mg q 2 days.
  √ Usually effective at 1.5–2.5 mg/day; doses up to 4.5 mg/day may be required for remission.

SPECIFIC PHOBIA

- Benzodiazepines may be used to provide acute symptom relief (e.g., before exposure to flying or dental or MRI procedure).

Side Effects

CENTRAL NERVOUS SYSTEM EFFECTS

Amnesia
- Anterograde amnesia especially with IV diazepam and lorazepam
- Directly related to the speed of onset

Behavior dyscontrol with irritability and impulsivity
- Paradoxical reactions are relatively uncommon (< 1%).

- Risk factors include high-potency agents (e.g., clonazepam), young or old age, and psychiatric status (e.g., personality disorders, other psychiatric conditions) with a history of alcohol abuse.
- Management
  √ Administer flumazenil 0.5 mg IV bolus followed by 0.1 mg until a desired response is achieved.
  √ Haloperidol 5 mg/IM may be a safe alternative.

Confusion, disorientation, clouded sensorium
- Occurs primarily in elderly, cognitively impaired, or brain-damaged patients.
- Increases risk of falls.
- Related to dose and high lipid solubility.
- Often reversible and misdiagnosed as dementia.

Incoordination, ataxia
- Occurs with high doses of benzodiazepines.
- Arises in 25% of patients on $\geq$ 10 mg/day of clonazepam.

Sedation
- Most common side effect; generally plateaus after 7–14 days.
- Management
  √ Increase dose slowly.
  √ Reduce dose.

EYES, EARS, NOSE, AND THROAT

Blurred vision
- Mild and rare
- Management: bethanechol 5–20 mg po tid or qid.

Nasal congestion
- *See* page 18.

GASTROINTESTINAL EFFECTS

Constipation
- *See* page 18.

Dry mouth
- *See* page 18.

RENAL EFFECTS

Urinary hesitancy or retention
- *See* page 20.

SEXUAL EFFECTS

Decreased libido, erectile dysfunction, anorgasmia
- Overall risk is low.

ANTIANXIETY AGENTS

• More common with high-dosage therapy and polypharmacy.
• Management
  √ Reduce dose.
  √ Switch to buspirone or a different benzodiazepine.

Drug and Food Interactions

Drug and Food Interactions with Benzodiazepines

Drugs (X) Interact with:	Benzodiazepines (B)[a]	Comments
Antacids, aluminmum hydroxide, magnesium hydroxide	B↓	Slow rate but not the extent of GI absorption; may delay onset of acute clinical effects.
Antiarrhythmics (e.g., amiodarone)	B↑	Decreased metabolism and increased plasma levels of benzodiazepines that are metabolized by oxidation.
Anticholinergics	B↓	Slow time to peak absorption but not the extent absorbed
Anticonvulsants		
Carbamazepine	B↓	Decreased alprazolam and clonazepam plasma levels by 20–50%.
Barbiturates	X↑B↓↑	Phenobarbital induces metabolism and reduces plasma concentrations of benzodiazepines; potentiate each other's effects.
Phenytoin	X↑↓	Increased phenytoin plasma level and toxicity reported with diazepam and chlordiazepoxide; decreased phenytoin level reported with clonazepam.
Valproate	B↑	Displacement of diazepam from protein binding sites. Unbound fraction of diazepam increased approximately 2-fold. May decrease metabolism of clonazepam and lorazepam.
Antidepressants		
MAO inhibitors	B↑	Increased benzodiazepine level and risk of toxicity
Nefazodone	B↑	Increased plasma levels of alprazolam and triazolam due to inhibited metabolism via CYP3A4
SSRIs (e.g., fluoxetine, fluvoxamine, sertraline)	B↑	Decreased metabolism of diazepam and alprazolam resulting in increased plasma level
Antifungals (e.g., fluconazole, itraconazole, ketoconazole)	B↑	Decreased metabolism of benzodiazepines via CYP3A4. Prescription of benzodiazepeines for patients receiving ketoconazole or itraconazole should be avoided.
Antiulcers (e.g., cimetidine, omeprazole)	B↑	Decreased clearance of benzodiazepines that are metabolized by oxidation; ranitidine and famotidine do not interact with benzodiazepines.
Beta-blockers (e.g., propranolol)	B↑	Increased half-life and decreased clearance of diazepam.
Cigarette smoking	B↓	Increased clearance of alprazolam and diazepam via enzyme induction
CNS depressants (e.g., barbiturates, antihistamines, alcohol)	X↑ B↑	Increased sedation; may lead to coma or fatal respiratory depression with high doses. Acute alcohol consumption increases the bioavailability of barbiturates. Chronic alcohol consumption decreases barbiturate bioavailability via enzyme induction.
Digoxin	X↑	Decreased metabolism and increased serum levels of digoxin; monitor levels.

Drugs (X) Interact with:	Benzodiazepines (B)[a]	Comments
Disulfiram	B↑	Decreased metabolism of benzodiazepenes that are metabolized by oxidation
Grapefruit juice	B↑	Decreased metabolism of diazepam, midazolam, and triazolam via CYP3A4, leading to increased peak concentration and bioavailability
Macrolide antibiotics (e.g., clarithromycin, erythromycin, troleandomycin)	B↑	Decreased metabolism and increased plasma levels of benzodiazepines metabolized by CYP3A4. No interaction with azithromycin.
Oral contraceptives	B↑↓	Oral contraceptives may inhibit the metabolism of oxidized benzodiazepines and induce the conjugative enzymes.

[a]↑ = increases; ↓ = decreases; ↑↓ = increases and decreases.

Special Populations

CHILDREN AND ADOLESCENTS

- Generally not recommended in view of tolerance and dependence risks.
- No compelling evidence to consider benzodiazepines as a first-line agent in the treatment of anxiety symptoms in children, but they may be useful as short-term adjuncts.
- Agents should be titrated slowly and tapered gradually in order to avoid drowsiness, disinhibition, and rebound anxiety.

WOMEN: PREGNANCY AND POSTPARTUM

Pregnancy Rating
Teratogenicity
   (1st trimester)

- Category D

- Case-controlled studies show a slightly increased risk of major malformations or oral cleft alone.

- Due to insufficient safety data, patients should discontinue benzodiazepines 3–4 weeks before attempting to conceive and should remain off them until the end of first trimester.

- When possible, use behavioral techniques, psychotherapy, and caffeine abstinence to manage anxiety.

- If medication is necessary, divide the daily dosage into at least two doses.

- Consider ultrasound screening in second trimester to rule out facial anomalies.

Direct Effect on
  Newborn (3rd
  trimester)

- High doses and/or prolonged use by mother may precipitate floppy infant syndrome (hypotonia, sucking difficulties, hypothermia, and cyanosis) and withdrawal symptoms in newborn.

ANTIANXIETY AGENTS

Lactation

- To avoid withdrawal, taper and discontinue benzodiazepines before delivery.
- Benzodiazepines are secreted into breast milk and may result in lethargy, poor suckling, and weight loss.
- Long-acting agents (e.g. diazepam) may accumulate in the infant; should be avoided.

LATE LIFE

- Clearance of benzodiazepines that undergo oxidative metabolism declines with age.
  √ Drug accumulation and excessive sedation may occur.
  √ Associated with adverse outcomes, including increased risk of falls and fractures, motor vehicle accidents, and cognitive impairment.
- Long-term use is discouraged due to risk of dependence.

Effects on Laboratory Tests

Effects of Benzodiazepines on Blood/Serum and Urine Tests

Generic Names	Blood/Serum Tests		Urine Tests	
	Marker	Results[a]	Marker	Results[a]
Diazepam	LFT[b]	↑	Urine glucose (using Diastix® or Clinistix®)	↓f
Oxazepam	Bilirubin	↑	None	
	Glucose (using Somogyi procedure)	↑f		
	Leukocytes	↓		

[a]↑ = increases; ↓ = decreases; f = falsely.
[b]LFT = liver function tests (AST/SGOT, ALT/SGPT, alkaline phosphatase, bilirubin, and LDH).

Discontinuation

Benzodiazepines have a significant potential for abuse and may cause physical and psychological dependence.

Discontinuation of a benzodiazepine may produce

- Withdrawal
  √ Occurs 1–2 days (short-acting) or 2–4 days (long-acting) following drug discontinuation.
  √ Peaks at 5–7 days and may last up to 2 weeks.
  √ Symptoms include anxiety, insomnia, headache, seizure, agitation, palpitations, sweating, GI distress, blurred vision, heightened sensory perception, muscle cramping, muscle twitches, and decreased appetite.

√ More severe with
- □ Short-acting benzodiazepines
- □ High doses for long duration
- □ Older age

- Rebound
  - √ Occurs 2–3 days following drug withdrawal; increased severity of anxiety symptoms beyond pretreatment levels reported.
- Relapse
  - √ Original anxiety symptoms may return within 3 months following drug discontinuation.

MANAGEMENT

Benzodiazepine withdrawal can be achieved by one of the following protocols:

- Gradual reduction in dosage
  - √ Reducing doses by a fixed percentage per unit of time rather than by a fixed dose per unit of time provides a more even and gradual taper.
    - □ For example, 10% reduction of the last dose q 3 days or 25% per week.
  - √ If the patient experiences abstinence effects after a reduction of dosage, the dose should be held at that level for a longer period before continuing the reduction at a slower rate.
- Substitution
  - √ Substitute the short-acting benzodiazepine with an equivalent dose of diazepam.
  - √ Once substitution is achieved, a gradual reduction of the diazepam dosage should follow.

Overdose: Toxicity, Suicide, and Treatment

A benzodiazepine overdose is rarely fatal when taken in isolation, and the majority of patients recover with minimal intervention. However, increased morbidity and mortality are associated with the combination of benzodiazepines and other CNS respiratory depressants in overdose.

Chronic benzodiazepine overdoses present with symptoms of

- Drowsiness
- Ataxia
- Slurred speech
- Vertigo
- Psychomotor impairment

Acute benzodiazepine overdoses manifest with chronic symptoms *and*

- Somnolence, confusion, lethargy, diminished reflexes
- Hypotension
- Hypotonia
- Coma

ANTIANXIETY AGENTS

- Cardiac arrest (extremely rare)
- Death (extremely rare)

The general management of benzodiazepine overdose includes the following:

- Clinical observation and supportive care
- Activated charcoal may provide adequate GI decontamination.
- Flumazenil, a specific benzodiazepine receptor antagonist, can reverse the effects of a benzodiazepine overdose.
  - √ Should only be considered when severe CNS depression is observed.
  - √ Contraindicated where there is history of co-ingestion of TCAs or benzodiazepine dependence. In such situations, administration of flumazenil may precipitate seizures.
- For hypotension
  - √ Norepinephrine 4–8 mg in 1000 ml 5% D/S or D/W by infusion, or
  - √ Metaraminol 10–20 mg sc/IM.
- Renal and extracorporeal elimination methods are not effective.

Precautions

Benzodiazepines are contraindicated in hypersensitive patients. Use cautiously with

- Elderly or debilitated patients
- Renal or hepatic insufficiency
- Limited pulmonary reserve
- Acute narrow-angle glaucoma
- History of alcohol and/or drug abuse
- Severely depressed patients, particularly if suicidal risk may be present

Key Points to Communicate to Patients and Families

- Medications are often best used in conjunction with cognitive–behavioral therapy and other psychological interventions.
- Use benzodiazepines for the shortest time possible (weeks rather than months).
- Before starting treatment, identify key symptoms and track their response to the medication.
- Particularly during the first few weeks, avoid or take extra care when driving or operating machinery.
- Benzodiazepines potentiate the effect of alcohol—one drink feels like two or three.
- Early side effects include daytime sleepiness, clumsiness, fuzzy thinking.
- Although symptom relief may occur early, remission of symptoms frequently requires higher doses.
- Try not to miss doses.
- Discontinuation effects may occur rapidly and resemble anxiety symptoms.
- Do not stop abruptly.
- Seizures and other discontinuation symptoms may occur.

NONBENZODIAZEPINES

Dosing, Dose Form, and Color

Profile of Nonbenzodiazepines

Generic Names	Therapeutic Dose Range (mg/day)	Geriatric Dose (mg/day)	Dose Form (mg)[a]	Color
		BETA-BLOCKERS		
Propranolol	30–80	30–60	t: 10/20/40/60/80	t: orange/blue/green/ pink/yellow
		ANTICONVULSANTS		
Divalproex sodium	750–3000		t: 500	t: gray
			t: 125/250/500	t: salmon–pink/ peach/lavender
			c: 125	c: blue-white
Gabapentin	900–3600	150–1200	c: 100/300/400	c: white/yellow/ orange
Pregabalin	200–600		c: 25/50/75/100/ 150/200/225/300	c: white/white/white– (different doses imprinted on each) orange/orange/ white/light orange/white–light orange/white– orange
Tiagabine	4–32		t: 2/4/12/16/20	t: orange–peach/ yellow/green/ blue/pink
Valproic acid	1000–2500	250–2000	c: 250/500 s: 250 mg/5 ml	c: orange/pale yellow s: red
		ANTIHISTAMINE		
Hydroxyzine	200–400	10–50	t: 10/25/50/100 s: 10 mg/5 ml c: 25/50/100 su: 25 mg/ml	t: orange/green/ yellow/red c: green/green– white/green–gray
		AZAPIRONE		
Busprione	30–45	15–30	t: 5/10	t: all white
		ANTIDEPRESSANTS		

Several SSRIs, clomipramine, and venlafaxine have indications for various anxiety disorders. These are discussed in Chapter 3.

ANTIPSYCHOTICS

Although none is indicated for the treatment of an anxiety disorder, adjunctive use is common.

[a]c = capsules; s = syrup; su = suspension; t = tablets.

Pharmacology

PHARMACOKINETICS

Buspirone
• Rapidly and almost completely absorbed following oral administration.
• Low bioavailability due to extensive first-pass metabolism.

- Food may decrease the rate of absorption and increase the amount of unchanged drug in the system.
- Clearance reduced by 2-fold in individuals with renal and hepatic impairment.

Hydroxyzine
- Readily absorbed from the GI tract.
- Distributes into the skin efficiently following an oral dose and sustains higher concentrations than in serum.
- Predominantly metabolized by the liver via oxidation.
- Increased half-life in the elderly and those with renal insufficiency.

Propranolol
- Rapidly and completely absorbed from the GI tract.
- Low bioavailability due to extensive first-pass metabolism.
- Co-administration of protein-rich food may enhance bioavailability by about 50%.
- Highly lipophilic and thus readily enters the brain.

Anticonvulsants
- Gabapentin
  - √ Bioavailability is highly variable and dose-dependent due to a saturable transport mechanism.
  - √ Eliminated primarily by renal excretion as unchanged drug.
    - ▫ Plasma clearance and renal clearance are directly proportional to creatinine clearance.
    - ▫ Dosage adjustment in patients with reduced renal function or undergoing hemodialysis is necessary.
- Pregabalin
  - √ Rapidly absorbed when administered in the fasting state; co-administration with food has no significant effect on the extent of absorption.
  - √ Elimination: similar pathway to gabapentin
- Valproate
  - √ *See* page 129.
- Tiagabine
  - √ Rapidly and completely absorbed from the GI tract; co-administration of a lipid-rich meal may decrease the rate, but not the extent, of absorption.
  - √ Predominantly metabolized by the liver.
    - ▫ Clearance is reduced by 60% in patients with moderate hepatic impairment.
  - √ A diurnal effect on the pharmacokinetics has been observed.

Pharmacokinetic Properties of Nonbenzodiazepines

Generic Names	Bioavailability (%)	Protein Binding (%)	Half-Life (h)	P450 Systems Substrate	P450 Systems Inhibitor	Excretion (%)[a]
Buspirone	4	95	2–11	3A4, 2C19, 2D6		30–60 R20–40 F
Divalproex sodium	100	90	6–16	2C9, UGT	2C9, 2C19, UGT	< 3 R or F
Gabapentin	60	< 3	5–7			97 R
Hydroxyzine	High	93	8–20		2D6	R/F
Pregabalin	≥ 90	0	6.3			99 R
Propranolol	26	80–95	2–6	2D6, 1A2	2D6	R
Valproic acid	78	60–95	5–20	2C9, UGT	2D6, 2C9, 2C19, UGT	
Tiagabine	90–95	96	7–9	3A4		25 R/63 F

[a]F = fecal; R = renal.
Note. Not all nonbenzodiazepines listed in the table at the top of p. 150 are included here. Additional agents are discussed in Chapter 3.

PHARMACODYNAMICS

Buspirone
• Acts as a full agonist at the presynaptic 5-HT$_{1A}$ autoreceptors and as a partial agonist at the postsynaptic 5-HT$_{1A}$ receptors.
• Chronic administration causes a down-regulation of 5-HT$_2$ receptors.
• Modulates dopaminergic activity via blockade at presynaptic D$_2$ receptors.
• Major metabolite—1-(2-pyrimidinyl)-piperazine (1-PP)—possesses central and peripheral α_2-adrenergic blocking activity.

Hydroxyzine
• Modest 5-HT$_2$ receptor antagonism in addition to H$_1$ and muscarinic blocking effects

Propranolol
• A nonselective β-blocker that acts on both β$_1$ (mainly heart) and β$_2$ (bronchial tissue) receptors.
• Possesses membrane-stabilizing properties in high doses.

Anticonvulsants
• Gabapentin
   √ Blocks voltage-gated sodium channels and calcium channels.
   √ Inhibits release of excitatory neurotransmitters (glutamate).
• Pregabalin
   √ Inhibits voltage-gated calcium channels.
     ▫ This results in a reduction in the release of excitatory neurotransmitters (glutamate).
• Valproate
   √ *See* page 130.
• Tiagabine
   √ Blocks the reuptake of synaptically released GABA.

Clinical Indications

GENERAL INFORMATION

- Although discrete diagnostic criteria are defined for each anxiety disorder, these disorders frequently overlap and are often comorbid with mood disorders (both major depressive disorder and bipolar disorder).
- There is most evidence to support first-line use of SSRIs for most anxiety disorders.
- However, symptom relief occurs more rapidly with benzodiazepines.
- The delay in symptom relief is particularly marked in the treatment of obsessive–compulsive disorder.
- An SSRI may take 6–12 weeks to be effective.
- Cognitive–behavioral therapy and other nonpharmacological interventions are frequently used alone or in combination with medications to treat anxiety disorders.

GENERALIZED ANXIETY DISORDER (GAD)

- Among the SSRIs, paroxetine, escitalopram, and sertraline were effective in large clinical trials, but other SSRIs may also be effective.
- Among the SNRIs, duloxetine and venlafaxine XR are both indicated for GAD.
  √ In one trial, venlafaxine was superior to both placebo and buspirone.
- Buspirone was comparable to benzodiazepines in several studies but may be less effective in patients with previous benzodiazepine exposure.
  √ Full effect often requires 4–6 weeks.
  √ Dose range 15–30 mg/day, but may increase to 60 mg/day.
- Early evidence supports the use of pregabalin for both somatic and psychological symptoms.
- Not effective in clinical trials and not recommended: propranolol.

OBSESSIVE–COMPULSIVE DISORDER (OCD)

- Most evidence for fluvoxamine, fluoxetine, paroxetine, and sertraline.
  √ Other SSRIs and venlafaxine XR may be effective; however, additional trials are needed.
- Clomipramine is as effective as SSRIs but has inferior tolerability.
- Doses of SSRI or clomipramine are often higher for the treatment of OCD than depression.
- Medications not effective in clinical trials and not recommended: desipramine, bupropion, clonidine, naltrexone, and buspirone.

PANIC DISORDER

- All available SSRIs and venlafaxine are used as first-line treatments for panic disorder.
- Although TCAs (clomipramine and imipramine) are equally effective, their use is limited by safety and tolerability concerns.
- Patients with panic disorder often experience serotonergically mediated side effects during the first week of SSRI or TCA therapy: insomnia, tremulousness, sweating.

√ Lower starting doses are recommended.
- The use of phenelzine is limited by safety and tolerability concerns associated with MAO inhibitors.
- There is some preliminary support for SGAs (olanzapine, quetiapine, and risperidone) in patients with refractory panic disorder.
- Medications not effective in clinical trials and not recommended: buspirone, trazodone, propranolol, carbamazepine.

PERFORMANCE ANXIETY

- Reduce physical symptoms of anxiety; not to be used before an athletic performance.
- Care must be taken in patients with
  √ Asthma
  √ Raynaud's phenomenon
  √ Diabetes
    □ On oral hypoglycemics or insulin (potential to mask hypoglycemic symptoms)
- May prescribe 2 h before nonathletic anxiety-provoking performance.
  √ Propranolol 10–80 mg
  √ Atenolol 30–100 mg

POSTTRAUMATIC STRESS DISORDER (PTSD)

- Fluoxetine, paroxetine, sertraline, and venlafaxine XR are first-line treatments.
- There is limited evidence to support the use of anticonvulsants (carbamazepine, lamotrigine, valproate, topiramate).
- Medications not effective in clinical trials and not recommended: olanzapine (as monotherapy), desipramine.

SOCIAL ANXIETY DISORDER

- SSRIs (with the exception of fluoxetine) and venlafaxine XR are used as first-line treatments for social anxiety disorder.
- Both gabapentin and pregabalin have demonstrated efficacy.
- Phenelzine has efficacy but its use is limited by safety and tolerability concerns.
- Medications not effective in clinical trials and not recommended: atenolol, propranolol, imipramine, and buspirone.

Side Effects

The common side effects of antipsychotics, antidepressants, and valproate are discussed in Chapters 1, 3, and 5, respectively.

CARDIOVASCULAR EFFECTS

Bradycardia
- Propranolol can cause bradycardia at modest doses.

√ Check pulse at rest and after brief exercise.

√ Consider decreased dose if resting pulse is under 60/min or exercise pulse is under 110/min.

Bronchospasm
- Do not give propranolol to asthmatics.
  - √ Stop propranolol if patient starts wheezing.
  - √ Consider a more selective agents (e.g., acetabutalol, atenolol, metoprolol, or betaxolol) if a beta-blocker is necessary.

Hypotension, dizziness, lightheadedness
- Propranolol can induce serious hypotension.
- Management
  - √ Measure BP before and during the first few days of propranolol, in both reclining and standing positions.
  - √ Increase dose more slowly.
  - √ Tell patient to
    - □ Sit for 60 seconds, or longer, if at all lightheaded.
    - □ Stand slowly while holding onto stable object (e.g., bed).
    - □ Wait for at least 30 seconds before walking.
  - √ *See* page 7 for further management.

Raynaud's phenomenon
- Cold fingers and toes
- Do not give beta-blocker if patient has history of Raynaud's.

CENTRAL NERVOUS SYSTEM EFFECTS

Daytime sedation, fatigue
- Observed at the onset of treatment and often resolves with time.
- Propranolol-induced fatigue is commonly mistaken for depression.
- Dose-related
  - √ Tolerable if therapy is started at lowest effective dose and titrated slowly over a period of a month or more.

Disorientation, clouded sensorium
- Reported with propranolol; not dose-related.
  - √ Can be due to chronic, relative hypotension (e.g., severe hypertensive corrected to "low normal").

Tremor
- Occurs with anticonvulsants (10%).
- Reduce dose.

EYES, EARS, NOSE, AND THROAT

Blurred vision
- *See* page 17.

GASTROINTESTINAL EFFECTS

Constipation
• *See* page 18.

Dry mouth
• *See* page 18.

Weight gain
• Gabapentin and pregabalin are associated with modest weight gain.
  √ Related to dose and duration of exposure.

HEMATOLOGIC EFFECTS

Leukopenia
• Reported in about 1% of patients treated with gabapentin.
• Gabapentin should be discontinued when the WBC count decreases to less than $3,000/mm^3$.

Thrombocytopenia
• Decrease in platelet count (20% below baseline and less than $150,000/mm^3$) has been observed with pregabalin.
• Tends to be mild and transient.
• No bleeding abnormalities were associated with the platelet decrease.

SEXUAL EFFECTS

• Propranolol doses >120 mg/day have been associated with decreased libido and erectile dysfunction.
• Buspirone (15–60 mg) prescribed on a regular basis may improve SSRI-related sexual dysfunction.

SKIN, ALLERGIES, AND TEMPERATURE

Angioedema
• Swelling of the face, mouth, and neck have been documented during initial and chronic treatment with pregabalin.
• Management
  √ Discontinue drug immediately.
  √ Do not prescribe to patients who
    ▫ Have had a previous episode of angioedema, or
    ▫ Are taking other drugs associated with angioedema (e.g., ACE inhibitors).

Drug and Food Interactions

• Pregabalin is unlikely to be involved in significant pharmacokinetic drug interactions.
• For information on valproate, *see* page 137.

Drug and Food Interactions with Nonbenzodiazepines

Drugs (X) Interact with:	Buspirone (B)[a]	Comments
Antidepressants		
MAO inhibitors	X↑	Case reports of elevated blood pressure; do not use together.
Antipsychotics		
Haloperidol	X↑	Increased plasma haloperidol level by 26% due to inhibited metabolism
Antiulcers		
Cimetidine	B↑	Associated with minor side effects (e.g., lightheadedness)
Food	B↓↑	Decreased rate of absorption but increased total amount in body

Drugs (X) Interact with:	Hydroxyzine (H)	Comments
Anticholinergics	X↑ H↑	Increased cholinergic effects
Antidepressants		
TCAs	X↑ H↑	CNS depression
MAO inhibitors	X↑	Case reports of elevated blood pressure; do not use together.
Antipsychotics	X↑ H↑	Hydroxyzine may block antipsychotic actions; increased CNS depression and anticholinergic effects.
CNS depressants (e.g., alcohol, narcotic sedatives)	X↑ H↑	CNS depression

Drugs (X) Interact with:	Propranolol (P)	Comments
Adrenergic agents		
Acebutolol	X↑ P↑	Increased antihypertensive effects of both drugs; adjust doses.
Clonidine	X↑	Beta-blockers can aggravate rebound hypertension in patients who have discontinued clonidine within 24–72 h. Symptoms include tremor, insomnia, nausea, flushing, and headaches. Patients should be discontinued from propranolol *before* starting clonidine. Metoprolol or another cardioselective beta-blocker may be preferable to propranolol.
Alcohol	P↑↓	May see variable changes in blood pressure; no special precautions. Slows rate of propranolol absorption.
Anesthetics	X↑	Beta-blockers and local anesthetics, particularly those containing epinephrine, can enhance sympathomimetic side effects. Acute discontinuation of blockers prior to local anesthesia may increase anesthetic side effects. Do not stop chronic beta-blockers before using local anesthetics. Avoid local anesthetics containing epinephrine in patients on propranolol.
Antacids (e.g., aluminum hydroxide, magnesium hydroxide)	P↓	Decreased level of beta-blockers, such as propranolol (60%), atenolol (35%), and metoprolol (25%). Avoid combination; otherwise, ingest antacids and propranolol 1h apart. Calcium carbonate may be okay.
Antiarrhythmics (e.g., amiodarone)	P↑	Bradycardia, arrhythmias
Antidepressants (i.e., MAO inhibitors, TCAs)	X↑↓	May exacerbate hypotensive effects of MAO inhibitors or TCAs. Depression occasionally worsens on β-blockers.
Antidiabetics	X↑	Propranolol may prevent the appearance of certain premonitory signs and symptoms (e.g., pulse rate and blood pressure changes) of acute hypoglycemia.
Antipsychotics	X↑	Increased levels of chlorpromazine, thioridazine, thiothixene resulting in increased risk of hypotension, toxicity, and seizures. Monitor serum levels or decrease dose.

Drugs (X) Interact with:	Propranolol (P)	Comments
Barbiturates	P↓	Barbiturates may lower propranolol.
Benzodiazepines	X↑	Increased half-life and decreased clearance of diazepam
Bronchodilators		
Albuterol	X↓ P↓	Decreased albuterol and β-adrenergic blocking effects. Avoid propranolol in bronchospastic disease; cardioselective agents safer.
Theophylline	X↑↓	Propranolol raises theophylline levels but antagonizes bronchodilation; cardioselective agents are safer.
Calcium channel blockers (e.g., bepridil, diltiazem, verapmil)	X↑ P↓	Decreased clearance of propranolol; may have additive effects, depressing myocardial contractility or atrioventricular conduction.
Catecholamine-depleting agents (e.g., reserpine, guanethidine)	X↑	May produce excessive reduction of resting sympathetic nervous activity, resulting in hypotension, bradycardia, vertigo, and syncopal attacks. Coadministration of reserpine and propranolol may also potentiate depression.
Cigarette smoking	P↓	Decreasd plasma level of propranolol via enzyme induction; may produce arrhythmias.
NSAIDs (e.g., indomethacin, naproxen)	P↓	Diminished antihypertensive effect of propranolol

Drugs (X) Interact with:	Gabapentin (G)	Comments
Antacids (e.g., aluminum hydroxide, magnesium hydroxide)	G↓	Reduced bioavailability of gabapentin by 20%
Antiulcers (e.g., cimetidine)	G↑	Decreased renal clearance of gabapentin
CNS depressants (e.g., alcohol, narcotic, sedatives)	X↑ G↑	CNS depression

Drugs (X) Interact with:	Tiagabine (T)	Comments
Anticonvulsants Carbamazepine, phenytoin, primidone	T↑	Increased clearance of tiagabine by 60% due to induction of CYP3A4.
Valproate	X↓	Slight decrease (about 10%) in steady-state of valproate concentrations.

[a] ↑ = increases; ↓ = decreases; ↑↓ = increases and decreases.

Special Populations

CHILDREN AND ADOLESCENTS

• Cognitive–behavioral therapy is the preferred first-line approach to preventing and treating anxiety disorders in children and adolescents.
• For moderately severe to severe symptoms, combination of cognitive–behavioral therapy and medication may provide rapid symptom relief and lasting remission.
  √ SSRIs are first-line option for long-term treatment.
  √ Consider buspirone for GAD and propranolol for performance anxiety.
  √ Avoid TCAs and antipsychotics.
• A subtype of pediatric OCD has been designated by the acronym PANDAS (pediatric autoimmune neuropsychiatric disorders associated with strepto-coccal infections).

√ This type of OCD is characterized by sudden symptom onset and a relapsing–remitting course of illness; exacerbation of symptoms occurs with throat infection and scarlet fever.

√ Better control of OCD symptoms can be achieved with combination of cognitive–behavioral therapy and an SSRI (e.g., fluoxetine).

WOMEN: PREGNANCY AND POSTPARTUM

Pregnancy Rating	• Buspirone: Category B
	• Others: Category C
Teratogenicity (1st trimester)	• Buspirone does not appear to be teratogenic in animals, but its risk in pregnant women has not been determined.
	• Hydroxyzine, gabapentin, pregabalin, and tiagabine are not recommended for use in the first trimester because they have been shown to cause birth defects in animal studies.
	• When possible, use behavioral techniques, psychotherapy, and caffeine abstinence to manage anxiety.
Direct Effect on Newborn (3rd trimester)	• Propranolol use is associated with decreased birth weight, intrauterine growth retardation, hypoglycemia, bradycardia, and respiratory depression at birth, and hyperbilirubinemia in neonates.
	√ If mother is already on propranolol, closely monitor infant for 24–48 h.
Lactation	• Buspirone, propranolol, gabapentin, and tiagabine are excreted in human milk.
	• Because the effect on the nursing infant is unknown, this class of agents should be avoided if clinically possible.

LATE LIFE

Buspirone
• Does not cause sedation or psychomotor slowing in the elderly.
• Dosage should be decreased in patients with reduced hepatic or renal function.

Hydroxyzine
• Anticholinergic effects are not well tolerated in the elderly and frequently result in bowel, bladder, and mental status changes.
• Elderly patients generally should be started on low doses and observed closely.

Propranolol
- Clearance of propranolol is reduced with aging due to decline in oxidation capacity; dose adjustment may be required.

Anticonvulsants
- Gabapentin and pregabalin can accumulate in patients with declining renal function.
  √ Monitor creatinine clearance and adjust dose as necessary.
- Safety and efficacy of tiagabine in geriatric patients have not been established.
- For information on valproate, *see* page 141.

Effects on Laboratory Tests

Effects of Nonbenzodiazepines on Blood/Serum and Urine Tests

Generic Names	Blood/Serum Tests		Urine Tests	
	Marker	Results[a]	Marker	Results[a]
Buspirone	LFT[b], WBC	↑	None	
Hydroxyzine	None		17-hydroxycorti-costeroids	↑f
Propranolol	LFT[b]	↑	None	
	T$_4$, rT$_3$, T$_3$	↑↑↓		
	BUN	↑		
	Antinuclear antibodies	↑		

[a]↑ = increases; ↓ = decreases; f = falsely.
[b]LFT = liver function tests (AST/SGOT, ALT/SGPT, alkaline phosphatase, bilirubin, and LDH).

Discontinuation

Buspirone

- Withdrawal effects have not been reported.

Hydroxyzine

- Does not produce physical dependence.
- REM rebound may cause disturbed sleep on discontinuation.
- Cholinergic rebound may produce flu-like syndrome.

Propranolol

- Usually safe to discontinue in psychiatric patients unless there are cardiac problems (e.g., hypertension, angina, or coronary artery disease).

Anticonvulsants

- Valproate (*see* p. 141)
- Abrupt discontinuation of gabapentin, pregabalin, and tiagabine may result in

A
N
T
I
A
N
X
I
E
T
Y

A
G
E
N
T
S

√ Pain and sweating
√ Nausea, diarrhea
√ Anxiety, insomnia, headache
√ Seizures

Overdose: Toxicity, Suicide, and Treatment

BUSPIRONE

• No fatal outcomes have been reported from overdose.
• Symptoms of overdose may include
  √ Nausea, vomiting, upset stomach
  √ Dizziness, drowsiness
  √ Miosis
• Management
  √ *See* page 24.
  √ Hemodialysis unnecessary.

HYDROXYZINE

Overdoses propagate side effects, especially drowsiness, GI hypomotility, occasional hypotension, and confusion/delirium.

• Management
  √ *See* page 24.
  √ Hemodialysis of little help.

PROPRANOLOL

Acute propranolol overdose symptoms and their treatment include:

• Bradycardia
  √ IV atropine 0.3–1.2 mg.
  √ If no response to vagal blockade, cautiously administer isoproterenol 1 mg (maximum 2 mg) in 500 ml 5% D/S or D/W by infusion. Injection can start at 0.2 mg/ml or take 5 ml dossette ampul.
• Cardiac failure
  √ Digitalis and diuretics
• Hypotension
  √ Epinephrine—drug of choice in anaphylactic shock
    ▫ 0.5 ml 1:1000 in 10 ml saline IV
    ▫ If no response, give 0.5 ml q 5–15 minutes.
  √ Levarterenol 4–8 mg in 1000 ml 5% D/S or D/W by infusion.

ANTICONVULSANTS

• Gabapentin
  √ Signs and symptoms include double vision, slurred speech, drowsiness, lethargy, and diarrhea.
  √ Management: Can be removed by hemodialysis.

- Pregabalin
  - √ No notable clinical consequences following overdose of up to 8000 mg.
  - √ Management
    - □ Elimination of unabsorbed drug may be attempted by emesis or gastric lavage.
    - □ Can be removed by hemodialysis.
- Valproate (*see* p. 141)
- Tiagabine
  - √ Signs and symptoms include drowsiness, slurred speech, poor coordination, confusion, and agitation.
  - √ Case reports of convulsive status epilepticus at plasma levels > 420 ng/ml (therapeutic 20–103 ng/ml).
  - √ Management
    - □ Elimination of unabsorbed drug may be attempted by emesis or gastric lavage.
    - □ Hemodialysis of little help.

Precautions

BUSPIRONE

- Sometimes triggers restlessness.
- Has no cross-tolerance with benzodiazepines and will not alleviate benzodiazepine withdrawal.
- Less effective for patients who have recently taken benzodiazepines.

HYDROXYZINE

- Should be used with caution in patients with
  - √ Narrow-angle glaucoma
  - √ Prostatic hyperplasia
  - √ Bladder neck obstruction
  - √ Asthma or chronic obstructive pulmonary disease (COPD).

PROPRANOLOL

- *Contraindicated* for patients with
  - √ Cardiogenic shock (systolic BP < 100 mm Hg)
  - √ Sinus bradycardia
  - √ Atrioventricular block (second- or third-degree)
  - √ Uncontrolled congestive heart failure
  - √ Asthma or COPD
  - √ Hypotension in myocardial infarction
- Give *cautiously* to patients with
  - √ Persistent angina, Wolff–Parkinson–White syndrome, or impaired myocardial functioning—all can become worse with propranolol.
    - □ Gradually withdraw propranolol from angina patients over a few weeks.
  - √ Glaucoma
    - □ Propranolol withdrawal may increase intraocular pressure.

ANTIANXIETY AGENTS

√ Hyperthyroidism, thyrotoxicosis
√ Diabetes mellitus
  □ Signs and symptoms of hypoglycemia may be masked.
√ Myasthenia gravis

ANTICONVULSANTS

• For information on precautions with valproate, *see* page 141.
• Use gabapentin and pregabalin cautiously in
  √ Geriatric patients
  √ Renal impairment
    □ Decrease dose and/or increase dosing interval if creatinine clearance ≤ 60 ml/min).
• Use tiagabine cautiously in patients with
  √ Previous evidence of generalized spike–wave discharges on EEG.
  √ History of status epilepticus
  √ Impaired liver function

Key Points to Communicate to Patients and Families

• Medications are often best used in conjunction with cognitive–behavioral and other psychological interventions.
• Before starting treatment, identify key symptoms and track their response to the medication.
• Expect several weeks before symptom relief occurs.
• Particularly during the first few weeks, avoid, or take extra care when, driving or operating machinery.
• These medications may potentiate the effect of alcohol—one drink feels like two or three.
• Early side effects include daytime sleepiness, clumsiness, fuzzy thinking.
• Although the starting dose may be adequate to achieve remission, dose alterations are often required.
• Do not stop abruptly; discontinuation symptoms may occur.

THERAPEUTIC APPLICATION

Initiation of Treatment

• Treatment options and dosing details are provided for each disorder under "Clinical Indications" (*see* pp. 164–165).
• In the case of benzodiazepines, start at lowest effective dose and use for the shortest time possible.
  √ Expect rapid symptom relief.
• With SSRIs or SNRIs, starting doses often need to be lower than in the treatment of major depressive disorder.
  √ For example, escitalopram 5 mg/day, sertraline 25 mg/day, or venlafaxine XR 37.5 mg/day
  √ Expect delayed symptom relief (6–12 weeks).
• For buspirone, initiate at 15–30 mg/day in divided doses and increase rapidly if required.

Treatment Resistance

- Typically defined as failure to respond to two different therapeutic trials at adequate dose for adequate duration.
- Often associated with comorbidity
  √ History and symptom profile should be reviewed with particular emphasis on substance abuse and mood disorders (especially bipolar disorder).
- In general, dose optimization and switching between classes are recommended as first strategies.
- Combination or augmentation therapies may be required, particularly with comorbid diagnoses.
  √ Emerging studies support an adjunctive role for second-generation antipsychotics (atypicals) in treatment-resistant anxiety disorders.

Maintenance

GENERAL INFORMATION

- Pharmacotherapy combined with cognitive–behavioral therapy may reduce the rate of relapse.
- Most studies confirm maintenance and relapse prevention benefits up to 1 year.
- Patients with recurrent and comorbid conditions are likely to require extended maintenance treatment.

GENERALIZED ANXIETY DISORDER (GAD)

- 20–40% of patients with GAD relapse within 6–12 months of discontinuing pharmacotherapy.
- Evidence for maintenance efficacy exists for escitalopram, paroxetine, and venlafaxine.

OBSESSIVE–COMPULSIVE DISORDER (OCD)

- Paroxetine, sertraline, and fluoxetine 60 mg were associated with decreased relapse rates over 1 year.
- Maintenance therapy for a minimum of 1–2 years is recommended.

PANIC DISORDER

- Alprazolam maintenance therapy for 2 years was effective, but up to one-third of patients was unable to discontinue.
- Citalopram, fluoxetine, paroxetine, sertraline, and venlafaxine XR were effective in studies up to 12 months.

POSTTRAUMATIC STRESS DISORDER (PTSD)

- Fluoxetine and sertraline are associated with improved response rates and relapse prevention over 6–12 months.

SOCIAL ANXIETY DISORDER

- Paroxetine, sertraline, and escitalopram are associated with improved response rates and relapse prevention over 6 months.

ANTIANXIETY AGENTS

7. Hypnotics

INTRODUCTION TO DRUG CLASSES

Insomnia is a pervasive symptom that is experienced not only by the majority of patients with a psychiatric disorder, but is also a significant problem for a large percentage of the general population. Although there is a continuing emphasis on nonpharmacological approaches to treating insomnia, including attention to sleep hygiene and the use of "natural products" (e.g., valerian, melatonin, or tryptophan), this chapter focuses mainly on prescription hypnotics.

Benzodiazepine hypnotics (estazolam, flurazepam, quazepam, temazepam, triazolam) and benzodiazepine receptor agonists (eszopiclone, zaleplon, zolpidem) are the most widely prescribed sleeping medications in the United States. Historically, barbiturates (e.g., pentobarbital and secobarbital) and barbiturate-like compounds (chloral hydrate and paraldehyde) were used for their hypnotic effects, but are no longer recommended because of high abuse potential and unfavorable adverse events. Ramelteon is a novel melatonin (MT_1 and MT_2) receptor agonist that is indicated as a hypnotic in the United States. Other agents, including melatonin, tryptophan, and sedating antidepressants, are also frequently used as hypnotics, although not approved for this use by the FDA.

Hypnotics by Chemical Class

Chemical Class	Generic Name	Trade Name
HYPNOTIC BENZODIAZEPINE AND SELECTIVE BENZODIAZEPINE-1 RECEPTOR AGONIST		
Benzodiazepine	Estazolam	ProSom
	Flurazepam	Dalmane
	Quazepam	Doral
	Temazepam	Restoril
	Triazolam	Halcion
Selective benzodiazepine-1 receptor agonist	Eszopiclone	Lunesta
	Zaleplon	Sonata
	Zolpidem	Ambien

Chemical Class	Generic Name	Trade Name
	SELECTIVE MELATONIN AGONIST	
	Ramelteon	Rozerem
	BARBITURATE AND BARBITURATE-LIKE COMPOUND[a]	
Barbiturate	Amobarbital	Amytal
	Butabarbital	Butisol
	Pentobarbital	Nembutal
	Phenobarbital	Various generics
	Secobarbital	Seconal
Barbiturate-like compounds	Chloral hydrate	Noctec, Aquachloral
	Paraldehyde	Paral

[a]Not recommended for use as hypnotics due to safety concerns and abuse potential.

HYPNOTIC BENZODIAZEPINES AND SELECTIVE BENZODIAZEPINE-1 RECEPTOR AGONISTS

Dosing, Dose Form, and Color

Profile of Hypnotic Benzodiazepines and Selective Benzodiazepine-1 Receptor Agonists

Generic Names	Therapeutic Dose Range (mg/day)	Geriatric Dose (mg/day)	Dose Form (mg)[a]	Color
		BENZODIAZEPINE		
Estazolam	1–2	0.5	t: 1/2	t: white/coral
Flurazepam	15–30	15	c: 15/30	c: orange–ivory/ red–ivory
Quazepam	7.5–15	7.5	t: 7.5/15	t: all light orange– white speckled
Temazepam	15–30	15	c: 15/30	c: maroon–pink/ maroon–blue
Triazolam	0.125–0.5	0.125	t: 0.125/0.25	t: white/blue
		SELECTIVE BENZODIAZEPINE-1 RECEPTOR AGONIST		
Eszopiclone	2–3	1–2	t: 1/2/3	t: light blue/white/ dark blue
Zaleplon	5–20	5–10	c: 5/10	c: opaque green– opaque pale green/ opaque green– opaque light green
Zolpidem	c: 5–20 cr: 12.5	c: 5 cr: 6.5	c: 5/10 cr: 6.25	c: pink/white cr: pink

[a]c = capsules; cr = controlled-release; t = tablets.

Pharmacology

The preceding chapter presented an overview of the pharmacology of benzodiazepines, with an emphasis on anxiolytic agents. The focus here is on hypnotic benzodiazepines.

PHARMACOKINETICS

Benzodiazepines
- Can be subclassified according to their pharmacokinetic profile:
  √ Short half-life (e.g., triazolam)
  √ Intermediate half-life (e.g., temazepam)
  √ Long half-life (e.g., flurazepam)
- Have carryover effects into the morning, such as excessive daytime sleepiness or drowsiness that are related to drug half-life, pattern of distribution, and dosage (*see also* p. 151).

Selective benzodiazepine-1 receptor agonists
- Are rapidly absorbed from the GI tract following oral administration.
  √ A high-fat meal may delay the rate of absorption.
- Are relatively short-acting with half-lives ranging from ultra-short (zaleplon) to intermediate (eszopiclone).
- Elimination half-life and dose are the primary determinants of duration of hypnotic effect.
- Parent compound is converted to inactive metabolites that are primarily eliminated by renal excretion.

Pharmacokinetic Properties of Hypnotic Benzodiazepines and Selective Benzodiazepine-1 Receptor Agonists

Generic Names	T_{max}[a] (h)	Half-life [Mean (range)] (h)	Onset of Action (min)	Duration of Action (h)[b]	Active Metabolites	P450 Substrate
BENZODIAZEPINE						
Estazolam	2	15 (10–24)	15–30	IA 6–8	4-hydroxy-estazolam	3A4
Flurazepam	0.5–1	67 (47–100)	30	LA > 40	N-desalkyl-flurazepam	2C, 2D6
Quazepam	0.5–2	25–40 (2–73)	30	LA 2–100	2-oxoquazepam, N-desalkyl-flurazepam	2D6
Temazepam	2–4	12 (9.5–20)	20–60	IA 6–20	None	Conjugated
Triazolam	0.5–1	2–4 (1.5–5.5)	20	SA < 6	None	3A4
SELECTIVE BENZODIAZEPINE-1 RECEPTOR AGONIST						
Eszopiclone	1	5–7	30	IA 8	None	3A4, 2E1
Zaleplon	1	1–2	20–30	SA 2–3	None	3A4
Zolpidem	1.6	2.5	20–30	SA < 6	None	3A4, 1A2, 2C9, 2C19, 2D6

[a]T_{max} = time to peak concentration.
[b]LA = long-acting; IA = intermediate; SA = short-acting.

PHARMACODYNAMICS

Benzodiazepines
- All benzodiazepine hypnotics exert similar effects on sleep patterns.
  √ Decrease sleep-onset latency.

√ Decrease the number and duration of awakenings and arousals.

√ Prolong non-rapid-eye-movement (NREM) stage 2.

√ Reduce NREM stages 3 and 4.

• Specific effects on REM sleep include:

√ Prolonged REM latency—except for flurazepam.

√ Decreased total duration of REM sleep—except for temazepam and low doses of flurazepam.

√ Increased frequency of REM cycles in the latter part of sleep.

Selective benzodiazepine-1 receptor agonists

• Bind selectively to $GABA_{A1}$ (omega 1) receptor.

• Increase total sleep time (except zaleplon) with a normal sleep stage distribution.

Clinical Indications

BENZODIAZEPINES

• Have demonstrated tolerability and efficacy in the treatment of transient and short-term insomnia.

• Clinicians tend to use long half-life benzodiazepines in patients who have difficulties maintaining sleep and short half-life benzodiazepines to treat sleep-onset insomnia.

• The use of these agents should be limited to short-term use (7–10 days) due to abuse potential and significant adverse events.

SELECTIVE BENZODIAZEPINE-1 RECEPTOR AGONISTS

• These agents are as effective as benzodiazepines in the treatment of transient and chronic insomnia.

• Although long-term hypnotic use is not generally recommended, sustained efficacy with nightly use up to 6 months has been demonstrated with no tolerance or rebound insomnia.

Side Effects

The adverse events associated with benzodiazepine hypnotics are the same as those discussed in the previous chapter for benzodiazepine antianxiety agents (*see* pp. 154–155).

However, note the following side effects:

RESPIRATORY DEPRESSION

• Patients with insomnia and chronic obstructive pulmonary disease, asthma, or other respiratory disorders should not receive benzodiazepine or barbiturate-like sleeping pills. They might intensify sleep apnea by increasing central effects or by slowing respiration. Risk factors for obstructive apnea include:

√ Snoring

√ Hypertension

√ Male

√ Obesity
√ Older age (> 55 yrs)
• Risk factors for central sleep apnea include:
  √ Older age
  √ Dementia
  √ Other general CNS disorders
• If a hypnotic is required, use trazodone, zolpidem, or zaleplon.

FALLS, FRACTURES

• Often follow *ataxia* and *confusion.*
• Can happen at night with any hypnotic.
• May occur during daytime with long-acting hypnotics (e.g., flurazepam).

HANGOVER EFFECTS

• Common
• Aggravated by
  √ Alcohol consumption
  √ Restricted fluid intake
• Management
  √ Reduce, discontinue, or switch hypnotic.
  √ Lower risk with shorter-acting hypnotic.

ANTEROGRADE AMNESIA

• May occur after a single dose.
• Particularly common with triazolam following overnight flights.
  √ On awakening, the patient has no memory of events occurring 6–11 h after ingesting triazolam.
  √ Memory loss is longer than sleep duration.
• Symptoms are exacerbated by alcohol.
  √ Behavior is otherwise normal.
• May also be seen with zolpidem or zaleplon, particularly in higher (≥ 20 mg) doses (that effect all benzodiazepine receptors).
  √ Usually occurs within 3 h.

Drug–Drug Interactions

Refer also to benzodiazepine interactions on page 156.

Drug Interactions with Benzodiazepine Receptor Agonists

Drugs (X) Interact with:	Benzodiazepine Receptor Agonists (B)[a]	Comments
Alcohol	X↑ B↑	Additive effect on psychomotor performance.
Antibiotics (e.g., clarithromycin, erythromycin, troleandomycin)	B↑	May increase plasma level of benzodiazepine receptor agonists due to inhibition of CYP3A4.

Drugs (X) Interact with:	Benzodiazepine Receptor Agonists (B)[a]	Comments
Anticonvulsants (e.g., phenytoin, carbamazepine, phenobarbital)	B↓	May decrease plasma level of benzodiazepine receptor agonists due to induction of CYP3A4.
Antidepressants (e.g., imipramine)	X↑↓ B↑	Co-administration with zaleplon demonstrated additive effects on decreased alertness and impaired psychomotor performance. Decreased plasma level of imipramine (by 20%) with zolpidem.
Antifungal (e.g., itraconazole, ketoconazole)	B↓	Increased plasma level and half-life of eszopiclone (by 1.4-fold and 1.3-fold, respectively) and expoure of zolpidem (by 34%) due to inhibition of CYP3A4. Dose reduction is recommended.
Antipsychotics (e.g., chlorpromazine, olanzapine, thioridazine)	X↑ B↑	Additive effects on decreased alertness and impaired psychomotor performance.
Antitubercular drugs (e.g., rifampin)	B↓	Decreased exposure of benzodiazepine receptor agonists (by up to 80%) due to induction of CYP3A4.
Antiulcer drugs (e.g., cimetidine)	B↑	Increased plasma level of zaleplon (by 85%) due to inhibited metabolism. An initial dose of 5 mg zaleplon should be given.
Protease inhibitors (e.g., ritonavir, nelfinavir)	B↑	May increase plasma level of benzodiazepine receptor agonists due to inhibition of CYP3A4.

[a]↑ = increases; ↓ = decreases.

Special Populations

CHILDREN AND ADOLESCENTS

• Benzodiazepines and selective benzodiazepine-1 receptor agonists are not recommended for children.
• If medication is necessary, the dose and duration of treatment must be kept to a minimum.

WOMEN: PREGNANCY AND POSTPARTUM

Pregnancy Rating

• Benzodiazepines: Category X

• Selective benzodiazepine-1 receptor agonists: Category C

Teratogenicity (1st trimester)

• Benzodiazepine hypnotics are *contraindicated* in pregnancy.
   √ Patients should discontinue these agents 3–4 weeks before attempting to conceive.

• Selective benzodiazepine-1 receptor agonists do not appear to be teratogenic in animals, but their risk in pregnant women has not been determined; *avoid* if possible.

Direct Effect on Newborn (3rd trimester)	• Use of benzodiazepine hypnotics during the last weeks of pregnancy may result in neonatal CNS depression.
	• No adequate data on selective benzodiazepine-1 receptor agonists.
Lactation	• Benzodiazepines are secreted into breast milk and may result in lethargy, poor suckling, and weight loss. √ Check infant benzodiazepine blood level to determine if level may be harmful to newborn. √ With longer-acting benzodiazepine, effects may persist 2–3 weeks in infants.
	• Small amounts of selective benzodiazepine-1 receptor agonists are excreted into milk, but the effects on an infant are unknown.

LATE LIFE

Benzodiazepines
• Clearance of benzodiazepines, which undergo oxidative metabolism, declines with age.
  √ Drug accumulation and excessive sedation may occur.
  √ Associated with adverse outcomes, including impairment of psychomotor performance.
• If a benzodiazepine hypnotic is used in the elderly, a drug with a short elimination half-life is an advantage.

Selective benzodiazepine-1 receptor agonists
• Preferred in the elderly due to their improved side effect profile.
• A lower dose is recommended.

Effects on Laboratory Tests

Effects of Benzodiazepines and Selective Benzodiazepine-1 Receptor Agonists on Blood/Serum and Urine Tests

Generic Names	Blood/Serum Tests		Urine Tests	
	Marker	Results[a]	Marker	Results
Benzodiazepines	WBC, RBC LFT[b]	↓r↓r ↑	None	
Selective benzodiazepine-1 receptor agonists	LFT[b]	↑	None	

[a]↑ = increases; ↓ = decreases; r = rarely.
[b]LFT = liver function tests (AST/SGOT, ALT/SGPT, alkaline phosphatase, bilirubin, and LDH).

Discontinuation

Benzodiazepines and selective benzodiazepine-1 receptor agonists produce similar discontinuation syndromes and are discussed in Chapter 6 (*see* p. 158).

Management

- Withdrawal from chronic drug dosing must be carried out via a program of gradual and careful dose reduction.
- A switch to diazepam is the preferred method, enabling mini-dose reductions over an extended period (*see* p. 159).

Overdose: Toxicity, Suicide, and Treatment

Benzodiazepines

- Benzodiazepine overdoses are discussed in Chapter 6.

Selective benzodiazepine-1 receptor agonists

- Overdoses are rarely fatal unless alcohol or other CNS-depressant drugs are simultaneously ingested.
- Signs and symptoms of an overdose may include:
  √ Sleepiness, confusion
  √ Dizziness, hypotension
  √ Difficult or slow breathing
  √ Coma
- Management (*see* p. 159)

Precautions

Benzodiazepine hypnotics are contraindicated in

- Hypersensitive patients
- Pregnant women

Use benzodiazepines and selective benzodiazepine-1 receptor agonists cautiously in

- Elderly or debilitated patients
- Renal or hepatic insufficiency
- Limited pulmonary reserve
- Acute narrow-angle glaucoma
- History of alcohol and/or drug abuse
- Severely depressed patients, particularly if suicidal risk may be present

Key Points to Communicate to Patients and Families

- Try new pharmacological options first.
- Short-acting benzodiazepines can be taken for 7–14 days during acute situational crises.
- Avoid long-term benzodiazepine use due to concerns about abuse potential and dependence.

- Triazolam, zolpidem (to a lesser extent), and zaleplon can cause traveler's amnesia.
- Insomnia is often part of a more complex psychiatric disorder, which requires other treatment.

SELECTIVE MELATONIN AGONIST

As of 2008, only ramelteon has an indication for sleep medication, although it is likely that agomelatine, with additional antidepressant properties, will also be used to improve sleep, particularly in depressed patients.

Dosing, Dose Form, and Color

Profile of Selective Melatonin Agonist

Generic Names	Therapeutic Dose Range (mg/day)	Geriatric Dose (mg/day)	Dose Form (mg)[a]	Color
Ramelteon	8	8	t: 8	t: pale orange–yellow

[a]t = tablets.

Pharmacology

PHARMACOKINETICS

- Well absorbed from GI tract following oral administration.
  - √ High-fat meal may delay the rate and the extent of absorption.
- Highly protein bound (70%)
- Low bioavailability ($< 2\%$) due to extensive first-pass metabolism and uptake by tissues
- Serum concentration of the pharmacologically active metabolite, M-II, is 20- to 30-fold greater than that of parent compound.
- Major route of excretion is via urine (84%).
  - √ Only a minor amount is found in feces (4%).

Pharmacokinetic Properties of Selective Melatonin Agonist

Generic Name	T_{max}[a] (h)	Half-Life (h)	Onset of Action (min)	Duration of Action (h)[b]	Active Metabolites	P450 Substrate
Ramelteon	0.5–1.5	0.8–2.6	30	SA	M-II	1A2, 2C, 3A4

[a]T_{max} = time to peak concentration.
[b]SA = short-acting.

PHARMACODYNAMICS

- A selective and potent melatonin MT_1 and MT_2 receptor agonist
- Activation of these receptors is believed to contribute to the sleep-promoting properties of ramelteon.

Clinical Indications

INSOMNIA

- Ramelteon has demonstrated efficacy for sleep induction in the treatment of both transient and chronic insomnia.
  √ It does not improve sleep maintenance.
- It is also under evaluation for use in the treatment of circadian rhythm disorders associated with shift work and transmeridian travel (jet lag).

Side Effects

- Adverse reactions have generally been similar in ramelteon and placebo treatment groups.
- No dose-related adverse events have been observed in the dose range of 4–32 mg/day.

CENTRAL NERVOUS SYSTEM EFFECTS

Dizziness, fatigue, somnolence
- Common

Headache
- Most common adverse event
- Take acetaminophen as needed.

Insomnia exacerbated
- Management
  √ Evaluate patient's medical condition.
  √ Switch to another hypnotic.

ENDOCRINE EFFECTS

The following hormonal disturbances have been reported:

- Abnormal morning cortisol levels
- Prolactin elevation
  √ Reported in females on daily doses ≥ 16 mg.
  √ No reported changes in menstrual patterns.
- Decrease in testosterone levels

GASTROINTESTINAL EFFECTS

Diarrhea
Nausea (common)

Drug and Food Interactions

Drug and Food Interactions with Selective Melatonin Agonist

Drugs (X) Interact with:	Ramelteon (R)[a]	Comments
Alcohol	X↑ R↑	Combined use may result in additive impairment of psychomotor skills.
Antibiotics (e.g., ciprofloxacin)	R↑	Increased plasma level of ramelteon due to inhibited metabolism via CYP1A2

Drugs (X) Interact with:	Ramelteon (R)[a]	Comments
Antidepressants (e.g., SSRIs—fluvoxamine)	R↑	Fluvoxamine increases plasma level of ramelteon (by 90-fold) due to inhibited metabolism via CYP1A2. *Avoid.*
Antifungal (e.g., ketoconazole, fluconazole)	R↑	Increased plasma level of ramelteon and metabolite M-II due to inhibited metabolism: *Use with caution.*
Antitubercular drugs (e.g., rifampin)	R↓	Decreased plasma level of ramelteon and metabolite M-II (by 80%) due to enzyme induction

[a]↑ = increases; ↓ = decreases.

Special Populations

CHILDREN AND ADOLESCENTS

• Safety and effectiveness have not been established in pediatric patients.
• Ramelteon has been associated with increased prolactin and decreased testosterone levels in adults.
  √ It is not known if ramelteon has an effect on reproductive development in children or adolescents.

WOMEN: PREGNANCY AND POSTPARTUM

Pregnancy Rating Teratogenicity (1st trimester)	• Category C
	• Ramelteon has been reported to be teratogenic and associated with physical and developmental delays in animals, but its risk in pregnant women has not been determined.
Direct Effect on Newborn (3rd trimester)	• No adequate data.
Lactation	• Breastfeeding is not recommended, as there are no adequate studies in women for determining infant risk.

LATE LIFE

• Ramelteon is well tolerated by elderly patients.
• Clearance is reduced in elderly compared with younger adults, resulting in increased systemic exposure; however, dosage adjustments are not necessary.

Effects on Laboratory Tests

Effects of Selective Melatonin Agonist on Blood/Serum and Urine Tests

	Blood/Serum Tests		Urine Tests	
Generic Names	Marker	Results[a]	Marker	Results
Ramelteon	Cortisol	↓	None	
	Prolactin	↑		
	Testosterone	↓		

[a]↑ = increases; ↓ = decreases.

Discontinuation

Ramelteon does not induce

- Dependence
- Tolerance
- Addiction
- Withdrawal

In clinical trials, ramelteon demonstrated no evidence of rebound insomnia. In addition, the reduction in sleep latency was maintained during the week following treatment discontinuation.

Overdose: Toxicity, Suicide, and Treatment

- No cases of ramelteon overdose were reported in clinical development.
- In an abuse liability trial, daily doses of up to 160 mg did not produce any signs of toxicity.
- Management
  √ Treat symptomatically and administer intravenous fluids as needed.
  √ If indicated, elimination of unabsorbed drug should be achieved by gastric lavage.
  √ Hemodialysis is ineffective in removal of ramelteon.

Precautions

Contraindicated in presence of

- Severe hepatic impairment
- Concurrent use of fluvoxamine
- Hypersensitivity to ramelteon

Use with *caution* in presence of

- Severe sleep apnea or COPD
- Moderate hepatic impairment
- Depression; worsening of depression or suicidal ideation may occur.
- Concurrent use of alcohol

Key Points to Communicate to Patients and Families

- Advise patient to take ramelteon within 30 minutes prior to bedtime.
  √ Do not take double or extra doses.
- Advise patient to avoid taking ramelteon with, or immediately after, eating a high-fat meal or snack.
  √ High-fat foods may alter the absorption of ramelteon into bloodstream.
- Patients should be cautioned not to consume alcohol when using ramelteon.
- Patients should consult a health care provider if they experience one of the following:

√ Worsening of insomnia
√ Cessation of menses or galactorrhea in females
√ Problems with fertility
• Keep medication away from bedside or any readily accessible place for safety reasons.

BARBITURATES AND BARBITURATE-LIKE COMPOUNDS

Dosing, Dose Form, and Color

Profile of Barbiturates and Barbiturate-Like Compounds

Generic Names	Therapeutic Dose Range (mg/day)	Geriatric Dose (mg/day)	Dose Form (mg)[a]	Color
BARBITURATES				
Amobarbital	65–200	65	p: 50 mg/ml	
Butabarbital	50–100	50	t: 15/30/50/100	t: lavender/green/orange/pink
Pentobarbital	50–200	50	c: 50/100 su: 30 p: 50 mg/ml	c: orange/yellow
Phenobarbital	15–600	16	Many generic doses	
Secobarbital	100–200	50	c: 100 p: 50 mg/ml	c: orange
BARBITURATE-LIKE COMPOUNDS				
Chloral hydrate	500–2000	500	c: 250/500 e: 500 mg/5 ml	c: both red
Paraldehyde	2000–15000	4000	e: 30 g/30 ml	

[a]c = capsules; e = elixir; p = parenteral; su = suppository; t = tablets.

Pharmacology

PHARMACOKINETICS

Barbiturates
• Well absorbed from GI tract after oral administration; food can delay the rate, but not the extent, of absorption.
• Highly lipophilic barbiturates (e.g., secobarbital) have
  √ Decreased latency to onset of activity
  √ Decreased duration of action
  √ A high degree of plasma protein binding
  √ Accelerated metabolic degradation by the liver
• Metabolic products are excreted in the urine and less commonly in the feces.

Chloral hydrate
• Rapidly and completely absorbed from the GI tract.
• Metabolized in the liver and erythrocytes by alcohol dehydrogenase to its major active metabolite, trichloroethanol.

• Trichloroethanol is highly protein bound (70–80%).
• Metabolic products are excreted in the urine.

Paraldehyde
• Rapidly absorbed from the GI tract following oral administration.
• Primarily metabolized by the liver (70–80%); small amounts are exhaled unchanged via the lungs or excreted in the urine.
  √ In hepatic disease, elimination rate is decreased and increased amounts are excreted through the lungs.
• The major metabolite, acetaldehyde, is pharmacologically inactive.

Pharmacokinetic Properties of Barbiturates and Barbiturate-Like Compounds

Generic Names	T_{max}a (h)	Half-life [Mean (range)] (h)	Onset of Action (min)	Duration of Action (h)b	Active Metabolites	P450 Substrate
BARBITURATES						
Amobarbital		25 (16–40)	45–60	IA 6–8	None	2C19
Butabarbital	3–4	34–24 (34–140)	45–60	IA 6–8	None	
Pentobarbital	30–60	22–50 (15-50)	15–60	SA 3–4	None	2C, 3A4
Phenobarbital	10–15	3–4 weeks	8–12	LA 80	None	2C19, 2C9, 2E1
Secobarbital	15–30	28–30 (15–40)	10–15	SA 3–4	None	
BARBITURATE-LIKE COMPOUNDS						
Chloral hydrate		4–14c	30–60		Trichloroethanol	2B, 2E1
Paraldehyde	0.5–1	3.4–9.8	10–15	IA 8–12	None	

aT_{max} = time to peak concentration.
bLA = long-acting; IA = intermediate; SA = short-acting.
cHalf-life for trichloroethanol—chloral hydrate's principal metabolite—is 7–10 h.

PHARMACODYNAMICS

• Barbiturates potentiate GABA-mediated chloride currents by binding to the $GABA_A$ receptor-ionophore complex.
  √ May stimulate $GABA_A$ receptors directly in the absence of GABA.
    □ This occurs at significantly higher concentrations than those required for therapeutic effect.
  √ Block glutamate (excitatory neurotransmitter) receptors in the CNS.
• The exact mechanisms of action of chloral hydrate and paraldehyde are unknown.

Clinical Indications

Barbiturate and barbiturate-like hypnotics are not recommended for the treatment of insomnia.

H
Y
P
N
O
T
I
C
S

• These medications are poor sleep inducers, cause rapid development of tolerance, produce REM rebound, and are lethal in overdose.
• Brief inpatient use of chloral hydrate for insomnia may be acceptable.

Intravenous amobarbital is occasionally used for "amytal interviews."

• Amobarbital (100–300 mg) is injected slowly over 5–10 minutes.
  √ Up to 500 mg if patient has tolerance to barbiturates or alcohol.
• Originally used during World War II to treat "combat fatigue."
• Subsequent use to facilitate diagnosis of a conversion disorder (e.g., blindness following witnessing a rape or murder).
• Patients with hysterical amnesia, paralyses, and other conversion symptoms sometimes experience spontaneous remission following the injection.
• Close observation for respiratory depression is required.

Side Effects

CENTRAL NERVOUS SYSTEM EFFECTS

Confusion, mental depression, unusual excitement
• May occur due to intolerance to, or high doses of, barbiturates.
  √ Particularly in elderly or debilitated patients.
• Confusion may lead to increased risk of falls.
• Management
  √ Monitor blood levels and make appropriate dosage adjustments.
  √ Switch hypnotic.

Drowsiness, hangover effects
• Common
• Dependent on drug dosage, half-life, and patient tolerance
• Aggravated by alcohol consumption
• Management
  √ Reduce, discontinue, or switch hypnotic.
  √ Reduce risk with short-acting hypnotic.

GASTROINTESTINAL EFFECTS

Nausea, vomiting
• Most frequent with choral hydrate.
• Management
  √ Administer capsule with a full glass of water or other liquid.

Unpleasant taste
• Occurs with paraldehyde.
• Odor may permeate breath.
• Management
  √ Take paraldehyde with a glass of milk or iced fruit juice.

RESPIRATORY EFFECTS

See page 180.

SKIN, ALLERGIES, AND TEMPERATURE

Rash, fever
- More commonly seen with phenobarbital (1–3%) than with the shorter-acting barbiturates.
- Usually mild and resolves quickly when the drug is discontinued.
- Very rarely, exfoliative dermatitis, erythema multiforme, or Stevens–Johnson syndrome has occurred.

Drug–Drug Interactions

Drug Interactions with Barbiturates and Barbiturate-Like Compounds

Drugs (X) Interact with:	Barbiturates (B)[a]	Comments
Anesthetics (e.g., halogenated hydrocarbon)	X↑↓	Barbiturates may increase the metabolism of enflurane, halothane, or methoxyflurane, leading to increased risk of hepatotoxicity. Chronic use of barbiturates prior to methoxyflurane may increase the formation of nephrotoxic metabolites, resulting in increased risk of nephrotoxicity.
Analgesics (e.g., methadone)	X↓	Increased metabolism of methadone, leading to decreased plasma level and opioid withdrawal symptoms.
Antiarrhythmics (e.g., disopyramide, propafenone, quinidine)	X↓	Decreased efficacy of antiarrhythmics due to increased metabolism
Antibiotics (e.g., doxycycline	X↓	Decreased efficacy of doxycycline due to increased metabolism; a higher dosage may be required.
Anticoagulants (e.g., dicumarol, warfarin)	X↓	Decreased efficacy of anticoagulants due to increased metabolism. Excess bleeding can occur on withdrawal.
Anticonvulsants (e.g., valproate)	B↑	Increased plasma level of barbiturate due to inhibited metabolism
Antidepressants		
MAO inhibitors	X↑ B↑	Enhanced sedative effects
TCAs	X↓	Decreased plasma level of TCAs due to enzyme induction; additive sedative effects.
Antifungals (e.g., griseofulvin)	X↓	Barbiturates may interfere with the absorption of orally administered griseofulvin, decreasing its blood level.
Beta-blockers (e.g., propranolol)	X↓	Reduced efficacy of propranolol due to enhanced metabolism
CNS depressants (e.g., alcohol, antihistamines, benzodiazpeines)	X↑ B↑	Increased CNS depression and psychomotor impairment. *Respiratory depression and coma may occur with high doses.*
Corticosteroids	X↓	Reduced efficacy of corticosteroids due to enhanced metabolism
Herbal preparations	X↑ B↑	*Avoid* evening primrose; seizure threshold decreased. *Avoid* valerian, St. John's wort, kava kava, gotu kola; may increase CNS depression.
Oral contraceptives	X↓	Reduced efficacy of oral contraceptives due to enhanced metabolism
Theophylline	X↓	Reduced efficacy of theophylline due to enhanced metabolism

Drugs (X) Interact with:	Chloral Hydrate (C)	Comments
Anticoagulants (e.g., dicumarol, warfarin)	X↑	Chloral hydrate displaces drugs that are protein-bound and may briefly accelerate hypoprothrombinemic response. Adverse clinical responses are uncommon, but bleeding may occur. Benzodiazepine hypnotics are preferred.
CNS depressants (e.g., alcohol)	X↑ C↑	This "Mickey Finn" combination yields CNS depression. Patients can have fainting, sedation, flushing, tachycardia, headache, hypotension, and amnesia. *Avoid* mixture, especially in cardiovascular problems.
Loop diuretics (e.g., furosemide)	X↑	Diaphoresis, hot flashes, and hypertension occur with IV furosemide. Give IV furosemide with caution to any patient on chloral hydrate in past 24 h.

Drugs (X) interact with:	Paraldehyde (P)	Comments
CNS depressants	X↑ P↑	Increased CNS depression
Disulfiram	P↑	Decreased metabolism of paraldehyde and increased blood concentrations of paraldehyde and acetaldehyde; an alcohol-like reaction will occur.

[a]↑ = increases; ↓ = decreases; ↑↓ = increases and decreases.

Special Populations

CHILDREN AND ADOLESCENTS

• Barbiturates
  √ May produce paradoxical excitement and hyperactivity or exacerbate existing hyperkinetic behavior.
  √ Rickets and osteomalacia have been reported following prolonged usage of barbiturates due to increased metabolism of vitamin D.
• Choral hydrate
  √ Used as a sedative for noninvasive procedures (e.g., MR imaging) in infants and children.
  √ Adverse reactions include hyperactivity, vomiting, and mild respiratory depression.
• Paraldehyde
  √ Infrequently used to control seizures in infants, including those refractory to phenobarbitone and phenytoin.

WOMEN: PREGNANCY AND POSTPARTUM

Pregnancy Rating	• Barbiturates: Category D
	• Barbiturate-like hypnotics: Category C
Teratogenicity (1st trimester)	• Barbiturates readily cross the placenta and are associated with increased incidence of congenital malformations and hemorrhagic disease of newborn.

• Chloral hydrate and paraldehyde have been shown to cross the placenta; no reports of congenital defects in newborn.

Direct Effect on Newborn
(3rd trimester)

• Barbiturate withdrawal has been reported in newborns and may be characterized by hypotonia, irritability, and vomiting.

• Use of paraldehyde during labor may cause respiratory depression in the newborn infant.

Lactation

• Small amounts of barbiturates and chloral hydrate are excreted in breast milk.
  √ Have generally been considered compatible with breastfeeding.

• Use of chloral hydrate by nursing mothers may cause drowsiness in the infant.

• Not known if paraldehyde excreted into breast milk.

LATE LIFE

• Increased risk of confusion, falls, cardiorespiratory depression, and apnea.
  √ Caution when combined with other CNS depressants.
• Lower doses should be given.

Effects on Laboratory Tests

Effects of Barbiturates and Barbiturate-Like Compounds on Blood/Serum and Urine Tests

	Blood/Serum Tests		Urine Tests	
Generic Names	**Marker**	**Results[a]**	**Marker**	**Results[a]**
Barbiturates	Bilirubin	↓	None	
	Phentolamine	↑ f		
Chloral hydrate	WBC	↓	Ketonuria	↑
			Glucose[b]	↑f
			Catecholamines[c]	↑↓
			17-hydroxycortico-steroids[d]	↑

[a]↑ = increases; ↓ = decreases; ↑↓ = increases and decreases; f = falsely.
[b]Use oxidative test instead of copper sulfate.
[c]Only fluorometric test.
[d]With Reddy, Jenkins, and Thorn procedure.

Discontinuation

Barbiturates and barbiturate-like hypnotics produce

• Dependence
• Tolerance

- Addiction
- Withdrawal

Signs and Symptoms of Barbiturate and Barbiturate-Like Hypnotic Withdrawal

Stage[a]	Signs and Symptoms	Timing for Alcohol Withdrawal	Untreated Patients (%)
"Shakes" (tremulousness)	Tremor, bad dreams, insomnia, morning sweats, apprehension, blepharospasm, agitation, ataxia, dilated pupils, labile BP, hypertension/hypotension, increased respiration and heart rate, nausea, vomiting, flushed; atypically have transient hallucinations and illusions; seizures—14%.[b]	5–10 h after last dose; peaks at 24–48 h; usually lasts 3–5 days but may last 2 weeks; may occur on any substance.	80
Hallucinations	Auditory hallucintations both vague (e.g., buzzes, hums) and specific (e.g., accusatory voices); visual hallucinations or perceptual disturbances may also occur; clear consciousness; fear, apprehension, panic, tinnitus; other atypical hallucinations and some clouded consciousness may arise; rum fits—3%.	Onset may happen on agent or up to 12–48 h (and infrequently up to 7 days) after last dose; typically persists 1 week, but can extend over 2 months.	5–25
Seizures	Single or multiple grand malconvulsions; occasionally status epilepticus; muscle jerks.	Appears 6–48 h after last dose; peaks at 12–24 h; seizures usually erupt 16 h into withdrawal.	10–25
Delirium tremens (DTs)	Delirium with clouded and fluctuating consciousness, confusion, disorientation, loss of recent memory; illusions and hallucinations (of all types, often scary), autonomic hyperactivity, hyperthermia, agitation, emotional stability, persecutory delusions, severe ataxia, coarse tremor; REM rebound (up to 3–4 months); death from DTs very rare with current aggressive treatments.	Appears 48–96 h after last dose; persists 4–7 days without complications; convulsions appear 16 h into withdrawal, and psychotic symptoms, 36 h into withdrawal.	15

[a]Stages may evolve gradually or leap ahead. May enter any stage without going through a previous stage.
[b]Seizures may occur during any stage. Stage III is associated with the most intense and frequent seizures. About 20% of patients with DTs have already had a seizure.

Overdose: Toxicity, Suicide, and Treatment

Barbiturates and barbiturate-like hypnotics

- Pose high suicide risks.
- About 10 times the daily dose of barbiturate can be severely toxic.
  √ Barbiturates with shorter half-lives (e.g., amobarbital) and high lipid solubility are more lethal.
- Death occurs in 0.5–12% of barbiturate overdoses. These fatalities may happen "on purpose" or in an "autonomous" state in which a heavily sedated

patient awakes in a fog, cannot remember how many pills have already been taken, and overconsumes.
• Patients may truly not remember overdosing secondary to retrograde amnesia.

CHLORAL HYDRATE

Chloral hydrate's lethal dose is 5–10 times its hypnotic dose of 1–2 g. Acute chloral hydrate overdoses display:

• Stomach distress
• Hypotension
• Hypothermia
• Respiratory depression
• Cardiac arrhythmias
• Coma

Management of chloral hydrate overdose:

• General management, as listed on page 184 for benzodiazepines
• Hemodialysis may eliminate the metabolite trichloroethanol.
  √ Peritoneal dialysis may assist.

PARALDEHYDE

• Acute paraldehyde overdose may produce
  √ Confusion
  √ Muscle tremors, severe weakness
  √ Shortness of breath or troubled breathing
  √ Slow heartbeat
• Diagnosis of paraldehyde overdose may be aided by the characteristic odor of the drug on the breath.

Toxicity and Suicide Data for Barbiturates and Barbiturate-Like Compounds

Generic Names	Toxic Doses Average (g)	Fatal Doses Average Lowest (g)	Toxic Levels[a] (μg/ml)	Fatal Levels[a] μg/ml
BARBITURATES				
Amobarbital	0.4	2–3	30–40	> 50
Butabarbital			40–60	> 50
Pentobarbital		2–3	10–15	> 30
Phenobarbital		6–10	50–80	> 80
Secobarbital		2–3	10–15	> 30
BARBITURATE-LIKE COMPOUNDS				
Chloral hydrate	30	10		

[a]*Toxic* levels produce coma, arousal difficulties, significant respiratory depression; *fatal* levels are usually lethal.

Precautions

Barbiturate and barbiturate-like hypnotics are *contraindicated* in patients with

• Hypersensitivity to hypnotic agents
• Pregnancy
• Sleep apnea

These agents should be *avoided* in patients with

• Liver impairment
• Alcoholism
• Renal conditions
• Porphyria
• Anticoagulant medication
• Suicidal ideation

Key Points to Communicate to Patients and Families

• Barbiturates and barbiturate-like compounds are no longer recommended for hypnotic use.
• These drugs can be lethal in overdose even with relatively small quantities of the medication.
• Abrupt withdrawal is extremely dangerous and likely to result in seizure or even death.
• A safer alternative prescription is recommended.

ADDITIONAL SLEEP-PROMOTING AGENTS

Other benzodiazepines (e.g., lorazepam, clonazepam), sedating antidepressants (e.g., trazodone, mirtazapine, amitriptyline), and second-generation antipsychotics (e.g., olanzapine, quetiapine) are frequently prescribed for off-label use in the management of insomnia.

TRAZODONE

• Originally licensed as a sedating antidepressant in a dose range between 200–600 mg
• Frequently prescribed for insomnia at sub-antidepressant doses.
  √ Hypnotic range: 25–150 mg hs
• Rapid absorption rate; peaks in 20-30 minutes.
• May also cause orthostatic hypotension.
• Priapism is a rare side effect (1:6000 males).
• Use is not recommended in elderly patients due to
  √ Moderately long half-life (12 h) resulting in daytime sedation
  √ Higher risks of postural hypotension and falls

Other OTC preparations are used for nighttime sedation.

MELATONIN

- A light-sensitive endogenous hormone secreted at night by the pineal gland.
- Available as over-the-counter preparations.
  - √ Isolated from pineal gland of nonhuman animals or synthetic.
- Limited evidence for melatonin in resetting circadian rhythm (e.g., jet lag, shift-work).
  - √ May reduce sleep-onset latency and increase total sleep time.
- Hypnotic dose range: 0.2–3 mg/day.
- Daytime sleepiness is a possible side effect.
- Claims of antioxidant effect; requires further investigation.

TRYPTOPHAN

- A natural amino acid (precursor of serotonin) that was formerly available in health food stores.
- Limited evidence to suggest delayed and mild hypnotic effects.
  - √ Hypnotic range: 2–6 g/day.
- Eosinophilia myalgia syndrome (EMS) was linked to a contaminated batch of the drug in 1989, leading to withdrawal of product from U.S. market.
- Prescription-grade tryptophan continues to be available in Canada and was not associated with EMS.
- High-dose SSRI–tryptophan combination has been associated with serotonin syndrome.

VALERIAN

- Dried root advocated for treating insomnia.
- Hypnotic dose varies between preparations.
  - √ 0.9–3.0 g valerian extract, standardized to contain 0.04–0.9% valerenic acid.
- Binds to GABA receptors.
- Hypnotic effects may not be apparent for 2–3 weeks; therefore, not recommended for the management of acute insomnia.
- Common side effects include morning sedation, headache, and GI distress.

THERAPEUTIC APPLICATION

Initiation of Treatment

- Transient insomnia may not require pharmacological intervention.
  - √ Review sleep hygiene with patient.
    - ▫ Avoid caffeine or other stimulants.
    - ▫ Create a more conductive environment for sleep.
    - ▫ Avoid daytime naps.
    - ▫ Apply cognitive–behavioral techniques.
- In the absence of a primary psychiatric or medical disorder, sustained insomnia of recent onset may be treated with a short-acting hypnotic.
  - √ Start at lowest recommended dose.
    - ▫ For example, zaleplon 5 mg, zolpidem 5 mg

√ Use every second or third night for a maximum of 4 weeks.

√ Dose increases may be required.

√ Longer-acting hypnotics may be required for patients who waken in the middle of the night.

    ▫ For example, temazepam 7.5 or 15 mg

• For chronic insomnia in patients with a history of nightly hypnotic benzodiazepine use, an attempt should be made to taper and switch to a nonbenzodiazepine alternative.

• For example, ramelteon, trazodone, mirtazapine

• Rebound insomnia may occur after discontinuation of hypnotic.

Treatment Resistance

• Review diagnosis and consider polysomnography.

• May require combination hypnotic therapy.

• Alternative therapies such as acupuncture, biofeedback, phase-shifting therapy, and light therapy have been suggested but not well evaluated.

Maintenance

• Although maintenance treatment is not recommended, some patients may benefit from continuation of hypnotic use.

• In the absence of abuse potential, ramelteon may be preferred as a maintenance medication.

8. Stimulants and Stimulant-Like Agents

INTRODUCTION TO DRUG CLASS

During the past decade, there has been accumulating evidence regarding the mechanism of action in stimulants. This knowledge base has provided a novel framework for categorizing psychostimulants. For example, conventional agents that block the reuptake and/or facilitate release of catecholamines include amphetamine-like compounds, whereas novel treatments (e.g., modafinil) primarily engage neuropeptide systems. Concern for abuse liability has provided the impetus to develop alternative agents that are less vulnerable to nontherapeutic usage, allowing for nonscheduled status by the Drug Enforcement Agency (DEA).

Two major developments regarding psychostimulants in the treatment of mental disorders includes their broadening therapeutic application and the approval of agents that are delivered through a variety of mechanisms that alter absorption and enhance pharmacokinetics and possibly pharmacodynamics. For example, psychostimulants are prescribed not only for attention-deficit/hyperactivity disorder, but also for treatment-resistant depression, cognitive impairment, as well as for bariatric use. This chapter aims to provide an up-to-date review of available psychostimulants with practical tactics and strategies for optimal and safe use.

Stimulants by Chemical Class

Chemical Class	Generic Name	Trade Name
FIRST-GENERATION		
Amphetamine	Amphetamine/dextroamphetamine salts	Adderall
	Dextroamphetamine	Dexedrine, Dextrostat
	Lisdexamfetamine	Vyvanse
Methylphenidate	Dexmethylphenidate	Focalin
	Methylphenidate	Ritalin, Concerta, Metadate, Methylin
	Methylphenidate transdermal system	Daytrana
SECOND-GENERATION		
	Atomoxetine	Strattera
	Modafinil	Provigil

FIRST-GENERATION STIMULANTS

Dosing, Dose Form, and Color

Profile of First-Generation Stimulants

Generic Names	Pediatric ADHD Dose (mg/kg/day)	Adult ADHD Dose (mg/day)[a]	Other Adult Doses (mg/day)	Dose Form (mg)[a]	Color
		AMPHETAMINE			
Amphetamine/ dextroamphetamine salts	0.25–1	t: 10–30 (bid or tid)	Narcolepsy: 5–60	t: 5/7.5/10/ 12.5/15/ 20/30	t: white (round)/ blue (oval)/ blue (round)/ orange (round)/ orange (oval)/ orange (round)/ orange (round)
		er: 10–30 (qd)		er:5/10/15/ 20/25/30	er: clear blue/ blue-blue/ blue–white/ orange-orange/ orange–white/ natural–orange
Dextroamphetamine	0.1–0.8	2.5–40 bid or tid (geriatric: 10–15)	Depression/ narcolepsy: 5–60	t: 5 e: 5 mg/5 ml sp: 5/10/15	t: orange e: orange sp: all brown (clear)
Lisdexamfetamine	30–70 mg/day (ages 6–12)			c: 30/50/70	c: white–orange/ white–blue/ blue–orange
		METHYLPHENIDATE			
Dexmethylphenidate	0.25–0.1	t: 5–20 (bid)		t: 2.5/5/10 er: 5/10/15/20	t: blue/yellow/white er: light blue/ light caramel/ green/white
Methylphenidate	0.5–2.0	t: 10–60 (qd or bid) (geriatric: 10–30)	Depression: 10–30 Narcolepsy: 10–60	t: 5/10/20 ch-t: 2.5/5/10 o: 5/10 mg/5 ml sr: 10/20/ 30/40 oc-t: 18/27/ 36/54	t: yellow/pale green/pale yellow ch-t: all white oc-t: yellow/gray/ white/red
Methylphenidate transdermal system	10–30			ts: 27.5/41.3/ 55/82.5 mg	

[a]c = capsule; ch-t = chewable tablets; e = elixir; er = extended-release capsules; o = oral solution; oc-t = osmotic-controlled-release tablets; sp = spansule; sr = sustained-release spansules; t = tablets; ts = transdermal system.

Pharmacology

PHARMACOKINETICS

Amphetamine/dextroamphetamine salts
• Rapidly absorbed from the GI tract; food may delay the rate but not the extent of absorption.
• Protein binding is approximately 20%.

- Extensively metabolized by the liver.
- Urinary excretion is highly pH-dependent; rate accelerated by acidification.

Lisdexamfetamine
- Rapidly absorbed from GI tract; food may delay the rate but not the extent of absorption.
- Converts to dextroamphetamine via first-pass intestinal and/or hepatic metabolism.
- Metabolites are primarily excreted by the kidneys.

Methylphenidate
- Rapidly absorbed from the GI tract following oral administration; food may delay time to peak concentration.
  √ Transdermal patch may yield a 1.9-fold higher plasma level than the once-daily oral formulations.
- Low plasma protein binding (15%)
- Low bioavailability (30%) due to extensive first-pass metabolism with high interindividual variation
  √ First-pass effect is decreased with transdermal administration; a lower dose (mg/kg) may produce higher exposure of parent compound compared to oral administration.
- Metabolites are primarily excreted by the kidneys.

Pharmacokinetic Properties of First-Generation Stimulants

Generic Names	T_{max}[a] (h)	Half-Life (h)	Onset of Action (h)	Duration of Action (h)	Metabolic Pathway	Excretion (%)[b]
Amphetamine salts/ dextroamphetamine	2–4	6–12	0.5–1	4–6	CYP2D6	20–70 R
Lisdexamfetamine	1[c]	< 1[c]			Hydrolysis	96 R/0.3 F
Methylphenidate/ dexmethylphenidate	1–3	2–4	0.5–1	3–6	De-esterification	90 R/3 F

[a]T_{max} = time to peak concentration.
[b]F = fecal; R = renal.
[c]Lisdexamfetamine is inactive until metabolized to dextroamphetamine, which has a T_{max} of 3.5 h and a mean half-life of 12 h.

PHARMACODYNAMICS

Amphetamine
- Promotes release of dopamine, norepinephrine, and serotonin into the synapse.
- Inhibits MAO to increase the quantity of biogenic amine available for release.

Methylphenidate
- Selectively blocks reuptake of dopamine and norepinephrine into the presynaptic neuron, thereby increasing synaptic levels of these catecholamines.
- Therapeutic effect is predominantly due to the *d*-enantiomer.

Clinical Indications

ATTENTION-DEFICIT/HYPERACTIVITY DISORDER (ADHD)

- Amphetamine and methylphenidate are recommended as first-line treatment for the core symptoms of ADHD.
  √ 70–80% of patients respond positively to stimulants, with substantial improvements in conduct, attentiveness, and academic performance.
  √ Efficacy and safety data have been well established.

NARCOLEPSY

- Stimulants (e.g., amphetamines, methylphenidate, and methamphetamine) have been recommended for patients with excessive sleepiness associated with narcolepsy.
  √ Prescribed as monotherapy or augmentation therapy
  √ Treatment may begin with standard, short-acting stimulants (e.g., methylphenidate 5 mg bid and titrate to 30 mg bid if necessary).

OFF-LABEL INDICATIONS

- Treatment-resistant depression

Side Effects

CARDIOVASCULAR EFFECTS

Hypertension, palpitations, tachycardia
- Management
  √ Monitor heart rate and blood pressure, especially after a dose increase.
  √ Cardiac evaluation recommended if patient exhibits
    □ Excessive increases in BP or pulse
    □ Exertional chest pain, or
    □ Unexplained syncope.

CENTRAL NERVOUS SYSTEM EFFECTS

Confusion, "dopey feeling"
- Especially arises with > 1 mg/kg/day of methylphenidate.

Dizziness

Dysphoria
- Occurs with all stimulants but especially with methylphenidate, which causes
  √ Mild dysphoria
  √ Subtle social withdrawal
  √ Dulled affect, emotional blunting
  √ Cognitive "overfocusing"
  √ Perseveration
- May be related to withdrawal effects; use sustained-release formulations.

Tourette's syndrome, tics
- Usually with higher doses.

Headache
- Most common 2–3 h after a dose.
- Tends to be transient; may take acetaminophen on a prn basis.

Insomnia
- Usually occurs at initiation of treatment.
- Affects 30% of children on moderately high stimulant doses.
- Management
  √ Give dose earlier in the day and/or
  √ Reduce dose.
  √ L-tryptophan (500–1000 mg), valerian (450–900 mg extract), or melatonin (0.5-1 mg) at bedtime may be useful.

Mania, psychosis
- At high doses can induce symptoms of mania and psychosis.
- Symptoms generally resolve within 2 days after discontinuation of the stimulant.
  √ Symptoms lasting 6 days or longer have been reported.

Restlessness
- Give dose earlier in the day and/or
- Reduce dose.

ENDOCRINE EFFECTS

Changes in libido
- Both increases and decreases reported.

Erectile dysfunction

Suppressed growth
- May suppress height and weight gain in some children.
- Related to dose and duration of drug use.
- Growth rebound appears during drug-free holidays.

GASTROINTESTINAL EFFECTS

Anorexia, weight loss
- Reduced appetite occurs in 30% of children given moderately high stimulant doses.
- Management
  √ Take medication with meals.
  √ Eat smaller meals more frequently.
  √ If weight loss exceeds 10%, consider switching to another agent.

Dry mouth
- Relieve by chewing sugarless gum or sucking on a piece of hard candy.

Drug and Food Interactions

Drug and Food Interactions with First-Generation Stimulants

Drugs (X) Interact with:	Dextroamphetamine (D)[a]	Comments
Acidifying agents (e.g., ascorbic acid, fruit juice, glutamic acid)	D↓	Decreased absorption and increased elimination of dextroamphetamine
Alkalinizing agents (e.g., potassium citrate, sodium bicarbonate)	D↑	Increased absorption and decreased elimination of dextroamphetamine
Antibiotic		
Furazolidone	D↑	Hypertensive crisis due to increased release of norepinephrine; *avoid.*
Anticonvulsants Phenobarbital, phenytoin	X↓↑	Intestinal absorption of phenobarbital or phenytoin may be delayed; co-administration may produce synergistic anticonvulsant effects.
Ethosuximide	X↓	Intestinal absorption of ethosuximide may be delayed.
Antidepressants		
MAO inhibitors	X↑	Hypertensive crisis due to increased release of norepinephrine. Tranylcypramine is the most dangerous MAO inhibitor. *Avoid.*
SSRIs	X↑ D↑	Increased agitation; may augment antidepressant effect. Fluoxetine and paroxetine may inhibit metabolism of dextroamphetamine via CYP2D6.
TCAs	X↑ D↑	Amphetamines may enhance TCA effect; can also produce arrhythmias, agitation, and psychosis. TCAs (desipramine, protriptyline) increase amphetamine levels.
Antihistamines	X↓	Decreased sedative effect of antihistamines
Antihypertensives	X↓	Decreased hypotensive effect of antihypertensive medication
Antipsychotics (e.g., chlorpromazine, haloperidol)	D↓	Counteract stimulant effects of amphetamines via dopamine and norepinephrine blockade. Chlorpromazine can be used to treat amphetamine overdose.
Lithium	D↓	Lithium blocks anorectic and stimulatory effects of amphetamines. No special precautions.
Narcotics		
Propoxyphene	X↑ D↑	Increased CNS symptoms in propoxyphene overdose, causing fatal convulsions
Opiates	X↑	Analgesic and anorectic effects may be potentiated.
Sibutramine	X↑	Hypertensive crisis; use with caution.

Drugs (X) Interact with:	Methylphenidate (M)[a]	Comments
Antibacterial		
Linezolid	X↑	Linezolid inhibits MAO; *avoid.*
Anticoagulants		
Warfarin	X↑	Decreased metabolism of anticoagulant; monitor INR.[b]
Anticonvulsants		
Carbamazepine	M↓	Decreased plasma level of methylphenidate via P450 induction

Drugs (X) Interact with:	Methylphenidate (M)[a]	Comments
Phenobarbital, phenytoin, primidone	X↑	Increased plasma level of phenobarbital phenytoin and primidone due to decreased metabolism; potential risk of toxicity—monitor.
Antidepressants		
MAO inhibitors	X↑	Hypertensive crisis due to accumulation of norepinephrine; *avoid*.
SNRI	X↑	Case report of serontonin syndrome from addition of methylphenidate to venlafaxine
SSRIs	X↑	Plasma level of SSRI may be increased.
TCAs	X↑	Increased plasma level of TCAs; may facilitate antidepressant and cardiovascular effects.
Antihypertensives	X↓	Decreased hypotensive effect of antihypertensive medication

[a]↑ = increases; ↓ = decreases.
[b]INR = international normalized ratio.

Special Populations

CHILDREN AND ADOLESCENTS

• Clinical evaluation for tics and Tourette's syndrome in children and their families before initiation of treatment is recommended.
• May exacerbate symptoms of thought disorder and behavior disturbance in children with psychosis.
• Chronic administration of stimulants may be associated with growth inhibition; monitor height and weight.

WOMEN: PREGNANCY AND POSTPARTUM

Pregnancy Rating	• Category C
Teratogenicity (1st trimester)	• There have been no well-controlled studies of stimulant use during pregnancy; therefore they should be discontinued.
	• Repeated high doses of amphetamine have suggested an embryotoxic and a teratogenic potential.
	• Methylphenidate is not associated with congenital defects.
Direct Effect on Newborn (3rd trimester)	• Stimulants can increase BP and worsen preeclampsia.
	• Stimulants are associated with premature delivery and low birth weight.

S
T
I
M
U
L
A
N
T
S

Lactation

- Amphetamines are excreted in human milk; breastfeeding is not recommended.
- Methylphenidate: no data.

LATE LIFE

- Lower doses and slower titration may be necessary to improve tolerability.
- Give with caution to patients with mild hypertension.
- Methylphenidate and dextroamphetamine have been demonstrated as useful adjuncts to antidepressant medications, particularly when apathy is prominent.

Effects on Laboratory Tests

Effects of First-Generation Stimulants on Blood/Serum and Urine Tests

	Blood/Serum Tests		Urine Tests	
Generic Names	**Marker**	**Results**[a]	**Marker**	**Results**
Dextroamphetamine	Corticosteroids, growth hormone, prolactin	↑	Steroid determinations	Interferes
Methylphenidate	RBC, WBC Growth hormone, prolactin	↓r↓r	None	

[a]↑ = increases; ↓ = decreases; r = rarely

Discontinuation

Stimulants can cause

- Psychological dependence
- Drug misuse

Stimulants less commonly cause

- Physical dependence
- Tolerance (more commonly in narcolepsy)
- Physical withdrawal

Common amphetamine and methylphenidate withdrawal symptoms include:

- Increased appetite, weight gain
- Increased need for sleep but often poor quality
- Decreased energy, psychomotor retardation
- Depression, paranoia, suicidal thoughts

Overdose: Toxicity, Suicide, and Treatment

Death rarely occurs from overdoses of prescribed stimulants, since they have a wide therapeutic range. Nevertheless, a 10-day supply taken at once can be very toxic, even lethal, especially in children.

Most amphetamine overdoses are from illegal, not clinically obtained, drugs.

Amphetamine overdoses produce

- Agitation
- Suicidal ideation
- Chest pain
- Hallucinations (auditory > visual)
- Confusion
- Dysphoria, weakness, lethargy
- Delusions

Other symptoms (< 5%) include

- Seizures, hyperreflexia, fever, tremor, rhabdomyolysis, hypertension or hypotension, stroke, aggression, headache, palpitations, abdominal pain, rashes, dyspnea, leg pain, and paresthesias.

For the general management of stimulant overdoses, *see* page 24. Other treatments for specific symptoms of stimulant overdoses include:

- For seizures
  √ Short-acting barbiturates (e.g., amobarbital) or
  √ IV diazepam
- For agitation
  √ Chlorpromazine: 1mg/kg body weight IM (children) or 100 mg IM (adults).
  √ If the amphetamine has been taken with a barbiturate, reduce the chlorpromazine dosage by half.
- For psychosis
  √ Isolate patient from environmental stimuli, which aggravate psychosis.

Precautions

Contraindications include

- Anxiety and agitation
- History of drug abuse (unless a solid clinical reason)
- Advanced arteriosclerosis, cardiovascular disease, hypertension
- Hyperthyroidism
- Allergy to stimulants
- Glaucoma
- Tics or Tourette's syndrome (in patients or family members)
- Concomitant treatment with MAO inhibitors
  √ Wait 14 days after MAO inhibitors discontinued.

Use *cautiously* in patients with prior history of seizures and EEG abnormalities.

- May lower the seizure threshold.

Key Points to Communicate to Patients and Families

- A 10-day supply of stimulants can be lethal for children.
- Most common temporary side effects are fast heartbeat, decreased appetite, headache, trouble sleeping, dizziness, stomach upset, weight loss, dry mouth.
  √ Slowing of growth (height and weight) in children may occur but is usually transient.
- Avoid applying external heat (e.g., heating pads, electric blankets, heated water beds) to the Daytrana patch, because it may result in increased release of methylphenidate.
- If a dose is missed
  √ Can take the medication up to 3 h later.
  √ Otherwise, wait for next dose.
  √ Never double the dose.
- Do not stop your medication suddenly because this may result in withdrawal symptoms such as sleep disturbances and changes in mood and behavior.
- Keep stimulants away from bedside or from any readily accessible place to deter accidental intake. Keep out of reach of children.

SECOND-GENERATION STIMULANTS

Dosing, Dose Form, and Color

Profile of Second-Generation Stimulants

Generic Names	Pediatric ADHD Dose	Adult ADHD Dose	Other Adult Doses	Dose Form (mg)[a]	Color
Atomoxetine	Up to 70 kg: 0.5–1.2 mg/ kg/day. Do not exceed 1.4 mg/kg or 100 mg, which- ever is less. Over 70 kg: 40–100 mg/day.	Over 70 kg: 40–100 mg/day		c: 10/18/25/ 40/60/80/ 100	c: white/ gold– white/ blue–white/ blue/blue– gold/brown– white/brown
Modafinil		100–300 mg/day	Narcolepsy, OSAHS[b], SWSD[c]: 200 mg/day	t: 100/200	t: all white

[a]c = capsule; t = tablets.
[b]OSAHS = obstructive sleep apnea–hypopnea.
[c]SWSD = shift-work sleep disorder.

Atomoxetine: Additional information

- In patients with moderate and severe hepatic insufficiency, doses should be reduced to 50% and 25% of the standard dose, respectively.
- If prescribed in combination with drugs that inhibit CYP2D6 (see Drug–Drug Interactions, p. 213): initiate dose, as above, but do not increase to the usual

target dose unless symptoms fail to improve *after 4 weeks* and the initial dose is well tolerated.

Pharmacology

PHARMACOKINETICS

Atomoxetine
- Well absorbed after oral administration with absolute bioavailability of 63%; high-fat meal may decrease the rate but not the extent of absorption.
- Predominantly eliminated by oxidative metabolism in the liver.
- Highly bound to plasma protein (98%).
- Excreted primarily as metabolites in the urine (80%) and to a lesser extent in the feces (17%).

Modafinil
- Rapidly absorbed from the GI tract; food may delay the rate but not the extent of absorption.
- Moderate protein binding (60%)
- Primarily metabolized by the liver, with less than 10% of the drug excreted unchanged.
- May induce its own metabolism after maintenance doses > 400 mg/day.

Pharmacokinetic Properties of Second-Generation Stimulants

Generic Names	T_{max}[a] (h)	Half-life (h)	Onset of Action (h)	Duration of Action (h)	Metabolic Pathway	Excretion (%)[b]
Atomoxetine	1–2	5	Delayed up to 4 weeks	24	CYP 2D6, CYP2C19	80 R
Modafinil	2–4	15	1.5–2	15	Hydrolytic deamination, S-oxidation, aromatic ring hydroxylation, glucuronide conjugation	80 R

[a]T_{max} = time to peak concentration.
[b]F = fecal; R = renal.

PHARMACODYNAMICS

Atomoxetine
- Increases extracellular levels of norepinephrine and dopamine in prefrontal cortex, but not in the nucleus accumbens or striatum.
- This mechanism of action suggests that atomoxetine is unlikely to have abuse potential or to cause motor tics.

Modafinil
- The precise mechanism through which it promotes wakefulness is unknown.
- Postulated to increase glutamate and decrease GABA levels in specific brain regions.

STIMULANTS

• May also stimulate postsynaptic α_1-adrenergic receptors and weakly block dopamine reuptake transporters.

Clinical Indications

ATTENTION-DEFICIT/HYPERACTIVITY DISORDER (ADHD)

• Atomoxetine is the first nonstimulant approved for the treatment of ADHD and the first drug to be licensed for the treatment of ADHD in adults.
  √ It is recommended as a second-line treatment if patient fails to respond or has intolerable side effects to stimulants or has a history of substance abuse.
• Modafinil has demonstrated effectiveness in the treatment of ADHD in children and adolescents.
  √ Particularly when anorexia or weight loss limits use of stimulants

Side Effects

CARDIOVASCULAR EFFECTS

Dizziness

Hypertension, palpitations
• Small increase in BP and pulse.
• Occur at start of treatment; usually plateau with time.
• Cardiac evaluation recommended if patient exhibits
  √ Excessive increases in BP or pulse
  √ Exertional chest pain, or
  √ Unexplained syncope.

CENTRAL NERVOUS SYSTEM EFFECTS

Drowsiness, fatigue

Emotional lability
• More frequently in children and adolescents
• Management
  √ Closely observe for clinical worsening as well as unusual changes in mood and behavior.
  √ Reduce dose.

Headache
• Transient and may resolve spontaneously.
• Administer acetaminophen prn.

Insomnia
• May experience delayed sleep onset.
• Usually transient at initiation of treatment.
• Management
  √ Reduce dose or
  √ Adjust time of dose to earlier in the day or morning.

ENDOCRINE AND SEXUAL EFFECTS

Sexual dysfunction
- Including erectile disturbance, erectile dysfunction, and abnormal orgasm
- Occurs in 2% of patients treated with atomoxetine.

Dysmenorrhea

EYES, EARS, NOSE, AND THROAT EFFECTS

Rhinitis (common)

GASTROINTESTINAL EFFECTS

Abdominal pain, nausea, vomiting
- Management
  √ Administer medication with food.
  √ Divide dose evenly to bid.

Dry mouth
- Relieve by chewing sugarless gum or sucking on sour candy, ice chips, or popsicles.

Constipation
- Relieve by increasing the amount of fiber and water intake in diet.

Loss of appetite
- Seen during initiation of atomoxetine, especially if dose titrated too rapidly.
- May lead to weight loss.

HEPATIC EFFECTS

Severe liver injury
- Rare

RENAL EFFECTS

*Urinary hesitation and/or urinary retention
and/or difficulty in micturition*

Drug–Drug Interactions

Drug Interactions with Second-Generation Stimulants

Drugs (X) Interact with:	Atomoxetine (A)[a]	Comments
Antiarrhythmics	A↑	Increased level of atomoxetine due to inhibited metabolism via CYP2D6
Antidepressants		
MAO inhibitor	X↑ A↑	Do not administer atomoxetine with a MAO inhibitor or within 2 weeks of discontinuing an MAO inhibitor.

Drugs (X) Interact with:	Atomoxetine (A)[a]	Comments
SSRI	A↑	Paroxetine and fluoxetine may increase plasma level and half-life of atomoxetine level due to inhibited metabolism via CYP2D6.
Antiparkinsonian agents (e.g., pergolide)	A↑	Increased level of atomoxetine due to inhibited metabolism via CYP2D6
Antiviral agents (e.g., ritonavir, delavirdine)	A↑	Increased level of atomoxetine due to inhibited metabolism via CYP2D6
Stimulants (amphetamines, methylphenidate)	X↑ A↑	May combine to augment response; possible potentiation of hypertension and tachycardia.

Drugs (X) Interact with:	Modafinil (M)	Comments
Benzodiazepines Triazolam	X↓	Decreased Cmax and AUC of triazolam (up to 60%)
Immunosuppressant Cyclosporin	X↓	Case of decreased cyclosporine blood level (by 50%); the interaction was postulated to be due to increased metabolism.
Oral contraceptives	X↓	Decreased plasma level of ethinyl estradiol due to induction of CYP3A4
Stimulants (dextroamphetamine, methylphenidate)	M↓	Concurrent use may delay absorption of modafinil.

[a]↑ = increases; ↓ = decreases.

Special Populations

CHILDREN AND ADOLESCENTS

Atomoxetine
- Associated with increased risk of suicidal thinking in children and adolescents.
  - √ Closely observe for clinical worsening as well as unusual changes in mood and behavior during the initial few months of therapy or at times of dose changes.
- Long-term therapy may suppress normal growth patterns.
  - √ Height and weight should be monitored throughout treatment.
- Pharmacokinetics in children and adolescents are similar to those in adults.

Modafinil
- Risk of developing severe and potentially life-threatening skin rash, including Stevens–Johnson syndrome.
- Mild and nonprogressive decreases in white blood cell counts have been reported in children.

WOMEN: PREGNANCY AND POSTPARTUM

- Pregnancy Category C; no adequate and well-controlled studies have been done in humans.
- Unknown if these agents are excreted in human milk.

LATE LIFE

- Clearance of modafinil may be reduced in elderly patients.
- Use with caution in patients with cardiovascular or liver dysfunction.

Effects on Laboratory Tests

- Atomoxetine and modafinil are not known to interact with commonly used clinical laboratory tests.

Discontinuation

- Abrupt discontinuation of atomoxetine or modafinil is not associated with symptom rebound or increases in adverse events in patients with ADHD.
- Tapering of doses is not necessary.

Overdose: Toxicity, Suicide, and Treatment

No reports of death involving overdose of atomoxetine alone (doses up to 1400 mg).

- Symptoms of overdose may include
  - √ Agitation
  - √ Drowsiness
  - √ Tachycardia, prolonged QT_c interval (rare)
  - √ Blurred vision, dry mouth
  - √ Seizures

No reports of fatal overdoses involving modafinil alone (doses up to 4500 mg).

- Symptoms of overdose may include:
  - √ Anxiety, irritability, aggressiveness
  - √ Confusion, nervousness, tremor
  - √ Palpitations
  - √ Sleep disturbances
  - √ Decreased prothrombin time

Management

- Supportive care should be given.
- Monitor cardiac and vital signs.
- If there are no contraindications, consider gastric lavage.
- Dialysis is not likely to provide benefit.

Precautions

ATOMOXETINE

- *Contraindicated* in patients with
  - √ Known hypersensitivity to atomoxetine

√ Concurrent MAO-inhibitor use
√ Narrow-angle glaucoma
  □ May increase risk of mydriasis.
• Use *cautiously* in patients with
  √ Hypertension or hypotension
  √ Tachycardia
  √ Cardiovascular or cerebrovascular disease
  √ Liver dysfunction

MODAFINIL

• *Contraindicated* in patients with
  √ Known hypersensitivity to modafinil
  √ Left ventricular hypertrophy
  √ Mitral valve prolapse
• Use *cautiously* in patients with
  √ Hypertension
  √ Unstable angina or a recent history of myocardial infarction
  √ Hepatic or renal impairment
  √ History of psychosis

Key Points to Communicate to Patients and Families

• Report to your doctor any changes in sleeping or eating habits or changes in mood or behavior.
• Modafinil may affect the effectiveness of birth control pills.
  √ This effect will last 1 month after stopping modafinil.
• Use caution when driving or engaged in potentially hazardous tasks.
• Do not discontinue or alter dose without consulting your doctor.
• Place away from bedside or any readily accessible area due to safety concerns. Keep out of reach of children.

THERAPEUTIC APPLICATION

Initiation of Treatment

• Stimulants as first-line treatment
  √ Most effective: 70–80%.
  √ 3–4% experience side effects causing discontinuation of medications.
  √ Long-acting agents
    □ Require one dose per day; eliminates the need for a midday dose.
    □ Improve medication adherence.
    □ Have less liability for abuse.
  √ Short-acting agents
    □ Require two to four doses per day.
    □ Suitable for patients who need augmentation for a particular task at a particular time of day.

- Atomoxetine as second-line treatment
  - √ Effective 50–60%.
  - √ Similar side effects to stimulants
  - √ Provides 24-hour coverage.
  - √ 1–3 weeks to reach effect.
  - √ Favorable in patients with comorbid substance use disorder.
- Baseline data on height, weight, blood pressure, and heart rate should be collected as well as a complete blood count.

Treatment Resistance

Symptoms that may not respond to stimulants in clinical practice include:

- Tics
- Irritability
- Severe sleep disorders: initial insomnia, parasomnias
- Oppositional and defiant behavior with parents
- Social difficulties with peers
- Inattention from other diagnoses (e.g., PTSD, depression)

Strategies for nonresponse

- If a patient does not show good response or has difficulty with side effects, first maximize the dosage or switch to another medication within the same class.
  - √ It is optimal to switch medication during long vacations or during the summer to avoid possible side effects that may impair school performance.
- If the patient does not respond to any of the first- or second-line medications,
  - √ Consider imipramine or bupropion.
  - √ Augmentation strategies might be helpful.
    - □ For severe oppositionality, add a low dose of second-generation antipsychotic.
    - □ For severe mood liability, add mood stabilizer.
    - □ Treat initial insomnia with behavioral plan, melatonin, clonidine, mirtazapine.

Maintenance

- Once dose is established, follow-up visits every 3–4 months are recommended.
- A dose may be effective for 1–2 years and then need adjusting.
  - √ A dose is not necessarily increased every year.

S
T
I
M
U
L
A
N
T
S

Appendix 1.
Drug Identification
by Generic Name

Generic Name	Trade Name	Chief Action[b]
acebutol	Sectral	β-blocker (CS)
acetaminophen[a]	Tylenol	analgesic
acetazolamide	Diamox	carbonic anhydrase inhibitor
acetophenazine	Tindal	neuroleptic
agomelatine	Valdoxan	antidepressant
albuterol	Proventil	sympathomimetic (DA) β
α-methyldopa	Aldomet	antihypertensive
alprazolam	Xanax	antianxiety
aluminum hydroxide[a]	Gelusil	antacid
amantadine	Symmetrel	antiparkinsonian, antiviral
ambenonium chloride	Mytelase	cholinomimetic
amiloride	Midamor	potassium-sparing diuretic
aminophylline	Mudrane	bronchodilator
amiodarone	Cordarone	antiarrhythmic (III)
amitriptyline	Elavil	TCA
amphetamine/ dextroamphetamine salts	Adderall	stimulant
amobarbital	Amytal	hypnotic
amoxapine	Asendin	HCA
anisotropine	Valpin	anticholinergic
antipyrine	Auralgan	analgesic (otic)
aripiprazole	Abilify	antipsychotic
astemizole	Hismanal	antihistamine (H1)
atenolol	Tenormin	β-blocker
atomoxetine	Strattera	SNRI
atropine	Atropine Sulfate	anticholinergic
azatadine	Optimine	antihistamine
azithromycin dihydrate	Zithromax	antibacterial (macrolide)
baclofen	Lioresal	skeletal muscle relaxant
beclomethasone	Vanceril	corticosteroid
benazepril hydrochloride	Lotensin	antihypertensive (ACE)
benztropine	Cogentin	antiparkinsonian
bepridil hydrochloride	Vascor	calcium-channel blocker, antianginal

(continued)

Generic Name	Trade Name	Chief Action[b]
bethanechol	Urecholine	cholinergic, anticholinesterase
biperiden	Akineton	antiparkinsonian, anticholinergic
bromocriptine	Parlodel	prolactin inhibitor, antiparkinsonian, dopamine agonist
bupropion	Wellbutrin	NDRI
buspirone	BuSpar	antianxiety
butabarbital	Butisol	antianxiety
caffeine	No Doz	CNS stimulant
calcium carbonate[a]	Tums	antacid
captopril	Capoten	antihypertensive (ACE)
carbamazepine	Tegretol	anticonvulsant, anticycling
carbidopa-levodopa	Sinemet	antiparkinsonian
carisoprodol	Soma	muscle relaxant
chorlal hydrate	Noctec	hypnotic
chloramphenicol	Chloromycetin	antibiotic
chlordiazepoxide	Librium	antianxiety
chlorothiazide	Diuril	thiazide diuretic
chlorpheniramine[a]	Chlortrimeton	antihistamine
chlorpromazine	Thorazine	neuroleptic
chlorprothixene	Taractan	neuroleptic
cholestyramine	Questran	hypolipidemic
cimetidine	Tagamet	h_2-receptor antagonist
citalopram	Celexa	SSRI
clarithromycin	Biaxin	antibacterial (macrolide)
clidinium bromide	Quarzan	anticholingeric
clomipramine	Anafranil	TCA
clonazepam	Klonopin	antianxiety, anticonvulsant
clonidine	Catapres	antihypertensive, α_2 agonist
clorazepate	Tranxene	antianxiety
clozapine	Clozaril	neuroleptic
cromolyn	Gastrocrom	mast cell stabilizer
cyclobenzaprine	Flexeril	muscle relaxant (tricyclic)
cyclosporine	Sandimmune	immunosuppressant
cyproheptadine	Periactin	antihistamine, serotonin antagonist
danazol	Danocrine	androgen derivative, gonadotropin inhibitor
dantrolene	Dantrium	skeletal muscle relaxant
desipramine	Norpramin	TCA
desvenlafaxine	Pristiq	SNRI
dexmethylphenidate	Focalin	stimulant
dextroamphetamine	Dexedrine	stimulant
dextromethorphan[a]	"DM" products	cough suppressor
diazepam	Valium	antianxiety
diclofenac sodium	Voltaren	anti-inflammatory (NSAID)
dicumarol	Dicumarol	anticoagulant (oral)
dicyclomine hydrochloride	Bentyl	anticholinergic
digoxin	Lanoxin	cardiac glycoside
diltiazem	Cardizem	calcium channel-blocker
diphenhydramine[a]	Benadryl	antihistamine
disopyramide	Norpace	antiarrhythmic (1)
disulfiram	Antabuse	alcohol blockade
divalproex	Depakote	anticonvulsant, mood stabilizer
dobutamine hydrochloride	Dobutrex	sympathomimetic (DA) $\alpha\beta$
donepezil	Aricept	enhances cholinergic function
dopamine	Intropin	sympathomimetic (DA) $\alpha\beta$
doxapram	Dopram	respiratory stimulant
doxepin	Sinequan	TCA
doxycycline	Vibramycin	tetracycline antibiotic
droperidol	Inapsine	antiemetic, antianxiety, neuroleptic
duloxetine	Cymbalta	SNRI
edrophonium chloride	Tensilon	cholinomimetic
enalapril	Vasotec	antihypertensive (ACE)
enflurane	Ethrane	anesthetic (general)
ephedrine[a]	Marax	vasoconstrictor
epinephrine[a]	Primatene	sympathetomimetic (DA) $\alpha\beta$

Generic Name	Trade Name	Chief Action[b]
erythromycin ethylsuccinate	Pediazole	antibacterial (macrolide)
escitalopram	Lexapro	SSRI
estazolam	ProSom	hypnotic
estrogens, conjugated	Premarin	estrogen
eszopiclone	Lunesta	hypnotic
ethacrynic acid	Edecrin	loop diuretic
ethchlorvynol	Placidyl	hypnotic
ethosuximide	Zarontin	anticonvulsant
famotidine	Mylanta, Pepcid	h_2-receptor antagonist
felbamate	Felbatol	anticonvulsant
fenfluramine	Pondimin	serotonergic anorectic
flecainide acetate	Tambocor	antiarrhythmic (1)
fludrocortisone	Florinef	mineral corticoid
fluoxetine	Prozac	SSRI
fluphenazine	Permitil	neuroleptic
fluphenazine	Prolixin	neuroleptic
flurazepam	Dalmane	hypnotic
fluvoxamine	Luvox	SSRI
fosinopril sodium	Monopril	antihypertensive (ACE)
furazolidone	Furoxone	antibiotic
furosemide	Lasix	loop diuretic
gabapentin	Neurontin	anticonvulsant
galantamine	Reminyl	cholinergic function enhanced
gemfibrozil	Lopid	hypolipidemic
glucagon	Glucagon	antihypoglycemic
glutethemide	Doriden	hypnotic
glyburide	Micronase	hypoglycemic
glycopyrrolate	Robinal	antihypoglycemic
griseofulvin	Fulvicin	antibiotic
guanadrel	Hylorel	antihypertensive
guanethidine	Ismelin	antihypertensive
halazepam	Paxipam	antianxiety
haloperidol	Haldol	neuroleptic
halothane	Fluothane	anesthetic
hydralazine	Apresoline	antihypertensive
hydrochlorthiazide	Aldoril	thiazide diuretic
hydroxyzine	Atarax, Vistaril	antihistamine, antianxiety
hyoscyamine sulphate	Levsin	anticholinergic, antispasmodic
ibuprofen[a]	Motrin	NSAID
imipramine	Janimine, Tofranil	TCA
indomethacin	Indocin	NSAID
ipratropium bromide	Bronkosol	bronchodilator
isocarboxazide	Marplan	MAOI
isoniazid	Rifamate	antibiotic
isoproterenol	Isuprel	sympathomimetc (DA) β
itraconazole	Sporanox	antifungal
ketamine	Ketalar	anesthetic (general)
ketoconazole	Nizoral	antifungal agent
ketoprofen	Orudis	NSAID
ketorolac tromethamine	Toradol	NSAID
labetalol	Normodyne	β-blocker (CS)
lamotrigine	Lamictal	anticonvulsant
levodopa	Larodopa	antiparkinsonian
lidocaine[a]	Xylocaine	anesthetic (local), antiarrhymic
liothyronine (T3)	Cytomel	thyroid hormone
lisdexamfetamine	Vyvanse	stimulant
lisinopril	Prinivil, Zestril	antihypertensive
lithium	Cibalith-S, Eskalith, Lithobid, Lithonate, Lithotab	mood regulator, anticycling
loperidide	Imodium	antidiarrheal
lorazepam	Ativan	antianxiety
loxapine	Loxitane	neuroleptic

(continued)

Generic Name	Trade Name	Chief Action[b]
magnesium hydroxide[a]	Maalox	antacid
maprotiline	Ludiomil	HCA
mazindol	Sanorex	anorectic agent
mebendazole	Vermox	anthelmintic agent
mefenamic acid	Ponstel	NSAID
melatonin	Bevitamel	enhances natural sleep process
memantine	Namenda	NMDA antagonist
meperidine	Demerol	narcotic analgesic
meprobamate	Miltown, Equanil	antianxiety
mesoridazine	Serentil	neuroleptic
metaproterenol	Alupent	sympathomimetic (DA) β
metaraminol	Aramine	sympathomimetic (MA) αβ
methabarbital	Mebaral	antianxiety
methadone	Dolophine	narcotic analgesic
methimazole	Tapazole	antithyroid drug
methotrimeprazine	Levoprome	CNS depressant
methyldopa	Aldomet	antihypertensive
methylphenidate	Concerta, Daytrana, Metadate, Methylin, Ritalin	stimulant
methyltestosterone	Android	androgen derivative
methylprylon	Noludar	hypnotic
metoclopramide	Reglan	dopamine blocking antiemetic
metoprolol	Lopressor	β-blocker (CS)
metronidazole	Flagyl	antibiotic
mirtazapine	Remeron	antidepressant
modafinil	Provigil	antinarcolepsy
molindone	Moban	neuroleptic
morphine	Roxanol	narcotic
nadolol	Corgard	β-blocker (CS)
naloxone	Narcan	narcotic antagonist
naltrexone	ReVia	narcotic antagonist
naproxen	Anaprox, Aleve	NSAID
nefazodone	Serzone	antidepressant
neostigmine	Prostigmin	anticholinesterase, cholinomimetic
nicotine (patch)	Habitrol	smoking deterrent
nifedipine	Procardia	calcium channel-blocker
nimodipine	Nimotop	calcium channel-blocker
nitrofurantoin	Macrobid	antibacterial agent
nitroprusside	Nipride	antihypertensive
nizatidine	Axid	NSAID
norepinephrine	Levophed	sympathomimetic (DA) αβ
nortriptyline	Aventyl, Pamelor	TCA
olanzapine	Zyprexa	antipsychotic
omeprazole	Prilosec	gastric acid pump inhibitor
ondansetron hydrochloride	Zofran	antiemetic
orphenadrine	Norflex	analgesic, anticholinergic
oxazepam	Serax	antianxiety
paliperidone	Invega	antipsychotic
pancuronium	Pavulon	neuromuscular blocker
paraldehyde	Paral	hypnotic
pargyline	Eutonyl	MAOI
paroxetine	Paxil	SSRI
pemoline	Cylert	stimulant
penbutalol	Levatol	β-blocer (NCS)
pentazocine	Talwin	narcotic agonist–antagonist
pentobarbital	Nembutal	hypnosedative
pentoxifylline	Trental	hematologic agent
pergolide	Permax	dopamine agonist
perphenazine	Trilafon	neuroleptic
phendimetrazine	Bontril, Plegin, Prelu-2	sympathomimetic amine
phenelzine	Nardil	MAOI
phenmetrazine	Preludin	anorectic agent
phenobarbital	Luminal	anticonvulsant, sedative

Generic Name	Trade Name	Chief Action[b]
phentermine	Fastin	sympathomimetic anorectic
phentolamine	Regitine	antihypertensive
phenylbutazone	Butazolidin	NSAID
phenylephrine[a]	Neo-Synephrine	sympathomimetic (MA) $\alpha\beta$
phenylpropanolamine[a]	Acutrim	sympathomimetic (IA) $\alpha\beta$, anorectic
phenytoin	Dilantin	anticonvulsant
physostigmine	Antilirium	anticholinesterase
pimozide	Orap	neuroleptic
pindolol	Visken	β-blocker (NCS)
piroxicam	Feldene	NSAID
prazepam	Centrax	antianxiety
prazosin	Minipress	antihypertensive
pregabalin	Lyrica	anticonvulsant
primidone	Mysoline	anticonvulsant
probenecid	Benemid	uricosuric agent, antigout
procainamide	Pronestyl	antiarrhythmic (IA)
prochlorperazine	Compazine	antiemetic, dopamine blocker
procyclidine	Kemadrin	antiparkinsonian, anticholinergic
promethazine	Phenergan	antihistamine, antiemetic
propantheline bromide	Pro-Banthine	anticholinergic
propoxyphene	Darvon	opioid analgesic
propranolol	Inderal	β-blocker (NCS)
protriptyline	Vivactil	TCA
pseudoephedrine[a]	Sudafed	sympathomimetic (IA) $\alpha\beta$
psyllium[a]	Metamucil	bulk laxative
quazepam	Doral	hypnotic
quinapril	Accupril	antihypertensive (ACE)
quetiapine	Seroquel	antipsychotic
quinidine	Quinidine	antiarrhythmic (IA)
quinine	Quinamm	skeletal muscle relaxant
ramelteon	Rozerem	hypnotic
ramipril	Altace	antihypertensive (ACE)
ranitidine	Zantac	h_2 blocker
reserpine	Serpasil	antihypertensive
rifampin	Rifadin	antibiotic
risperidone	Risperdal	antipsychotic
rivastigmine	Exelon	cholinersterase inhibitor
scopolamine	Transderm Scop	anticholinergic, antiemetic
secobarbital	Seconal	hypnotic
selegiline	Eldepryl	MAOI-B
sertaline	Zoloft	SSRI
spectinomycin	Trobicin	antibiotic (macrolide)
spironolactone	Aldactone	potassium-sparing diuretic
succinulcholine	Anectine	neuromuscular blocker
sulfamethoxazole	Gantanol	antibacterial
sulindac	Clinoril	NSAID
sumatriptan succinate	Imitrex	antimigrane agent, $5HT_3$ agent
tacrine	Cognex	cholinergic, antidementia
temazepam	Restoril	hypnotic
terbutaline	Brethine	sympathomimetic (DA) β
terfenadine	Seladane	antihistamine
tetrabenazine		depletes and blocks dopamine
tetracycline	Achromycin	antibiotic
theophylline[a]	Bronkaid	bronchodilator
tiagabine	Gabitril	anticonvulsant
thiopental	Pentothal	anesthetic (general)
thioridazine	Mellaril	neuroleptic
thiothixene	Navane	neuroleptic
ticarcillin disodium	Ticar	antibacterial
timolol maleate	Blocadren	β-blocker (NCS)
tocainide	Tonocard	antiarrhythmic (1)
topiramate	Topamax	antiseizure
tranylcypromine	Parnate	MAOI

APPENDIX 1

(continued)

Generic Name	Trade Name	Chief Action[b]
trazodone	Desyrel	atypical antidepressant
triamterene	Dyrenium	potassium-sparing diuretic
triazolam	Halcion	hypnotic
trifluoperazine	Stelazine	neuroleptic
trihexyphenidyl	Artane	antiparkinsonian, anticholinergic
trimipramine	Surmontil	TCA
troleandomycin	Tao	antibacterial (macrolide)
tubocurarine	Tubocurarine	neuromuscular blocker
tyramine		sympathomimetic (IA) $\alpha\beta$
valproic acid	Depakene	anticonvulsant
vecuronium bromide	Norcuron	neuromuscular blocker
venlafaxine	Effexor	SNRI
verapamil	Isoptin	calcium channel-blocker
warfarin	Coumadin	anticoagulant (oral)
yohimbine[a]	Yocon	presynaptic α_2 antagonist
zaleplon	Sonata	hypnotic, anticonvulsant
zidovudine	Retrovir	antiviral
ziprasidone	Geodon	neuroleptic
zolpidem	Ambien	hypnotic, anticonvulsant

[a]Can be sold in nonprescription drug.
[b]ACE = angiotensin converting enzyme; CS = cardioselective; DA = direct acting; HCA = heterocyclic antidepressant; IA = indirect acting; MA = mixed acting; MAOI = monoamine oxidase inhibitor; NCS = noncardioselective; NDRI = norepinephrine and dopamine reuptake inhibitor; NSAID = nonsteroidal anti-inflammatory drug; SNRI = serotonin and norepinephrine reuptake inhibitor; SSRI = selective serotonin reuptake inhibitor; TCA = tricyclic antidepressant.

Appendix 2.
Drug Identification
by Trade Name

Trade Name	Generic Name	Chief Action
Abilify	aripiprazole	antipsychotic
Accupril	quinapril	antihypertensive (ACE)
Achromycin	tetracycline	antibiotic
Acutrim	phenylpropanolamine[a]	sympathomimetic (IA) αβ, anorectic
Adderall	amphetamine/ dextroamphetamine salts	stimulant
Akineton	biperiden	antiparkinsonian, anticholinergic
Aldactone	spironolactone	potassium-sparing diuretic
Aldomet	α-methyldopa	antihypertensive
Aldomet	methyldopa	antihypertensive
Aldoril	hydrochlorthiazide	thiazide diuretic
Altace	ramipril	antihypertensive (ACE)
Alupent	metaproterenol	sympathomimetic (DA) β
Ambien	zolpidem	hypnotic, anticonvulsant
Amytal	amobarbital	hypnotic
Anafranil	clomipramine	TCA
Anaprox, Aleve	naproxen	NSAID
Android	methyltestosterone	androgen derivative
Anectine	succinulcholine	neuromuscular blocker
Antabuse	disulfiram	alcohol blockade
Antilirium	physostigmine	anticholinesterase
Apresoline	hydralazine	antihypertensive
Aramine	metaraminol	sympathomimetic (MA) αβ
Aricept	donepezil	enhances cholinergic function
Artane	trihexyphenidyl	antiparkinsonian, anticholinergic
Asendin	amoxapine	HCA
Atarax, Vistaril	hydroxyzine	antihistamine, antianxiety
Ativan	lorazepam	antianxiety
Atropine Sulfate	atropine	anticholinergic
Auralgan	antipyrine	analgesic (otic)
Aventyl, Pamelor	nortriptyline	TCA
Axid	nizatidine	NSAID

(continued)

225

Trade Name	Generic Name	Chief Action
Benadryl	diphenhydramine[a]	antihistamine
Benemid	probenecid	uricosuric agent, antigout
Bentyl	dicyclomine hydrochloride	anticholinergic
Bevitamel	melatonin	enhances natural sleep process
Biaxin	clarithromycin	antibacterial (macrolide)
Blocadren	timolol maleate	β-blocker (NCS)
Bontril, Plegin, Prelu-2	phendimetrazine	sympathomimetic amine
Brethine	terbutaline	sympathomimetic (DA) β
Bronkaid	theophylline[a]	bronchodilator
Bronkosol	ipratropium bromide	bronchodilator
BuSpar	buspirone	antianxiety
Butazolidin	phenylbutazone	NSAID
Butisol	butabarbital	antianxiety
Capoten	captopril	antihypertensive (ACE)
Cardizem	diltiazem	calcium channel-blocker
Catapres	clonidine	antihypertensive, α_2 agonist
Celexa	citalopram	SSRI
Centrax	prazepam	antianxiety
Chloromycetin	chloramphenicol	antibiotic
Chlortrimeton	chlorpheniramine[a]	antihistamine
Cibalith-S, Eskalith, Lithobid, Lithonate, Lithotab	lithium	mood regulator, anticycling
Clinoril	sulindac	NSAID
Clozaril	clozapine	neuroleptic
Cogentin	benztropine	antiparkinsonian
Cognex	tacrine	cholinergic, antidementia
Compazine	prochlorperazine	antiemetic, dopamine blocker
Concerta, Daytrana, Metadate, Methylin, Ritalin	methylphenidate	stimulant
Cordarone	amiodarone	antiarrhythmic (III)
Corgard	nadolol	β-blocker (CS)
Coumadin	warfarin	anticoagulant (oral)
Cylert	pemoline	stimulant
Cymbalta	duloxetine	SNRI
Cytomel	liothyronine (T3)	thyroid hormone
Dalmane	flurazepam	hypnotic
Danocrine	danazol	androgen derivative, gonadotropin inhibitor
Dantrium	dantrolene	skeletal muscle relaxant
Darvon	propoxyphene	opioid analgesic
Demerol	meperidine	narcotic analgesic
Depakene	valproic acid	anticonvulsant
Depakote	divalproex	anticonvulsant, mood stabilizer
Desyrel	trazodone	atypical antidepressant
Dexedrine	dextroamphetamine	stimulant
Diamox	acetazolamide	carbonic anhydrase inhibitor
Dicumarol	dicumarol	anticoagulant (oral)
Dilantin	phenytoin	anticonvulsant
Diuril	chlorothiazide	thiazide diuretic
"DM" products	dextromethorphan[a]	cough suppressor
Dobutrex	dobutamine hydrochloride	sympathomimetic (DA) $\alpha\beta$
Dolophine	methadone	narcotic analgesic
Dopram	doxapram	respiratory stimulant
Doral	quazepam	hypnotic
Doriden	glutethemide	hypnotic
Dyrenium	triamterene	potassium-sparing diuretic
Edecrin	ethacrynic acid	loop diuretic
Effexor	venlafaxine	SNRI
Elavil	amitriptyline	TCA
Eldepryl	selegiline	MAOI-B
Ethrane	enflurane	anesthetic (general)
Eutonyl	pargyline	MAOI

Trade Name	Generic Name	Chief Action
Exelon	rivastigmine	cholinersterase inhibitor
Fastin	phentermine	sympathomimetic anorectic
Felbatol	felbamate	anticonvulsant
Feldene	piroxicam	NSAID
Flagyl	metronidazole	antibiotic
Flexeril	cyclobenzaprine	muscle relaxant (tricyclic)
Florinef	fludrocortisone	mineral corticoid
Fluothane	halothane	anesthetic
Focalin	dexmethylphenidate	stimulant
Fulvicin	griseofulvin	antibiotic
Furoxone	furazolidone	antibiotic
Gabitril	tiagabine	anticonvulsant
Gantanol	sulfamethoxazole	antibacterial
Gastrocrom	cromolyn	mast cell stabilizer
Gelusil	aluminum hydroxide[a]	antacid
Geodon	ziprasidone	neuroleptic
Glucagon	glucagon	antihypoglycemic
Habitrol	nicotine (patch)	smoking deterrent
Halcion	triazolam	hypnotic
Haldol	haloperidol	neuroleptic
Hismanal	astemizole	antihystamine (H1)
Hylorel	guanadrel	antihypertensive
Imitrex	sumatriptan succinate	antimigrane agent, 5HT$_3$ agent
Imodium	loperidide	antidiarrheal
Inapsine	droperidol	antiemetic, antianxiety, neuroleptic
Inderal	propranolol	β-blocker (NCS)
Indocin	indomethacin	NSAID
Intropin	dopamine	sympathomimetic (DA) αβ
Invega	paliperidone	antipsychotic
Ismelin	guanethidine	antihypertensive
Isoptin	verapamil	calcium channel-blocker
Isuprel	isoproterenol	sympathomimetc (DA) β
Janimine, Tofranil	imipramine	TCA
Kemadrin	procyclidine	antiparkinsonian, anticholinergic
Ketalar	ketamine	anesthetic (general)
Klonopin	clonazepam	antianxiety, anticonvulsant
Lamictal	lamotrigine	anticonvulsant
Lanoxin	digoxin	cardiac glycoside
Larodopa	levodopa	antiparkinsonian
Lasix	furosemide	loop diuretic
Levatol	penbutalol	β-blocker (NCS)
Levophed	norepinephrine	sympathomimetic (DA) αβ
Levoprome	methotrimeprazine	CNS depressant
Levsin	hyoscyamine sulphate	anticholinergic, antispasmodic
Lexapro	escitalopram	SSRI
Librium	chlordiazepoxide	antianxiety
Lioresal	baclofen	skeletal muscle relaxant
Lopid	gemfibrozil	hypolipidemic
Lopressor	metoprolol	β-blocker (CS)
Lotensin	benazepril hydrochloride	antihypertensive (ACE)
Loxitane	loxapine	neuroleptic
Ludiomil	maprotiline	HCA
Luminal	phenobarbital	anticonvulsant, sedative
Lunesta	eszopiclone	hypnotic
Luvox	fluvoxamine	SSRI
Lyrica	pregabalin	anticonvulsant
Maalox	magnesium hydroxide[a]	antacid
Macrobid	nitrofurantoin	antibacterial agent
Marax	ephedrine[a]	vasoconstrictor
Marplan	isocarboxazide	MAOI
Mebaral	methabarbital	antianxiety
Mellaril	thioridazine	neuroleptic

(continued)

Trade Name	Generic Name	Chief Action
Metamucil	psyllium[a]	bulk laxative
Micronase	glyburide	hypoglycemic
Midamor	amiloride	potassium-sparing diuretic
Miltown, Equanil	meprobamate	antianxiety
Minipress	prazosin	antihypertensive
Moban	molindone	neuroleptic
Monopril	fosinopril sodium	antihypertensive (ACE)
Motrin	ibuprofen[a]	NSAID
Mudrane	aminophylline	bronchodilator
Mylanta, Pepcid	famotidine	h$_2$-receptor antagonist
Mysoline	primidone	anticonvulsant
Mytelase	ambenonium chloride	cholinomimetic
Namenda	memantine	NMDA antagonist
Narcan	naloxone	narcotic antagonist
Nardil	phenelzine	MAOI
Navane	thiothixene	neuroleptic
Nembutal	pentobarbital	hypnosedative
Neo-Synephrine	phenylephrine[a]	sympathomimetic (MA) αβ
Neurontin	gabapentin	anticonvulsant
Nimotop	nimodipine	calcium channel-blocker
Nipride	nitroprusside	antihypertensive
Nizoral	ketoconazole	antifungal agent
No Doz	caffeine	CNS stimulant
Noctec	chorlal hydrate	hypnotic
Noludar	methylprylon	hypnotic
Norcuron	vecuronium bromide	neuromuscular blocker
Norflex	orphenadrine	analgesic, anticholinergic
Normodyne	labetalol	β-blocker (CS)
Norpace	disopyramide	antiarrhythmic (1)
Norpramin	desipramine	TCA
Optimine	azatadine	antihistamine
Orap	pimozide	neuroleptic
Orudis	ketoprofen	NSAID
Paral	paraldehyde	hypnotic
Parlodel	bromocriptine	prolactin inhibitor, antiparkinsonian, dopamine agonist
Parnate	tranylcypromine	MAOI
Pavulon	pancuronium	neuromuscular blocker
Paxil	paroxetine	SSRI
Paxipam	halazepam	antianxiety
Pediazole	erythromycin ethylsuccinate	antibacterial (macrolide)
Pentothal	thiopental	anesthetic (general)
Peri-Colace	casanthranol[a]	laxative
Permax	pergolide	dopamine agonist
Permitil	fluphenazine	neuroleptic
Phenergan	promethazine	antihistamine, antiemetic
Placidyl	ethchlorvynol	hypnotic
Pondimin	fenfluramine	serotonergic anorectic
Ponstel	mefenamic acid	NSAID
Preludin	phenmetrazine	anoretic agent
Premarin	estrogens, conjugated	estrogen
Prilosec	omeprazole	gastric acid pump inhibitor
Primatene	epinephrine[a]	sympathetomimetic (DA) αβ
Prinivil, Zestril	lisinopril	antihypertensive
Pristiq	desvenlafaxine	SNRI
Pro-Banthine	propantheline bromide	anticholinergic
Procardia	nifedipine	calcium channel-blocker
Prolixin	fluphenazine	neuroleptic
Pronestyl	procainamide	antiarrhythmic (IA)
ProSom	estazolam	hypnotic
Prostigmin	neostigmine	anticholinesterase, cholinomimetic
Proventil	albuterol	sympathomimetic (DA) αβ
Provigil	modafinil	antinarcolepsy

Trade Name	Generic Name	Chief Action
Prozac	fluoxetine	SSRI
Quarzan	clidinium bromide	anticholingeric
Questran	cholestyramine	hypolipidemic
Quinamm	quinine	skeletal muscle relaxant
Quinidine	quinidine	antiarrhythmic (IA)
Regitine	phentolamine	antihypertensive
Reglan	metoclopramide	dopamine blocking antiemetic
Remeron	mirtazapine	antidepressant
Reminyl	galantamine	cholinergic function enhanced
Restoril	temazepam	hypnotic
Retrovir	zidovudine	antiviral
ReVia	naltrexone	narcotic antagonist
Rifadin	rifampin	antibiotic
Rifamate	isoniazid	antibiotic
Risperdal	risperidone	antipsychotic
Robinal	glycopyrrolate	antihypoglycemic
Roxanol	morphine	narcotic
Rozerem	ramelteon	hypnotic
Sandimmune	cyclosporine	immunosuppressant
Sanorex	mazindol	anorectic agent
Seconal	secobarbital	hypnotic
Sectral	acebutol	β-blocker (CS)
Seladane	terfenadine	antihistamine
Serax	oxazepam	antianxiety
Serentil	mesoridazine	neuroleptic
Seroquel	quetiapine	antipsychotic
Serpasil	reserpine	antihypertensive
Serzone	nefazodone	antidepressant
Sinemet	carbidopa-levodopa	antiparkinsonian
Sinequan	doxepin	TCA
Soma	carisoprodol	muscle relaxant
Sonata	zaleplon	hypnotic, anticonvulsant
Sporanox	itraconazole	antifungal
Stelazine	trifluoperazine	neuroleptic
Strattera	atomoxetine	SNRI
Sudafed	pseudoephedrine[a]	sympathomimetic (IA) $\alpha\beta$
Surmontil	trimipramine	TCA
Symmetrel	amantadine	antiparkinsonian, antiviral
Tagamet	cimetidine	h_2-receptor antagonist
Talwin	pentazocine	narcotic agonist–antagonist
Tambocor	flecainide acetate	antiarrhythmic (1)
Tao	troleandomycin	antibacterial (macrolide)
Tapazole	methimazole	antithyroid drug
Taractan	chlorprothixene	neuroleptic
Tegretol	carbamazepine	anticonvulsant, anticycling
Tenormin	atenolol	β-blocker
Tensilon	edrophonium chloride	cholinomimetic
Thorazine	chlorpromazine	neuroleptic
Ticar	ticarcillin disodium	antibacterial
Tindal	acetophenazine	neuroleptic
Tonocard	tocainide	antiarrhythmic (1)
Topamax	topiramate	antiseizure
Toradol	ketorolac tromethamine	NSAID
Transderm Scop	scopolamine	anticholinergic, antiemetic
Tranxene	clorazepate	antianxiety
Trental	pentoxifylline	hematologic agent
Trilafon	perphenazine	neuroleptic
Trobicin	spectinomycin	antibiotic (macrolide)
Tubocurarine	tubocurarine	neuromuscular blocker
Tums	calcium carbonate[a]	antacid
Tylenol	acetaminophen[a]	analgesic
Urecholine	bethanechol	cholinergic, anticholinesterase
Valdoxan	agomelatine	antidepressant

(continued)

Trade Name	Generic Name	Chief Action
Valium	diazepam	antianxiety
Valpin	anisotropine	anticholinergic
Vanceril	beclomethasone	corticosteroid
Vascor	bepridil hydrochloride	calcium-channel blocker, antianginal
Vasotec	enalapril	antihypertensive (ACE)
Vermox	mebendazole	anthelmintic agent
Vibramycin	doxycycline	tetracycline antibiotic
Visken	pindolol	β-blocker (NCS)
Vivactil	protriptyline	TCA
Voltaren	diclofenac sodium	anti-inflammatory (NSAID)
Vyvanse	lisdexamfetamine	stimulant
Wellbutrin	bupropion	NDRI
Xanax	alprazolam	antianxiety
Xylocaine	lidocaine[a]	anesthetic (local), antiarrhymic
Yocon	yohimbine[a]	presynaptic α_2 antagonist
Zantac	ranitidine	h_2 blocker
Zarontin	ethosuximide	anticonvulsant
Zithromax	azithromycin dihydrate	antibacterial (macrolide)
Zofran	ondansetron hydrochloride	antiemetic
Zoloft	sertaline	SSRI
Zyprexa	olanzapine	antipsychotic

[a]Can be sold in nonprescription drug.
[b]ACE = angiotensin converting enzyme; CS = cardioselective; DA = direct acting; HCA = heterocyclic antidepressant; IA = indirect acting; MA = mixed acting; MAOI = monoamine oxidase inhibitor; NCS = noncardioselective; NDRI = norepinephrine and dopamine reuptake inhibitor; NSAID = nonsteroidal anti-inflammatory drug; SNRI = serotonin and norepinephrine reuptake inhibitor; SSRI = selective serotonin reuptake inhibitor; TCA = tricyclic antidepressant.

Appendix 3.
Drug Interactions—Cytochrome P450 Enzymes

P450 ENZYME SYSTEM

Function: Oxidation of substances (drugs) to make them more hydrophilic and easily eliminated.

Coding subtypes: Each human P450 enzyme is the expression of a unique gene. Most P450 enzymes involved in drug metabolism belong to three distinct gene families (1, 2, 3—or I, II, III). A special coding system is used. For example: P450 2D6 is a very specific subtype where *2* is first number, *D* is first letter, and *6* is second number.

- First number—represents families with > 40% amino acid sequence homology.
- First letter—represents subfamilies with > 55% amino acid homology.
- Second number—represents the single gene that controls the enzyme's expression.

There are four P450 enzymes (1A2, 2D6, 3A3, and 3A4) that control a majority of the drug metabolism of psychiatric drugs. 3A3 and 3A4 are essentially the same enzymes, each controlled by a different gene, and are often descriptively condensed to 3A3/4. Other P450 enzymes (e.g., 2C19) also play an important role.

Definition of Substrates, Inhibitors, and Inducers of P450 Enzymes

Substrates: Drugs metabolized by the specific enzyme.

Inhibitors: Drugs that interfere with the enzyme's oxidation of substrates and raise plasma levels of drugs that depend on that enzyme.

Competitive inhibitors: Drugs that are substrates of the enzyme but compete with other substrates. All substrate drugs have the potential to be inhibitors if they compete with another substrate drug.

Noncompetitive inhibitors: Drugs that are not metabolized by the particular enzyme that they inhibit.

Inducers: Drugs that increase a specific enzyme's activity and lower levels of substrates metabolized by that drug.

Appendix 4.
Measurement-Based Care

Measurement-based care refers to systematic and objective measuring of symptom response to treatment. In addition, the quantification of treatment-emergent adverse events and safety concerns (e.g., movement disorders, metabolic indices) is considered a standard of care.

Measurement-based tools can be broadly divided into (1) screening tools, (2) symptom measures, and (3) adverse-event rating scales. Below, commonly employed and recommended tools for clinical practice are listed.

1. Screening Tools

• Mood Disorder Questionnaire (MDQ) for bipolar disorder
• Mini Mental Status Examination (MMSE) for dementia

2. Psychopathology Measures

DEPRESSION

Clinician-rated
• Montgomery Asberg Depression Rating Scale (MADRS)
• Hamilton Rating Scale—17 Item (HAMD-17)
• Hamilton Rating Scale—7 Item (HAMD-7)
• Inventory of Depressive Symptomatology (IDS-30)

Patient-rated
• Quick Inventory of Depressive Symptomatology—16-item (QIDS-16)
• Beck Depression Inventory—I/II (BDI-I/II)
• Patient Health Questionnaire—9 (PHQ-9)

MANIA

- Young Mania Rating Scale (YMRS)
- Clinician-Administered Rating Scale for Mania (CARS-M)

ANXIETY

- Liebowitz Social Anxiety Scale
- Hamilton Anxiety Rating Scale (HAM-A)
- Yale–Brown Obsessive Compulsive Scale (YBOCS)

PSYCHOSES

- Positive and Negative Symptoms Scale (PANSS)
- Schedule for the Assessment of Negative Symptoms (SANS)
- Schedule for the Assessment of Positive Symptoms (SAPS)
- Brief Psychiatric Rating Scale (BPRS)

ATTENTION-DEFICIT-HYPERACTIVITY DISORDER (ADHD)

- Swanson, Nolan, and Pelham—Fourth Edition (SNAP-IV)
- Conners Parent Rating Scale—Revised (CPRS-R)

3. Adverse-Event Rating Scales

- Abnormal Involuntary Movement Scale (AIMS)
- Sex Effects Scale (Sex-FX)

Bibliography

ANTIPSYCHOTICS

Berk, M., & Dodd, S. (2005). Efficacy of atypical antipsychotics in bipolar disorder. *Drugs, 65,* 257–269.

Food and Drug Administration (Public Health Advisory). (2005). *Deaths with antipsychotics in elderly patients with behavioral disturbances.* FDA advisory. Retrieved November 4, 2005, from www.fda.gov/cder/drug/advisory/antipsychotics.htm.

Kapur, S., & Seeman, P. (2001). Does fast dissociation from the dopamine D(2) receptor explain the action of atypical antipsychotics?: A new hypothesis. *American Journal of Psychiatry, 158,* 360–369.

Kennedy, S. H., & Lam, R. W. (2003). Enhancing outcomes in the management of treatment resistant depression: A focus on atypical antipsychotics. *Bipolar Disorders, 5*(Suppl 2), 36–47.

McIntyre, R., & Katzman, M. (2003). The role of atypical antipsychotics in bipolar depression and anxiety disorders. *Bipolar Disorders, 5*(Suppl 2), 20–35.

McIntyre, R. S., & Konarski, J. Z. (2005). Tolerability profiles of atypical antipsychotics in the treatment of bipolar disorder. *Journal of Clinical Psychiatry, 66*(Suppl 3), 28–36.

AGENTS FOR TREATING MOVEMENT DISORDERS

Burgyone, K., Aduri, K., Ananth, J., & Parameswaran, S. (2004). The use of antiparkinsonian agents in the management of drug-induced extrapyramidal symptoms. *Current Pharmaceutical Design, 10*(18), 2239–2248.

Gareri, P., De Fazio, P., De Fazio, S., Marigliano, N., Ferreri, I. G., & De Sarro, G. (2006). Adverse effects of atypical antipsychotics in the elderly: A review. *Drugs Aging, 23*(12), 937–956.

Gentile, S. (2007). Extrapyramidal adverse events associated with atypical antipsychotic treatment of bipolar disorder. *Journal of Clinical Psychopharmacology, 27*(1), 35–45.

Pierre, J. M. (2005). Extrapyramidal symptoms with atypical antipsychotics: Incidence, prevention, and management. *Drug Safety, 28*(3), 191–208.

Trosch, R. M. (2004). Neuroleptic-induced movement disorders: Deconstructing extrapyramidal symptoms. *Journal of the American Geriatrics Society, 52*(Suppl 12), S266–S271.

235

Weiden, P. J. (2007). EPS profiles: The atypical antipsychotics are not all the same. *Journal of Psychiatric Practice*, *13*(1), 13–24.

ANTIDEPRESSANTS

Bresnahan, D. B., Pandey, G. N., Janicak, P. G., Sharma, R., Boshes, R. A., Chang, S. S., et al. (1990). MAO inhibition and clinical response in depressed patients treated with phenelzine. *Journal of Clinical Psychiatry*, *51*(2), 47–50.

Clayton, A. H., & Montejo, A. L. (2006). Major depressive disorder, antidepressants, and sexual dysfunction. *Journal of Clinical Psychiatry*, *67*(Suppl 6), 33–37.

Davis, J. M., Janicak, P. G., & Bruning, A. K. (1987). The efficacy of MAO inhibitors in depression: A meta-analysis. *Psychiatric Annals*, *17*(12), 825–831.

Detke, M. J., Lu, Y., Goldstein, D. J., Hayes, J. R., & Demitrack, M. A. (2002). Duloxetine, 60 mg once daily, for major depressive disorder: A randomized double-blind placebo-controlled trial. *Journal of Clinical Psychiatry*, *63*(4), 308–315.

Dewan, M. J., & Anand, V. S. (1999). Evaluating the tolerability of the newer antidepressants. *Journal of Nervous and Mental Disease*, *187*(2), 96–101.

Fava, M. (2003). Diagnosis and definition of treatment-resistant depression. *Biological Psychiatry*, *53*(8), 649–659.

Fava, M., Rush, A. J., Wisniewski, S. R., Nierenberg, A. A., Alpert, J. E., McGrath, P. J., et al. (2006). A comparison of mirtazapine and nortriptyline following two consecutive failed medication treatments for depressed outpatients: A STAR*D report. *American Journal of Psychiatry*, *163*(7), 1161–1172.

Glassman, A. H. (1998). Cardiovascular effects of antidepressant drugs: Updated. *Journal of Clinical Psychiatry*, *59*(Suppl 15), 13–18.

Himmelhoch, J. M., Thase, M. E., Mallinger, A. G., & Houck, P. (1991). Tranylcypromine versus imipramine in anergic bipolar depression. *American Journal of Psychiatry*, *148*(7), 910–916.

Kennedy, S. H. (2007). Agomelatine: An antidepressant with a novel mechanism of action. *Future Neurology*, *2*(2), 145–151.

Kennedy, S. H., Andersen, H. F., & Lam, R. W. (2006). Efficacy of escitalopram in the treatment of major depressive disorder compared with conventional selective serotonin reuptake inhibitors and venlafaxine XR: A meta-analysis. *Journal of Psychiatry and Neuroscience*, *31*(2), 122–131.

Kent, J. M. (2000). SNaRIs, NaSSAs, and NaRIs: New agents for the treatment of depression. *Lancet*(9207), *355*, 911–918.

Mayers, A. G., & Baldwin, D. S. (2005). Antidepressants and their effect on sleep. *Human Psychopharmacology*, *20*(8), 533–559.

Nierenberg, A. A., Fava, M., Trivedi, M. H., Wisniewski, S. R., Thase, M. E., McGrath, P. J., et al. (2006). A comparison of lithium and T(3) augmentation following two failed medication treatments for depression: A STAR*D report. *American Journal of Psychiatry*, *163*(9), 1519–1530.

Pande, A. C., Birkett, M., Fechner-Bates, S., Haskett, R. F., & Greden, J. F. (1996). Fluoxetine versus phenelzine in atypical depression. *Biological Psychiatry*, *40*(10), 1017–1020.

Patkar, A. A., Pae, C. U., & Masand, P. S. (2006). Transdermal selegiline: The new generation of monoamine oxidase inhibitors. *CNS Spectrums*, *11*(5), 363–375.

Quitkin, F., Rifkin, A., & Klein, D. F. (1979). Monoamine oxidase inhibitors: A review of antidepressant effectiveness. *Archives of General Psychiatry*, *36*(7), 749–760.

Quitkin, F. M., McGrath, P. J., Stewart, J. W., Harrison, W., Tricamo, E., Wager, S. G., et al. (1990). Atypical depression, panic attacks, and response to imipramine and phenelzine. A replication. *Archives of General Psychiatry*, *47*(10), 935–941.

Rosenbaum, J. F., Fava, M., Hoog, S. L., Ascroft, R. C., & Krebs, W. B. (1998). Selective serotonin reuptake inhibitor discontinuation syndrome: A randomized clinical trial. *Biological Psychiatry, 44*(2), 77–87.

Rubino, A., Roskell, N., Tennis, P., Mines, D., Weich, S., & Andrews, E. (2007). Risk of suicide during treatment with venlafaxine, citalopram, fluoxetine, and dothiepin: Retrospective cohort study. *British Medical Journal, 334*(7587), 242.

Rush, A. J., Trivedi, M. H., Wisniewski, S. R., Stewart, J. W., Nierenberg, A. A., Thase, M. E., et al. (2006). Bupropion-SR, sertraline, or venlafaxine-XR after failure of SSRIs for depression. *New England Journal of Medicine, 354*(12), 1231–1242.

Shulman, K. I., & Walker, S. E. (1999). Refining the MAOI diet: Tyramine content of pizzas and soy products. *Journal of Clinical Psychiatry, 60*(3), 191–193.

Smith, D., Dempster, C., Glanville, J., Freemantle, N., & Anderson, I. (2002). Efficacy and tolerability of venlafaxine compared with selective serotonin reuptake inhibitors and other antidepressants: A meta-analysis. *British Journal of Psychiatry, 180,* 396–404.

Thase, M. E., Entsuah, A. R., & Rudolph, R. L. (2001). Remission rates during treatment with venlafaxine or selective serotonin reuptake inhibitors. *British Journal of Psychiatry, 178,* 234–241.

Thase, M. E., & Howland, R. H. (1994). Refractory depression: Relevance of psychosocial factors and therapies. *Psychiatric Annals, 24,* 232–240.

Trivedi, M. H., Fava, M., Wisniewski, S. R., Thase, M. E., Quitkin, F., Warden, D., et al. (2006). Medication augmentation after the failure of SSRIs for depression. *New England Journal of Medicine, 354*(12), 1243–1252.

Trivedi, M. H., Rush, A. J., Wisniewski, S. R., Nierenberg, A. A., Warden, D., Ritz, L., et al. (2006). Evaluation of outcomes with citalopram for depression using measurement-based care in STAR*D: Implications for clinical practice. *American Journal of Psychiatry, 163*(1), 28–40.

DEMENTIA-TREATING AGENTS

Auriacombe, S., Pere, J. J., Loria-Kanza, Y., & Vellas, B. (2002). Efficacy and safety of rivastigmine in patients with Alzheimer's disease who failed to benefit from treatment with donepezil. *Current Medical Research and Opinion, 18*(3), 129–138.

Cohen-Mansfield, J. (2003). Nonpharmacologic interventions for psychotic symptoms in dementia. *Journal of Geriatric Psychiatry and Neurology, 16*(4), 219–224.

Emre, M., Aarsland, D., Albanese, A., Byrne, E. J., Deuschl, G., De Deyn, P. P., et al. (2004). Rivastigmine for dementia associated with Parkinson's disease. *New England Journal of Medicine, 351*(24), 2509–2518.

Evans, J. G., Wilcock, G., & Birks, J. (2004). Evidence-based pharmacotherapy of Alzheimer's disease. *International Journal of Neuropsychopharmacology, 7*(3), 351–369.

McKeith, I., Del Ser, T., Spano, P., Emre, M., Wesnes, K., Anand, R., et al. (2000). Efficacy of rivastigmine in dementia with Lewy bodies: A randomised, double-blind, placebo-controlled international study. *Lancet, 356*(9247), 2031–2036.

Overshott, R., & Burns, A. (2005). Treatment of dementia. *Journal of Neurology, Neurosurgery, and Psychiatry, 76*(Suppl 5), v53–v59.

Overshott, R., Byrne, J., & Burns, A. (2004). Nonpharmacological and pharmacological interventions for symptoms in Alzheimer's disease. *Expert Review of Neurotherapeutics, 4*(5), 809–821.

Schneider, L. S., Olin, J. T., Doody, R. S., Clark, C. M., Morris, J. C., Reisberg, B., et al. (1997). Validity and reliability of the Alzheimer's Disease Cooperative Study—Clinical Global Impression of Change. The Alzheimer's Disease Cooperative Study. *Alzheimer Disease and Associated Disorders, 11*(Suppl 2), S22–S32.

Tariot, P. N., Farlow, M. R., Grossberg, G. T., Graham, S. M., McDonald, S., & Gergel, I. (2004). Memantine treatment in patients with moderate to severe Alzheimer disease already receiving donepezil: A randomized controlled trial. *Journal of the American Medical Association, 291*(3), 317–324.

MOOD STABILIZERS

Baldessarini, R. J., Pompili, M., & Tondo, L. (2006). Suicide in bipolar disorder: Risks and management. *CNS Spectrum, 11*, 465–471.

Baldessarini, R. J., Tondo, L., & Hennen, J. (1999). Effects of lithium treatment and its discontinuation on suicidal behavior in bipolar manic–depressive disorders. *Journal of Clinical Psychiatry, 60*(Suppl 2), 77–84.

Bauer, M. S., & Mitchner, L. (2004). What is a "mood stabilizer"? An evidence-based response. *American Journal of Psychiatry, 161*, 3–18.

Bowden, C. L., Calabrese, J. R., Sachs, G., Yatham, L. N., Asghar, S. A., Hompland, M., et al. (2003). A placebo-controlled 18-month trial of lamotrigine and lithium maintenance treatment in recently manic or hypomanic patients with bipolar I disorder. *Archives of General Psychiatry, 60*, 392–400.

Dunner, D. L. (2003). Drug interactions of lithium and other antimanic/mood-stabilizing medications. *Journal of Clinical Psychiatry, 64*(Suppl 5), 38–43.

Ernst, C. L., & Goldberg, J. F. (2002). The reproductive safety profile of mood stabilizers, atypical antipsychotics, and broad-spectrum psychotropics. *Journal of Clinical Psychiatry, 63*(Suppl 4), 42–55.

Gitlin, M. (1999). Lithium and the kidney: An updated review. *Drug Safety, 20*, 231–243.

Goldberg, J. F., & Citrome, L. (2005). Latest therapies for bipolar disorder: Looking beyond lithium. *Postgraduate Medicine, 117*, 25–32, 35.

Hahn, C. G., Gyulai, L., Baldassano, C. F., & Lenox, R. H. (2004). The current understanding of lamotrigine as a mood stabilizer. *Journal of Clinical Psychiatry, 65*, 791–804.

Ketter, T. A., & Wang, P. W. (2002). Predictors of treatment response in bipolar disorders: Evidence from clinical and brain imaging studies. *Journal of Clinical Psychiatry, 63*(Suppl 3), 21–25.

Ketter, T. A., Wang, P. W., Becker, O. V., Nowakowska, C., & Yang, Y. S. (2003). The diverse roles of anticonvulsants in bipolar disorders. *Annals of Clinical Psychiatry, 15*, 95–108.

Manji, H. K., Moore, G. J., & Chen, G. (2000). Clinical and preclinical evidence for the neurotrophic effects of mood stabilizers: Implications for the pathophysiology and treatment of manic–depressive illness. *Biological Psychiatry, 48*, 740–754.

Rybakowski, J. (2007). Long-term pharmacological treatment of bipolar disorders. *Neurology and Endocrinology Letters, 28*(Suppl 1), 71–93.

Scott, J., & Pope, M. (2002). Nonadherence with mood stabilizers: Prevalence and predictors. *Journal of Clinical Psychiatry, 63*, 384–390.

Silverstone, P. H., McGrath, B. M., & Kim, H. (2005). Bipolar disorder and myoinositol: A review of the magnetic resonance spectroscopy findings. *Bipolar Disorders, 7*, 1–10.

Yatham, L. N., Kennedy, S. H., O'Donovan, C., Parikh, S., Macqueen, G., McIntyre, R., et al. (2005). Canadian Network for Mood and Anxiety Treatments (CANMAT) guidelines for the management of patients with bipolar disorder: Consensus and controversies. *Bipolar Disorders, 7*(Suppl 3), 5–69.

Yonkers, K. A., Wisner, K. L., Stowe, Z., Leibenluft, E., Cohen, L., Miller, L., et al. (2004). Management of bipolar disorder during pregnancy and the postpartum period. *American Journal of Psychiatry, 161*, 608–620.

ANTIANXIETY AGENTS

Allgulander, C. (1999). Paroxetine in social anxiety disorder: A randomized placebo-controlled study. *Acta Psychiatrica Scandinavica, 100*(3), 193–198.

Allgulander, C., Dahl, A. A., Austin, C., Morris, P. L., Sogaard, J. A, Fayyad, R, Kutcher, S. P., & Clary, C. M. (2004). Efficacy of sertraline in a 12-week trial for generalized anxiety disorder. *American Journal of Psychiatry, 161*(9), 1642–1649.

Allgulander, C., Mangano, R., Zhang, J., Dahl, A. A., Lepola, U., Sjödin, I., & Emilien, G. (2004). Efficacy of Venlafaxine ER in patients with social anxiety disorder: A double-blind, placebo-controlled, parallel-group comparison with paroxetine. *Human Psychopharmacology, 19*(6), 387–396.

Ball, S. G., Kuhn, A., Wall, D., Shekhar, A., & Goddard, A. W. (2005). Selective serotonin reuptake inhibitor treatment for generalized anxiety disorder: A double-blind, prospective comparison between paroxetine and sertraline. *Journal of Clinical Psychiatry, 66*(1), 94–99.

Bakker, A., van Balkom, A., & Spinhoven, P. (2002). SSRIs vs. TCAs in the treatment of panic disorder: A meta-analysis. *Acta Psychiatrica Scandinavica, 106*(3), 163–167.

Barlow, D. H., Gorman, J. M., Shear, M. K., et al. (2000). Cognitive–behavioral therapy, imipramine, or their combination for panic disorder: A randomized controlled trial. *Journal of the American Medical Association, 238*(19), 2529–2536.

Bergeron, R., Ravindran, A. V., Chaput, Y., Goldner, E., Swinson, R., van Ameringen, M. A., Austin, C., & Hadrava, V. (2002). Sertraline and fluoxetine treatment of obsessive-compulsive disorder: Results of a double-blind, 6-month treatment study. *Journal of Clinical Psychopharmacology, 22*(2), 148–154.

Bielski, R. J., Bose, A., & Chang, C. C. (2005). A double-blind comparison of escitalopram and paroxetine in the long-term treatment of generalized anxiety disorder. *Annals of Clinical Psychiatry, 17*(2), 65–69.

Bradwejn, J., Ahokas, A., Stein, D. J., Salinas, E., Emilien, G., & Whitaker, T. (2005). Venlafaxine extended-release capsules in panic disorder: Flexible-dose, double-blind, placebo-controlled study. *British Journal of Psychiatry,187,* 352–359.

Brady, K., Pearlstein, T., Asnis, G. M., Baker, D., Rothbaum, B., Sikes, C. R., & Farfel, G. M. (2000). Efficacy and safety of sertraline treatment of posttraumatic stress disorder: A randomized controlled trial. *Journal of the American Medical Association, 283*(14), 1837–1844.

Davidson, J. R., Dupont, R. I., Hedges, D., et al. (1999). Efficacy, safety and tolerability of venlafaxine extended-release and buspirone in outpatients with generalized anxiety disorder. *Journal of Clinical Psychiatry, 60*(8), 528–535.

Davidson, J. R., Rothbaum, B. O., van der Kolk, B. A., Sikes, C. R., & Farfel, G. M. (2001). Multicenter, double-blind comparison of sertraline and placebo in the treatment of posttraumatic stress disorder. *Archives of General Psychiatry, 8*(5), 485–492.

Davidson, J., Yaryura-Tobias, J., DuPont, R., Stallings, L., Barbato, L. M., van der Hoop, R. G., & Li, D. (2004). Fluvoxamine-controlled release formulation for the treatment of generalized social anxiety disorder. *Journal of Clinical Psychopharmacology, 24*(2), 118–125.

Denys, D., van der Wee, N., van Megen, H. J., & Westenberg, H. G. (2003). A double-blind comparison of venlafaxine and paroxetine in obsessive-compulsive disorder. *Journal of Clinical Psychopharmacology, 23*(6), 568–575.

DeVeaugh-Geiss, J., Landau, P., & Katz, R. (1989). Preliminary results from a multicenter trial of clomipramine in obsessive–compulsive disorder. *Psychopharmacology, 25*(1), 36–40.

Hale, W. E., May, F., Moore, M., et al. (1988). Meprobamate use in the elderly: A report from the Dunedin Program. *Journal of the American Geriatric Society, 36*(11), 1003–1005.

Herman, J. B., Rosenbaum, J. F., & Brotman, A. W. (1987). The alprazolam to clonazepam switch for the treatment of panic disorder. *Journal of Clinical Psychopharmacology, 7*(3), 175–178.

Hollander, E., Allen, A., Steiner, M., Wheadon, D. E., Oakes, R., & Burnham, D. B. (2003). Acute and long-term treatment and prevention of relapse o obsessive-compulsive disorder with paroxetine. *Journal of Clinical Psychiatry, 64*(9), 1113–1121.

Kavirajan, H. (1999). The amobarbital interview revisited: A review of the literature since 1966. *Harvard Review of Psychiatry, 7*(3), 153–165.

Lepola, U., Arato, M., Zhu, Y., & Austin, C. (2003). Sertraline versus imipramine treatment of comorbid panic disorder and major depressive disorder. *Journal of Clinical Psychiatry, 64*(6), 654–662.

Lepola, U., Bergtholdt, B., St Lambert, J., Davy, K. L., & Ruggiero, L. (2004). Controlled-release paroxetine in the treatment of patients with social anxiety disorder. *Journal of Clinical Psychiatry, 65*(2), 222–229.

Liebowitz, M. R., Gelenberg, A. J., & Munjack, D. (2005). Venlafaxine extended release vs. placebo and paroxetine in social anxiety disorder. *Archives of General Psychiatry, 62*(2), 190–198.

McDougle, C. J., Naylor, S. T., Cohen, D. T., et al. (1996). A double-blind placebo-controlled study of fluvoxamine in adults with autistic disorder. *Archives of General Psychiatry, 53*(11), 1001–1008.

Pande, A. C., Davidson, J. R., Jefferson, J. J., et al. (1999). Treatment of social phobia with gabapentin: A placebo-controlled study. *Journal of Clinical Psychopharmacology, 19*(4), 341–348.

Phillips, K. A., Albertini, R. S., & Rasmussen, S. A. (2002). A randomized placebo-controlled trial of fluoxetine in body dysmorphic disorder. *Archives of General Psychiatry, 59*(4), 381–388.

Rickels, K., Zaninelli, R, McCafferty, J., Bellew, K., Iyengar, M., & Sheehan, D. (2003). Paroxetine treatment of generalized anxiety disorder: A double-blind, placebo-controlled study. *American Journal of psychiatry, 160*(4), 749–756.

Sheehan, D. V., Burnham, D. B., Iyengar, M. K., & Perera, P. (2005). Efficacy and tolerability of controlled-release paroxetine in the treatment of panic disorder. *Journal of Clinical Psychiatry, 66*(1), 34–40.

Spiegel, D. A. (1999). Psychological strategies for discontinuing benzodiazepine treatment. *Journal of Clinical Psychopharmacology, 19*(Suppl 2), 17S–23S.

Stein, D. J., Davidson, J., Seedat, S., & Beebe, K. (2003). Paroxetine in the treatment of posttraumatic stress disorder: Pooled analysis of placebo-controlled studies. *Expert Opinion on Pharmacotherapy, 4*(10), 1829–1838.

Tesar, G. E., & Rosenbaum, J. F. (1986). Successful use of clonazepam in patients with treatment-resistant panic disorder. *Journal of Nervous and Mental Disease, 174*(8), 447–482.

HYPNOTICS

Almeida Montes, L.G., Ontiveros Uribe, M.P., Cortés Sotres, J., & Heinze Martin, G. (2003). Treatment of primary insomnia with melatonin: A double-blind, placebo-controlled, crossover study. *Journal of Psychiatry and Neuroscience, 28*(3), 191–196.

Dorsey, C.M., Lee, K.A., & Scharf, M.B. (2004). Effect of zolpidem on sleep in women with perimenopausal and postmenopausal insomnia: A 4-week, randomized, multicenter, double-blind, placebo-controlled study. *Clinical Therapeutics, 26*(10), 1578–1586.

Erman, M., Seiden, D., Zammit, G., Sainati, S., & Zhang, J. (2006). An efficacy, safety, and dose–response study of ramelteon in patients with chronic primary insomnia. *Sleep Medicine, 7*(1), 17–24.

Feren, S., Katyal, A., & Walsh, J. K. (2006). Efficacy of hypnotic medications and other medications used for insomnia. *Sleep Medicine Clinics, 1,* 387–397.

Gelenberg, A. (2000). Zaleplon: A new nonbenzodiazepine hypnotic. *Biological Therapies in Psychiatry, 23,* 5–6.

Griffiths, R. R., & Johnson, M.W. (2005). Relative abuse liability of hypnotic drugs: A conceptual framework and algorithm for differentiating among compounds. *Journal of Clinical Psychiary, 66*(Suppl 9), 31–41.

Hajak, G., & Bandelow, B. (1998). Safety and tolerance of zolpidem in the treatment of disturbed sleep: A post-marketing surveillance of 16,944 cases. *International Clinical Psychopharmacology, 13*(4), 157–167.

Hertzman, P. A., Blevins, W. L., Mayer, J., Greenfield, B., Ting, M., & Gleich, G. J. (1990). Association of the eosinophilia–myalgia syndrome with the ingestion of tryptophan. *New England Journal of Medicine, 322*(13), 869–873.

Houghton, P. J. (1999). The scientific basis for the reputed activity of valerian. *Journal of Pharmacy and Pharmacology, 51*(5), 505–512.

Kales, A. (1990). Quazepam: Hypnotic efficacy and side effects. *Pharmacotherapy, 10*(1), 1–10.

Kato, K., Hirai, K., Nishiyama, K., Uchikawa, O., Fukatsu, K., Ohkawa, S., et al. (2005). Neurochemical properties of ramelteon (TAK-375), a selective MT1/MT2 receptor agonist. *Neuropharmacology, 48*(2), 301–310.

Krystal, A. D., Walsh, J. K., Laska, E., Caron, J., Amato, D. A., Wessel, T. C., et al. (2003). Sustained efficacy of eszopiclone over 6 months of nightly treatment: Results of a randomized, double-blind, placebo-controlled study in adults with chronic insomnia. *Sleep, 26*(7), 793–799.

McKernan, R. M., Rosahl, T. W., Reynolds, D. S., Sur, C., Wafford, K. A., Atack, J. R., et al. (2000). Sedative but not anxiolytic properties of benzodiazepines are mediated by the GABA(A) receptor alpha-1 subtype. *Nature Neuroscience, 3*(6), 587–592.

Mendelson, W. B. (2005). A review of the evidence for the efficacy and safety of trazodone in insomnia. *Journal of Clinical Psychiatry, 66*(4), 469–476.

Novel, P. D., Mazumdar, S., Buysse, D. J., Dew, M. A., & Reynolds, C. F. (1997). Benzodiazepines and zolpidem for chronic insomnia: A meta-analysis of treatment efficacy. *Journal of the American Medical Association, 278*(24), 2170–2177.

Ringdahl, E. N., Pereira, S. L., & Delzell, J. E., Jr. (2004). Treatment of primary insomnia. *Journal of the American Board of Family Practice, 17*(3), 212–219.

Roehrs, T., & Roth, T. (2006). Safety of insomnia pharmacotherapy. *Sleep Medicine Clinics, 1,* 399–407.

Roth, T., Seiden, D., Sainati, S., Wang-Weigand, S., Zhang, J., & Zee, P. (2006). Effects of ramelteon on patient-reported sleep latency in older adults with chronic insomnia. *Sleep Medicine, 7*(4), 312–318.

Roth, T., Stubbs, C., & Walsh, J. K. (2005). Ramelteon (TAK-375), a selective MT1/MT2-receptor agonist, reduces latency to persistent sleep in a model of transient insomnia related to a novel sleep environment. *Sleep, 28*(3), 303–307.

Roth, T., Walsh, J.K., Krystal, A., Wessel, T., & Roehrs, T. A. (2005). An evaluation of the efficacy and safety of eszopiclone over 12 months in patients with chronic primary insomnia. *Sleep Medicine, 6*(6), 487–495.

Savic, M. M., Obradovic, D. I., Ugresic, N. D., & Bokonjic, D. R. (2005). Memory effects of benzodiazepines: Memory stages and types versus binding-site subtypes. *Neural Plasticity, 12*(4), 289–298.

Sproule, B. A., Busto, U. E., Buckle, C., Herrmann, N., & Bowles, S. (1999). The use of non-prescription sleep products in the elderly. *International Journal of Geriatric Psychiatry, 14*(10), 851–857.

Walsh, J. K., Pollak, C. P., Scharf, M. B., Schweitzer, P. K., & Vogel, G. W. (2000). Lack of residual sedation following middle-of-the-night zaleplon administration in sleep maintenance insomnia. *Clinical Neuropharmacology, 23*(1), 17–21.

Walsh, J. K., Roth, T., Randazzo, A., Erman, M., Jamieson, A., Scharf, M., et al. (2000). Eight weeks of non-nightly use of zolpidem for primary insomnia. *Sleep, 23*(8), 1087–1096.

Walsh, J. K., Vogel, G. W., Scharf, M., Erman, M., Erwin, C., Schweitzer, P. K., et al. (2000). A five week, polysomnographic assessment of zaleplon 10 mg for the treatment of primary insomnia. *Sleep Medicine, 1*(1), 41–49.

STIMULANTS

Anderson, V. R., & Keating, G. M. (2007). Spotlight on methylphenidate controlled-delivery capsules (Equasym XL, Metadate CD) in the treatment of children and adolescents with attention-deficit hyperactivity disorder. *CNS Drugs, 21*, 173–175.

Arnsten, A. F. (2006). Stimulants: Therapeutic actions in ADHD. *Neuropsychopharmacology, 31*, 2376–2383.

Brown, R. T., Amler, R. W., Freeman, W. S., Perrin, J. M., Stein, M. T., Feldman, H. M., et al. (2005). Treatment of attention-deficit/hyperactivity disorder: Overview of the evidence. *Pediatrics, 115*, e749–e757.

Gibson, A. P., Bettinger, T. L., Patel, N. C., & Crismon, M. L. (2006). Atomoxetine versus stimulants for treatment of attention deficit/hyperactivity disorder. *Annals of Pharmacotherapy, 40*, 1134–1142.

King, S., Griffin, S., Hodges, Z., Weatherly, H., Asseburg, C., Richardson, G., et al. (2006). A systematic review and economic model of the effectiveness and cost-effectiveness of methylphenidate, dexamfetamine, and atomoxetine for the treatment of attention deficit hyperactivity disorder in children and adolescents. *Health Technology Assessment, 10*, iii–146.

Lopez, F. A. (2006). ADHD: New pharmacological treatments on the horizon. *Journal of Developmental and Behavioral Pediatrics, 27*, 410–416.

McIntyre, R. S., Fallu, A., & Konarski, J. Z. (2006). Measurable outcomes in psychiatric disorders: Remission as a marker of wellness. *Clinical Therapy, 28*, 1882–1891.

Nair, J., Ehimare, U., Beitman, B. D., Nair, S. S., & Lavin, A. (2006). Clinical review: Evidence-based diagnosis and treatment of ADHD in children. *Modern Medicine, 103*, 617–621.

Prince, J. B. (2006). Pharmacotherapy of attention-deficit hyperactivity disorder in children and adolescents: Update on new stimulant preparations, atomoxetine, and novel treatments. *Child and Adolescent Psychiatry Clinics of North America, 15*, 13–50.

Pritchard, D. (2006). Attention deficit hyperactivity disorder in children. *Clinical Evidence*, 331–344.

Sulzer, D., Sonders, M. S., Poulsen, N. W., & Galli, A. (2005). Mechanisms of neurotransmitter release by amphetamines: a review. *Progress in Neurobiology, 75*, 406–433.

Weiss, M. D., Gadow, K., & Wasdell, M. B. (2006). Effectiveness outcomes in attention-deficit/hyperactivity disorder. *Journal of Clinical Psychiatry, 67*(Suppl 8), 38–45.

Index

side effects of, 186
therapeutic application of, 199
rash
on anticonvulsants, 135, 147
on carbamazepine/lamotrigine, 135
on phenobarbital, 192
Raynaud's phenomenon, 165, 166
rebound
after benzodiazepine withdrawal, 159
cholinergic, 98
of extrapyramidal side effects, 57
insomnia, 180, 199
REM, 171, 191
receptor antagonists/agonists, 64
clinical indications for, 94
discontinuation of, 98–99
dosing, dose form, and color, 93
drug–drug interactions with, 97
effects on laboratory tests, 98
key points for patients and families,
74–75
overdose: toxicity, suicide, and
treatment, 99
side effects of, 94–97
relapse
after benzodiazepine withdrawal, 159
cognitive–behavioral therapy
reduces rate of, 175
risk of, on antipsychotics, 46
risk of, on lithium, 147
SSRIs reduce rates in
obsessive–compulsive disorder,
175
remission rates
of dual-action agents compared to
SSRIs, 100
with first antidepressant, 79
renal side effects
of antiparkinsonian drugs, 53
of antipsychotics, second-generation,
36
of benzodiazepines, 155
of cholinesterase inhibitors, 108
of lithium, 123
of memantine, 112
on transporter inhibitors, 86
resistance, *see* treatment
respiratory depression
on barbiturate-like drugs, 180, 192
on benzodiazepines, 180
restless legs syndrome (RLS), differs
from akathisia, 9
rigidity, cogwheel, 41
on lithium, 121

treating with antiparkinsonian drugs,
51–52
rimantadine, avoid with memantine,
112
risperidone, 27
haloperidol versus, 43
as mood stabilizer, 118, 144
movement disorders and, 31
rivastigmine, 104
pharmacology of, 105–6
randomized controlled trials (RCTs)
for, 106
starting dose, 114
Schedule for the Assessment of
Negative Symptoms (SANS), 45
schizoaffective disorder, 44, 45
schizophrenia
antipsychotics (first-generation)
treating, 5
antipsychotics (second-generation)
treating, 29
poor outcome predictors for, 42
treatment resistance in, 43–44
secobarbital, 189
sedation
on agomelatine, 95
on antipsychotics, first-generation,
13
on antipsychotics, second-
generation, 32
benzodiazepine side effect,
154, 158
in children and adolescents on
antipsychotics (first-generation),
22
on MAO inhibitors, 68
on mirtazapine, 95
on transporter inhibitors, 84
on trazodone, 94, 95, 97
seizures
and abrupt discontinuation of
anticonvulsants, 142
antipsychotic (first-generation)
overdose and, 25
on antipsychotics, second-
generation, 32, 40
clozapine increases risk of, 43
on lithium, 121
and MAO inhibitors, 68–69
oxcarbazepine treating, 138
on stimulants, first-generation, 209
on transporter inhibitors, 84, 92
selective melatonin agonist, 185 (*see
also* ramelteon)

I
N
D
E
X